I,

WHO

A SWEEPING STORY OF LOSS, REDEMPTION, AND FATE

DID NOT

ZAHED HAFTLANG & NAJAH ABOUD

WITH MEREDITH MAY

DIE

Regan Arts.

NEW YORK

Regan Arts.

65 Bleecker Street
New York, NY 10012

First Regan Arts hardcover edition, March 2017

Library of Congress Control Number: 2016955005

ISBN 978-1-68245-011-6

Interior design by Nancy Singer
Cover design by Richard Ljoenes

Printed in the United States of America

10 9 8 7 6 5 4 3 2 1

For Alyaa, Amjad, Mina, Daryoosh,
and all those who did not survive
the Iran-Iraq War to tell their stories

"Be certain that in the religion of Love
there are no believers and unbelievers.
Love embraces all."

—*Maulana Jalaluddin Rumi*

For the first time, on the road north of Tampico,
I felt the life sliding out of me,
a drum in the desert, harder and harder to hear.
I was seven, I lay in the car
watching palm trees swirl a sickening pattern past the glass.
My stomach was a melon split wide inside my skin.

"How do you know if you are going to die?"
I begged my mother.
We had been traveling for days.
With strange confidence she answered,
"When you can no longer make a fist."

Years later I smile to think of that journey,
the borders we must cross separately,
stamped with our unanswerable woes.
I who did not die, who am still living,
still lying in the backseat behind all my questions,
clenching and opening one small hand.

—Naomi Shihab Nye, "Making a Fist," 1952

CONTENTS

FOREWORD

by Pierre Razoux

The Iran-Iraq War was the longest and most brutal conventional war of the twentieth century, yet remarkably, many American and European history classrooms are silent on the subject. Firsthand accounts and books about this pivotal war are few, yet this eight-year conflict is the matrix of the geopolitical situation that prevails in the Persian Gulf today.

Only now, with witness testimonies like that of Zahed Haftlang and Najah Aboud, are we beginning to get a glimpse of this "forgotten war," and to start to understand what lies behind the current firefights ravaging Aleppo, Mosul, and Raqqa.

The Iran-Iraq War, from 1980–1988, relied on national and religious ideology to sway civilians and soldiers alike, and its military strategy condensed the most violent tactics of previous wars. Like World War I, it was marked by large-scale trench combat and bayonet charges, and extensive use of chemical weapons, such as mustard gas, against Iranian troops and Kurdish civilians. It combined the massive use of armored vehicles and fighter jets common to World War II, and missiles and aerial duels over the desert like those of the Arab-Israeli conflict. Troops also fought in swampy marshes similar to what soldiers faced in Vietnam, and engaged in arid and snowy mountain battles in Kurdistan reminiscent of wars in Algeria and Afghanistan.

The death and destruction left in the wake of this ruthless war were colossal, with soldiers buried in mass battlefield graves and entire villages reduced to dust. No one was unscathed. Nearly 40 percent of the adult male population in the two countries was swept up in the fighting. Up to 700,000 lives were lost, among them 80,000 Iranian child soldiers who fought on the front lines. These boys were members of the volunteer Basij youth militia, which recruited from local mosques, schools, and workplaces. Most child soldiers joined the war at age twelve or thirteen, and some were used as human minesweepers to clear the fields in advance of the armed Islamic Revolutionary Guards. Another two million people were wounded or mutilated, and victims are still dying today from the long-term effects of poison gas attacks. Another one million were uprooted during the course of the bombings, which destroyed some 1,800 border villages and towns, most notably Khorramshahr and Adaban, where the world's largest oil refinery was severely damaged. In Iraq, Basra was decimated.

The overall cost of the war is estimated at $1.1 trillion in 1988 dollars with Iran accounting for about 60 percent of the loss. Material damages added another combined $350 billion. Together, the belligerents lost 5,000 tanks and 500 combat aircraft. In the aftermath, the economies of both countries were plunged into multimillion dollar debt, economic development came to a standstill, and much of the oil industry throughout the region was decimated by air raids.

In the end, nothing changed. Both sides eventually wore down and agreed to a ceasefire that included no reparations or boundary changes. And, unlike any conflict before it, prisoners-of-war were held indefinitely by both sides; more than 115,000 broken and forgotten men slowly released over a ten-year period after the war.

But the permanent cost was a deepening of the complex power struggles, historical hatreds, and persistent fears that stem directly from this unforgiving war. These same complex forces persist today, fueling the ranks of the Islamic State in Iraq and Syria (ISIS) and animosities between Iran and Saudi Arabia, Russia and the United States.

The Iran-Iraq War ultimately was a battle of wills between Saddam

Hussein and the Ayatollah Khomeini, the latest chapter in an ancient rivalry between neighboring countries that dates back to the Ottoman Turkish Empire and the Persian Empire of the 1500s. Then, as in the 1980s, the longtime enemies argued over religion, politics, and borders, in particular, a section of waterway where the Tigris and Euphrates rivers join and flow into the Persian Gulf. Control of that section of waterway meant power—and control of the tanker ships that exported oil through the area.

But the Iran-Iraq War was not just about territory—it was a violent manifestation of two opposing worldviews. Hussein believed Arab nationalism tied all the different religious sects together—Sunni and Shia, Christian and Muslim, Kurd and Arab. He positioned himself as the undisputed leader of a secular, pan-Arab empire that would replace Iran as the most powerful Persian Gulf state.

This ran contradictory to the religious ideology of Ayatollah Khomeini, who was swept into power during the 1979 Islamic Revolution that ousted the Shah. Backed by a large Shia following, Khomeini vowed to eradicate state nationalism, insisting there should be no division between religion and politics, because the highest unifying entity was Islam. He positioned himself as the leader of a borderless, Islamic empire that would encompass the entire Middle East.

Khomeini began radio broadcasts in Iraq aimed at the country's long-suppressed Shia majority, encouraging the overthrow of Hussein's regime and the takeover of Iraq's holy Shia cities of Karbala and Najaf.

Hussein, whose Baathist Party was comprised of minority Sunnis, feared the Islamic Revolution would spill over into Iraq and encourage widespread Shia riots, a revival of the armed Kurdish secessionist movement, and ultimately civil war. He abruptly deported thousands of Iraqi Shia citizens. Then he attacked the source of Shia inspiration—the Khomeini regime.

Iraqi troops invaded Iran in September 1980. Hussein anticipated a quick fight, assuming his armies would meet little resistance from a disbanded and disorganized Iranian army that Khomeini had yet to rebuild after the Islamic Revolution. And it appeared that way at the outset, as Iraq quickly captured several border cities, including Khorramshahr. But, although Iraq had more firepower, Iranian troops had more patriotic fervor. While Hussein was fighting for power, Khomeini positioned Iran as fighting for Allah, and a holy war easily coalesced around a common enemy. Young Iranian men and boys were told not to fear death because as martyrs they would join the prophets in heaven, and their families would be given compensation, food rations, and access to better schools and jobs.

What the outside world saw was religious fanaticism taken to the extreme. Disturbing images of child soldiers thrown into frontline battle, bloodied trenches, refineries aflame, gassed corpses, and humiliated prisoners. Why would anyone join this war?

Najah and Zahed allow us to understand the reasons are more nuanced than they appear. Their stories show us that, contrary to popular prejudice that mixes all Muslims—Sunnis, Shiites, Arabs, Kurds, and Persians—into one extremist and violent religion, most Iraqi and Iranian soldiers did not form hordes of fanatic zombies, but battalions of poor citizens courageously carrying arms because they simply had no other choice. Desertion would have immediately earned them the firing squad. Like so many of his fellow Basij child soldiers who volunteered to serve as cannon fodder for the Islamic Revolutionary Guards, Zahed's reasons have nothing to do with religious fervor, ideological indoctrination, or adoration of Ayatollah Khomeini. They are more prosaic: the taste for adventure, the will to escape the ferocity of a violent father and to assert himself as a man in the eyes of the family, the seduction of a girlfriend, and a kid's ingrained attraction to weapons. And above all, a prevailing sense of duty to country and family—some of the very same reasons young people of all origins are joining the ranks of ISIS today.

Iraq and Iran gained nothing after eight years of bloodshed besides exhaustion and ruin. To this day, no peace treaty has ever been signed. And with each year that passes, there are fewer witnesses to tell the world what really happened.

Here are two.

PIERRE RAZOUX is Research Director at IRSEM (Institute for Strategic Research) in Paris and author of *The Iran-Iraq War* (Harvard University Press/Belknap), which was awarded as the Best Book of the Year by the Military History Society in 2016.

PROLOGUE

KHORRAMSHAHR, IRAN, MAY 1982—Crawling on my belly in the sand, I felt it before it happened: a low rumble like the moment before an earthquake, or maybe it was Satan himself howling from below. Then a massive boom and I was airborne. Grains of sand needled into my pores, and for the briefest moment, I was suspended above the battlefield. All sound stopped, all the shelling, all the screaming for Allah, all of it was silenced, and the orange flashes of mortar fire looked almost pretty in the darkness. Like candles flickering above the desert.

When I crashed back to earth, I had no more faith in anything. I didn't believe in God, in humanity, or in Saddam's war. There was no time for such devotions, as blood seeped from my forehead and chest, and all around me men were being executed as they begged for their lives. There was only one truth left: I was going to rot in a mass grave with hundreds of other forgotten Iraqi soldiers.

It's true what they say about your whole life flashing by as you wait for death to come sit next to you. It happens fast, like Kodachrome slides snapping into view—all these images of yourself in moments of pure joy. I closed my eyes and saw my brothers and me climbing trees to pick dates. I felt my fingers close around the fur of our big German shepherd as we wrestled in the family courtyard, and heard my mother's voice singing from the kitchen. I tasted the falafel my sister and I fried in our restaurant, and I saw my fiancée's *abaya* fluttering in the wind as she held our newborn son. The last thing I saw was my family together, celebrating the thirtieth birthday I would never have.

Then I felt a presence near me. I opened my eyes and saw a child soldier pointing a rifle at my temple. He was so small that he had to roll up the sleeves and pant legs of his uniform. This Persian boy had been brainwashed to hate me. I spoke as softly as I could.

"Please," I said, "I'm a Muslim, just like you."

He backed up a step and cocked the rifle. He either couldn't understand Arabic or he didn't care to chat before pulling the trigger.

"Muslim! Muslim!" I pleaded.

The boy took aim.

I reached into my jacket pocket to show him my Koran, and the boy lunged, grabbing it from me. He rustled through the pages, stopping when he discovered the photo of my fiancée holding our baby. He studied the image, as if he recognized them. He glanced at me and back to the photo again. I think I saw him gently touch her face with his finger.

He snapped the book shut and turned toward me with an expression of utter blankness. I silently said good-bye to everyone I loved. Then the boy slid the Koran back into my pocket. He knelt down and gave me water from his canteen. Then he leaned in close and put his finger to his lips.

"Shhhhhh."

ONE

ZAHED

Most kids in Masjed Soleyman had bicycles, even the slum kids who lived on the ugly side of town inside crumbling mud houses all stacked on top of each other. But we lived in a real brick house with a corrugated tin roof built for the oil company workers, so I should have had a bicycle, at least. Your own set of wheels meant you always had a way to escape the kind of heat that sinks down into your bones. You could pedal away from the dusty roads to the relief of the Karun River, say, or up a red dirt path in the Zagros Mountains and look over practically all of western Iran to clear your head from the clang of too many neighbors stirring up trouble in everybody else's business.

But Baba said I didn't deserve a bicycle. I was not sure why, other than I sometimes got in trouble at school for shoving the boys or chasing the girls, but I thought it had to do with my ten brothers and sisters. My father could easily have bought one bike because he had money from his mechanic job at the British Petroleum company. But I suppose if Baba had bought me a bicycle, he'd have had to buy ten more, and he for sure couldn't afford that. He always reminded us how much it cost to put food in eleven mouths—twelve, if you counted Maman. Liquor made him more likely to demonstrate how bad our money problems were by shoving the person closest to him. So on the days he stopped for a drink on his way home from work, we all rushed to the dinner table in the courtyard; no one wanted to be last and have to sit next to him.

Money troubles were the reason why, in our family, playing was a sin. As soon as my brothers and sisters and I could walk, Baba put a rag in our hands and gave us jobs in his garage. That's where he worked on cars for extra cash. It wasn't a real auto shop with a lift or anything, and he barely had any tools besides what anyone else would have in their house—pliers and scissors and screwdrivers and a hammer. But he managed with salvaged parts from junked cars and by borrowing a real tool when he could, so neighbors came to him because he charged less than real shops and he could get the work done fast because of his free labor force.

One day my job was to grind the valves on an eight-cylinder carburetor head. Baba handed me a stiff wire and a piece of thin plastic, and told me to cover the wire tip with the plastic and scrape the valves clean with it. Normally, this is done with a power tool, but we did everything by hand. Before me was a pile of thirty-two valves crusted with who knows how many years of calcium crud. Of all us kids I was the only one who really did want to be a mechanic, so before I was even old enough to work, I used to watch and memorize Baba's movements around a car. He taught me that when the valves get dirty, they don't form a tight seal in the carburetor, so the engine will leak.

"The customer is coming for his car this evening, so every valve needs to be smooth by the time I get home," he said.

The heat inside the garage was like a snake charmer, coaxing vapor out of the oil spills on the floor. The sweet smell of grease hung in the air and sweat trickled between my shoulder blades as I stared out the door at the neighborhood kids on their bicycles. I didn't need a thermometer to know it was the hottest day of the year so far; all I had to do was squint my eyes to see waves ripple up from the earth, making my friends look like they were pedaling underwater.

The gunk on the valve stems was stubborn, and I couldn't get all of it off. I turned the tubes over and over, working each one, and in no time I had the hands of an old person, full of cramps. I could tell by the sun that half the afternoon was already gone and there was no way I would be able to finish by the time Baba returned. My only option was to use what little money I had from customer tips to hire some of the kids outside to help me. For the price of a *gaz* nougat candy each, I hired three helpers, but they were useless, wandering off when their hands started to ache. By the time Baba's shadow stretched from the doorway over to me, I had only cleaned half of the valves.

His dark eyes turned to pinpoints, and I could hear the breath coming out of his nose.

"This? This is it?"

"My hands hurt, Baba. And it's too hard with just this wire. I need a real tool."

He turned away from me and grabbed a grooved radiator belt from a peg in the wall.

"How about this tool?" he said, lifting it over his head.

At first I didn't understand what he meant. You can't clean a valve with a strip of rubber. Then he brought his arm down and the belt made a ripping noise through the air. When it laced across my back, it sounded like a wet fish slapping on the table. I inhaled sharply and for the first few seconds felt absolutely nothing, as if time had frozen in place. Then the pain, like a wolf scratching its claws across my back, woke my body, and a scream tore from my throat.

"Baba, no!"

"Is this tool good enough for you?"

I scrambled to my feet and ran for the door, but not fast enough. The belt sliced my back a second time. Baba followed me into the courtyard, his weapon a lasso now. The black loop whirled toward me again, and this time I reached for it, stopping it just before it lashed my head. I yanked back, and suddenly I was the one with the whip in my hands. I threw it with all my might onto the roof of the garage, out of his reach.

"You little . . ."

Baba ran toward me, and stupidly, I just stood there. When he kicked me square in the tailbone, the pain shot straight to my molars. I crumpled to the ground, unable to hold myself up on legs that no longer had any sensation. I could hear my mother's screams, but it sounded like she was deep at the bottom of a well. Or maybe I was in the well and she was high above, screaming for someone to get me out, but there was nobody to hear her. She was so tiny, and Baba was mightier than Godzilla and John Wayne put together. He walked right past her and picked up a wooden four-by-four to finish me off.

As I closed my eyes to wait for the impact, I heard someone running and shouting. It was Mostafa, the truck driver who lived next door, who wrapped his muscled arms around my father.

"What are you doing? He's just a twelve-year-old kid!" Mostafa hollered.

"Teaching him to be a man," Baba panted.

By now a crowd of neighbors had gathered. The last thing I saw before everything went black was my friend Ghaffor, standing near the water tank, pretending not to look.

That night when Maman rolled out the sleeping cots, I took my usual place between my two older sisters but asked them to please sleep close like books on a shelf so I wouldn't roll onto my back. Every time my tailbone touched anything, it felt like I had been kicked again. Sleep wouldn't come. But then I was overtaken by a floating feeling like being in a boat. Somewhere on this journey to nowhere, a beautiful girl joined me. She had a pleated white dress, and her golden hair caught the moonbeams and turned them into diamonds.

"What is your name?" I asked.

"I don't need one," she said.

She reached for my hands, and I could feel a message in her fingertips, a promise that she would protect me. I told her my name was Zahed.

"I'd like to call you Dadna," I said.

She didn't answer; she kissed me on the forehead and flew away.

When the swelling and bruises had gone down enough that I looked mostly like myself again, I ventured outside. I wanted Ghaffor to tell me what he had seen of the fight. I found him in his usual spot, sprawled out on a rug watching a Hollywood action movie on a TV that was buried in a cave of VHS tapes. Ghaffor was three years younger than me and still sucked his thumb. That was the only clean part of his body; the rest of him was always covered in a layer of dirt. Probably all that dust settled on him because he so rarely moved from his position in front of the TV's glow.

"You're not dead," he said, removing his thumb from his mouth.

"Maybe I'm back from the dead," I said, gingerly taking a seat next to him on the thick carpet. Ghaffor was adopted, and his new parents never hit him, not once. He didn't have to work on cars, and he knew all the names of the American celebrities because he studied movies all day. Ghaffor was smart; he had the kind of mind that could come up with ideas no one else had. From all those movies, he had learned many ways to kill someone and get away with it.

"The one who needs to be dead," I whispered, "is Baba."

He lowered his voice and looked at me sideways. His eyes were the color of honey.

"You can't kill anyone." He laughed. "You're too scrawny."

I stood in front of the TV so Ghaffor had to pay attention to me. I may have been small, but my mind was fierce, especially when I had decided to do something.

"What makes you think I won't steal a knife from the kitchen, wait until he falls asleep, and then stab him in the chest?"

"*Beee-cause* you are scrawny. And also, apparently, deaf and retarded."

I pounced on Ghaffor and we wrestled like tumbleweeds in a cowboy movie, rolling from wall to wall. I was about to win the match and force him to kiss my feet in apology, when he sank his teeth into my shoulder.

"Ow! That's not playing fair!" I shouted, hopping off him.

Ghaffor turned the TV volume up extra loud to hide our voices. Then he leaned in close and asked, "You really want to kill your dad?"

"God willing," I said, rubbing my shoulder.

"Scorpion tails boiled in his tea."

The plan was so smart, so simple, that I couldn't believe I hadn't thought of it. Scorpions were everywhere in Masjed Soleyman, hiding in the cracks of mud walls and holes in the ground. I nicked a pair of needle-nose pliers from Baba's workshop and spent the next couple days hunting at the dump pile. There was a curve in the road that was out of sight of the homes, and that's where people tossed all sorts of stuff they didn't want—old blankets and tires and rusty pieces of metal. The junk pile made for a nice, protected cave for scorpions, but when the sun went down and it started to cool down, the scorpions came skittering out to hunt. When the first black scorpion emerged, I clamped the pliers over its head and squeezed. When its body stopped moving and I was certain it was dead, I used the pliers to separate the tail, being careful not to touch it as I dropped it into a jar. After a couple hours, I had collected three tails. When I put them in boiling water, they came alive again, wriggling and bumping into each other, looking for their bodies. I added some tea, closed the lid, and let it stew.

It couldn't have been more than ten minutes, but the wait seemed endless. I thought of all the things I didn't say when Baba hit me, how all of us were living in fear of him, and that as the oldest boy in the family, it was my job to do something. He was getting older, weaker, and one day I would be too big for him to push around anymore. But I couldn't wait any longer. I was going to save my whole family from this misery now, because I was braver than Baba could ever imagine. Once he was gone, we were going to be a happy family like Ghaffor's. I'd free all of us from work so we could watch movies and play after school like normal kids.

I lifted the lid off the teapot and wrinkled my nose. The tails had turned a milky white, and the tea was cloudy. I strained the brew into a cup, put in a lump of sugar to mask any strange taste, and dumped the tails behind the fence. I arranged the pot and teacup on a tray, next to a small plate with sugar cubes, and delivered it like an English butler to my father as he bent over the open hood of a car. He stood up when he heard me approach and wiped his hands on a rag. His shoulders relaxed when he saw me with what he thought was a peace offering.

"Ah, I see you are ready to learn the proper way to grind a valve," he said, blowing his nose into the greasy rag.

He took one sip of the tea and frowned. "Tastes bad," he said, setting it down.

"Try more sugar," I suggested, dropping in another piece.

He swallowed a few more times and then returned the cup with a little bit of tea left in the bottom. "Still don't like it."

Baba turned his attention back to the car. I watched him tinker for a few minutes, and eventually he dropped his wrench. He cursed, bent over to pick it up, and then lost his balance, grabbing the bumper to break his fall. He swore again, and then put both hands on the engine to steady himself. Until this moment, my murder plan had been just a fantasy, like one of Ghaffor's movies. I didn't really think it would work, but fighting back against evil made me feel so good, like a superhero, that I didn't give much thought to what would happen if Baba actually died. But now that it was real, I wanted to rewind the tape. I needed more time to think about this. All of a sudden I could see there was a world of difference between being angry and being a murderer. When Baba turned to face me, his cheeks were an ashy color, like the tea, and he was sweating. He opened his mouth to say something, then collapsed. I screamed and ran to get Ghaffor.

"I changed my mind! Come quick, I changed my mind!"

Ghaffor and I raced to Baba's side, and Ghaffor put his ear to Baba's chest. Baba's breath was coming out in little wheezes, like it did when he was sleeping off too many beers.

"He's not dead yet."

I wanted to take everything back. Saving him would mean more beatings, but letting him die would mean my brothers and sisters would have no one to take care of them. I might not like Baba, but maybe some of my siblings did. It wasn't right for me to make this choice for them.

"What am I going to do?"

"Go get your mother," Ghaffor said.

"Are you crazy? Tell her that I poisoned Baba?"

"No, stupid. You leave that part out. Tell her he got bit by a scorpion. Hurry."

We were lucky that the hospital was only a five-minute drive away, because the doctor said Baba could have died if we'd waited much longer. They gave him medicine that stopped the venom, and he had to stay in the hospital for a month while they changed all his blood. While he was recovering, I would steal away to the top of the hill behind our house, where I had found a den dug by stray dogs. I crawled down into the dirt hole and cried as loud as I wanted, asking Baba to forgive me for my wickedness. I still didn't like Baba, but I liked the idea of being a boy without a father even less.

I tried to be good after that. At school, I stopped pulling the girls' hair so much and tried to pay more attention in class. When I raised my hand to answer the teacher's question once, she looked stunned, as if I had suddenly turned into a chicken.

One day my class let out early after morning tests, and as I neared the house, I saw Baba scurry out of the storage shed and into his car, the tires kicking up pebbles as he stepped on the gas. I crept into the shed to see if I could tell what he had been doing. I scanned the shelves and my gaze stopped on the gramophone, with its brass speaker shaped like a trumpet. It had been moved from its usual spot two shelves lower. Upon further examination, I saw that the screws holding it together were loose—another sign that some guiding force was directing me to take it apart.

Inside was more money than I had ever seen, a pile of purple bills—rials—with the face of Mohammad Reza Shah and his father on them. Each rial note was worth about one and a half American dollars. And there were more than I could count, maybe more than a thousand of them. Underneath the bills I found gold rings, a watch, and a fistful of coins. My mouth watered at the idea of finally being able to buy sugar crystal candy sticks after school with the other kids. But if I took too much, Baba would surely notice, so I just took one bill. I put everything back just as it was, stashed the money in my pocket, and walked toward town, my brain beginning to work on the delicious problem of how to spend it.

I knew I couldn't buy myself a gift, because as soon as anything new came into the house, the whole family had to inspect and discuss it. I needed a temporary luxury. I wandered with the bounce of freedom in my stride until I reached the cinema, where I stopped in front of a movie poster. They were showing *Sholay*, the Indian action film about a sheriff who seeks revenge against the bandit who murdered his family by hiring two petty criminals to kill him.

"I heard the girl in that movie does a belly dance."

I turned around and saw Ali, my friend from school.

"Oh yeah?" I asked.

"Yeah. She does it barefoot. On broken glass."

She was on the poster: A dark-haired beauty with her hands crossed above her head and dozens of bracelets tracing her arms. She was flanked by the two heroes, one in a white suit and the other in a black muscle T-shirt, both brandishing rifles. Behind them was a wall of roaring orange flames.

I peeled the bill from my front pocket and let Ali get a good, long look. "You coming inside?" I asked.

After purchasing our tickets, we strode to the snack counter.

"Give us four shawarmas and four Coca-Colas," I said, acting like I said these sorts of things all the time. It was a little disappointing when the clerk didn't even blink.

We went to our seats, and I sank back into the seat cushions and inhaled the steam coming off our lamb sandwiches, letting the cinema lull me with color and music and the promise that for the next three hours, I was a boy with zero problems. After the first showing, we hid in the bathroom and returned to the theater to watch it again. Right in the middle of one of the best scenes, the gunfight on top of a moving train, the volume suddenly went up and the gunfire got louder. I looked at Ali to see if he had noticed anything, but he was absorbed in the shootout.

"Did you feel that?" I asked.

"What?"

"My seat. It's shaking."

Suddenly a slice of yellow light interrupted the dark of the theater, and everyone started shouting at once and running for the doors. Ali and I ran with the crowd, gathering more runners as we went. I heard someone say that the Iraqi planes had been aiming for the oil refinery but missed and hit my elementary school next door instead. Parents called out the names of their children as they ran, and begged Allah to spare them. It was about three in the afternoon, and school was already out for the day, but often kids stayed to do homework or play soccer. Was there a soccer match today? I tried to remember, but my mind wasn't working. In my panic, I couldn't even recall what day of the week it was.

We made it to the edge of the soccer field, and then we saw it. From this distance it looked like ants were crawling over a burning hill, there were so many people running in all directions. My school was smashed, with flames shooting out of it. Some kids were rolling on the ground to get the fire off them; others were walking around dazed. I looked closer and saw that some of my classmates would never be getting up off the ground again.

The Iraqis had been dropping bombs on Masjed Soleyman for about a year, and I was getting used to seeing buildings broken into pieces, hearing the ambulances and the women wailing. I had learned to step around puddles of blood. But now it seemed as if Saddam Hussein was aiming his guns right at me.

"A curse on you and all the Arabs!" I shouted.

Ali tugged at my elbow and said, "C'mon, let's go home. Your curses won't help anybody."

I ran to my street and was relieved to find Ghaffor and Mostafa's son Omid out on their bicycles. Maman saw me first, and she came running out the door and collected me in her arms, as if I was a baby. I tried to squirm out, not wanting my friends to see her smoothing my hair and kissing me on the cheeks. But I'm embarrassed to say that I almost started crying with her. Something about being held that way made me think of how easily it could have been my body that was blown apart. Some of my classmates would never feel their mother's breath on their faces again. I stopped wriggling and let myself go limp into the softness of her embrace. For the briefest of moments, my racing brain paused.

"Thank you, blessed Allah, you are safe," she said, whisking me into the house. "We were so worried; we looked for you at the school. Where *were* you?"

She set me down, and the coins jangled in my pants pocket. In the panic of the afternoon, I'd forgotten to get rid of the evidence.

"I was j-just out walking," I stammered.

"Well, go wash up. Dinner is almost ready. We're all accounted for, so we might as well eat."

Baba gave me a look that let me know I'd hear more about this later, and gestured for me to sit down. Maman poured me a glass of *doogh*, and the carbonated water and yogurt soothed my throat, which was dry from sprinting home. She set a plate of lamb, grilled tomatoes, and rice before me, and I pretended I was ravenous. My sister Leyla eyed me suspiciously, the beginnings of a smile pulling at the corners of her mouth.

"So, Zahed, if you weren't in school today, where were you living it up?" she asked.

"Swallow your tongue!" Maman hissed.

But Leyla wouldn't let it go.

"I'm surprised you still have an appetite, after eating so much at the cinema," Leyla said, her eyes triumphant. The neighborhood kids must have told her already, and she was obviously jealous that I hadn't invited her. You could never keep a secret in Masjed Soleyman, not even if you tied a rock to it and threw it deep into the bottom of the Karun River. I shot her hot daggers with my eyes.

Before I could stop her, Leyla reached into my pants pocket and tossed the coins I'd stolen on the table. They landed with a sickening clunk.

Baba jumped to his feet and slapped me, and my fork went flying. At the same instant, I wet my pants.

"Tell me where this came from, right now," he boomed. "And if you lie, I'll brand you."

I pleaded with my eyes to Maman, but to her, thieves were lower than worms.

"Did you hear that?" she shouted. "We'll brand you!"

I opened my mouth . . . and lied. It was the weakest, most half-hearted, unoriginal thing I could muster: "Leyla is lying."

I felt myself being dragged to the kitchen by the back of my shirt and heard the gas stove ignite. While Baba held me down, he ordered Maman to bring him a kebab skewer. He held it in the flame until it glowed red, as I thrashed, trying to break free. But I was a fly caught in a jar, frantically slamming into the glass with no chance of escape.

"You stupid idiot! You think you can lie to me? Where did you steal this? You know what happens to thieves? They get their hands cut off!"

I screamed as he brought the skewer toward me and Maman begged him to stop, but Baba was so mad his ears had shut down. The burn was coming, I knew that, so I covered my face with my hands and clenched my teeth. Then I heard the sizzle and felt a sharp sting on the outside of my left ankle, and I let out a howl like a desert jackal's. That's the last thing I remember—that my voice sounded not like mine but like an animal's.

When I awoke, I was in a strange bed. Not a hospital bed, but some-one else's. I stood on my good foot and hopped over to the wall to look at the framed photos. I was in our neighbor Mostafa's house. I hopped back to bed and passed out from the pain. I don't know how long I was asleep—minutes, days, weeks—when the door jostled and I ducked under the covers, terrified it might be Baba.

"Zahed."

A woman's voice. I peeked out to find Mostafa's wife, Fatemah, and Omid with a tray of food. The kindness made me embarrassed, and my tears came before I could hide them.

"You did a bad thing, but your mother and father did something worse," she said, laying a warm hand on my shoulder. "Your parents and I have discussed it, and we think you should live with us for a while."

She was pretty, like Raquel Welch times a thousand. My mouth was so dry, but I managed a raspy "Thank you." My wish to be safe was stronger than my wish not to be pitied. Omid stayed behind as I nibbled at the rice.

"That was stupid to steal from your father," he said. I shrugged my shoulders. There was nothing to say, anyway. Everyone knew what went on in my house. I gave up on the rice, and Omid took my tray and then turned back in the door frame. "Don't worry. If you are lonely, tell me, and I will bring my mattress and sleep in this room with you."

When my foot eventually healed, Mostafa asked if I'd like to help him make deliveries in his truck. School was still closed because of the bombing, so I had nothing better to do. His trips sometimes were as long as three weeks, hauling produce and construction supplies between the ports and the major cities. I always wondered what adventures he was having on the road in his red Mack truck and what it would be like to sleep in the bunk beds in the cabin behind the driver's seat. I could hear that truck's rumble coming from way down the street, and loved watching Mostafa part the sea of kids with it, its radiator grille gleaming like shark teeth.

Mostafa tugged at his mustache as he waited for me to speak. He had tanned skin and a rough beard, yet eyes that were kind and welcoming. He kept his hair long, and started each morning before the mirror carefully combing it to the side with oil that smelled like mangoes. I always thought he would make a good judge, because he had a face that people automatically trusted. I told him that I wanted to see what there was in the world beyond Masjed Soleyman. That I would do anything to put distance between my father and me.

We left the next day for Bandar Abbas, a port city on the Strait of Hormuz, fourteen hours away. We stopped in several cities along the way to pick up and deliver water pipes and concrete and shipping containers. My job was to help Mostafa tie our cargo down with straps, to change the cassette tapes, and to fry onions and meat on a camp stove propped between my feet on the passenger side. That first night, after I ran out of jobs and darkness took away the view, I lulled myself to sleep watching a silver necklace with the word *Allah* sway from the rearview mirror. I only woke when the truck grumbled to a halt. When I opened my eyes, Mostafa was pouring bottled water over his face, arms, and feet and scrubbing with a towel.

"Where are we?"

"Time to pray," he said.

"What?"

He went to the sleeping cabin and unrolled a small rectangular carpet, kneeled down on it, and indicated for me to do the same next to him.

"That's the doorway to Allah's house in Mecca," he said, pointing to an archway woven into the silk fibers. "Your head goes there."

"That's OK; you go ahead," I said. I watched him recite Arabic verses from the Koran and kneel forward, placing his head on a small, round piece of clay. We had never prayed in my house, and I didn't understand a word he was saying, but whatever he was doing, he looked like he really meant it. In the distance, I heard a wolf howl. The night was so, so black, and I said my own secret prayer for Mostafa to hurry up so we could get back on the road. My prayer was answered in about ten minutes.

"Talk to me so I can stay awake," Mostafa said as he accelerated through the gears.

"OK," I said, but I couldn't think of a thing to say. Instead I just fiddled with my slingshot. "Why do you pray like that?" I asked finally.

"I was not always a good Muslim, Zahed."

"Mmmm?"

"I was a man without God. So I know things that, if I tell you, will save you a lot of trouble. Listen to me; I never want to see you smoking, doing drugs, or gambling. I do not want you to do anything wrong, so you must pray."

I wasn't so sure about religion, but I respected Mostafa. He bought me clothes and shoes. And he gave me a small salary for helping him with deliveries. He treated me like a son, so I listened to his stories from the Koran and from the Bible. Mostly they were boring, but I did like the ones about the Prophet Solomon because that guy could speak to animals and control the wind.

"Zahed, if somebody steals from you, you should forgive them because they might have been in need. If someone speaks behind your back, say nothing because you must be the bigger person. When you fall in love, give all your heart to your beloved and don't ever doubt."

Maybe he was trying to tell me that he understood why I stole from Baba. I wasn't sure, but I nodded anyway.

"But if someone hurts your feelings intentionally, be merciless!" he said.

"Merciless!" I shouted, pulling the rubber back on my slingshot and pretending to aim at his temple. In one swift move he whisked my weapon from my grasp and hid it under his enormous thigh.

"Be careful with that thing," he said.

Over the next year, I watched him pray several times a day. I wasn't sure if I would keep my promise to pray, but I was certain of this: I felt happy with Mostafa and wanted to be with him. And where else was I going to go? It didn't look like my school was coming back anytime soon, unless you counted the tent where students were now supposed to pick up math and grammar worksheets and do them on their own. No classmates I knew even bothered. My life was better now, traveling with Mostafa, but how much longer could I keep saying thank you—for the meals, for the clothes, and for the lessons from the Koran? Eventually I would need a future that was my own. How would I ever become a man if I was always somebody's sidekick?

One day our route took us to a military camp near Darkhovin, close to the Iran-Iraq border, where soldiers were fighting. I still didn't understand why Saddam Hussein and Ayatollah Khomeini had started the war almost eighteen months before. Khomeini said we were in a jihad against Iraq to save Islam, but I didn't have much use for a holy war. The battle was something adults talked about into the night, but to me it was something out there, something make-believe, like *Sholay*. Now I was going to see it for myself. We were going to visit a real battle zone to deliver produce and bullets to the Basij, a militia of volunteer boy soldiers, some of whom were thirteen, the same age as me.

I had no idea they'd be carrying Kalashnikovs, semiautomatic pistols, and even machine guns, but there they were, walking as casually as if they were carrying a book. I felt like a little boy next to them. They had hard jaws already, but when one looked me in the eye as I handed him a box of ammunition, I tried to start a conversation by asking his name.

"What do you want from me?" he replied. His voice was fast and direct, like a boxer landing punches.

"How did you come to the front?" I asked.

"I forged a permission letter from my father."

"That's it?"

He nodded.

"In the village, I was nothing. This," he said, sweeping his hand over the cluster of barracks encircled by barbed wire, "this is where my life finally started."

I couldn't get that soldier out of my mind after that. It took Mostafa and me almost a week to get back, and when we finally reached the house, I practically flung myself out of the passenger-side door. Omid was eagerly awaiting my report from the front lines. I told him about the rows of tents and campfires, the hundreds of boys who already had muscles and mean stares, and described the guns in fearsome detail. For good measure, I threw in a few explosions that didn't actually happen.

His eyes widened, and he admitted that he already had a secret plan to run away and join the Basij. It was all I needed to hear. I leaned toward Omid and lowered my voice: "Why don't we leave tomorrow?"

TWO

NAJAH

I didn't need an alarm clock to wake me up at four in the morning; the army trained me to sleep with one eye open, at the ready. At least I could thank the military for that. Oh, and the relentless jogging in formation and hiking into the mountains of Kurdistan had turned my body into something I could count on. Otherwise, eight tedious years patrolling the Iraqi border for opium smugglers was a duty that was finally, joyfully receding into my past.

I was a free man now, at twenty-six. And my kingdom was Shula, one of the crummiest neighborhoods of Baghdad, where in 1979 cars were still brought to a standstill by muddy potholes in the rainy season and family wealth was determined by which households could afford shoes. But in the predawn before you could really see it, Shula was almost beautiful.

Guided by moonlight, I walked down the middle of the dirt road, my arms wrapped around a fifty-pound bowl of uncooked falafel paste my sister Samera had prepared the night before. By now, I knew the way to her husband's restaurant by sound and smell. I followed the incense wafting from the homes toward the low murmurings of the men bowing inside the mosque for the predawn prayer, then took a left at the scent of fish-shaped *samoon* loaves baking, then a right at the sound of the trickling wastewater in the open trenches lining the street. The shushing of the date palm fronds in the breeze told me I was near the bus stop, which meant only a few more steps to reach my castle.

The metal retracting door clacked as I pushed it up, and with a flick of a switch the outdoor floodlight lit up the deserted street like a theater stage. That sudden explosion of light was the best part of my daily routine, like an invisible emcee promoting a show to an audience that had yet to arrive: "Ladies and gentlemen, I give you Najah Aboud and his Bruce Lee Restaurant!"

There was no name on the awning, but customers had started calling it that after I redecorated the walls with Bruce Lee movie posters. Men and schoolboys alike were taken with the martial arts hero, and the posters of him twirling nunchucks and flexing his abs were good for business. Long after they finished their falafel sandwiches, people stayed late into the night drinking rivers of tea and rehashing the plots of *Fist of Fury* or *Enter the Dragon*. Having seen all of Bruce Lee's movies, I was only too happy to join in.

That wasn't the only change I made since my brother-in-law handed me the keys and offered me half the profits if I would save this albatross on a dead-end street. All this place needed was a few fresh ideas—and breakfast.

I set the falafel down in the kitchen and turned on the propane burners to heat water for tea. I slid a tape in the cassette player, and the speakers crackled with the lulling sound of a man's voice reciting the Koran. This cheap tape was my fishing lure, drawing the hungry faithful out of the mosques after their early morning prayer. It also worked on people waiting at the bus stop, soldiers on their way to duty, and the insomniacs. It didn't take long before even the classier people from the side of town with paved streets began crossing the park to pick up a few sandwiches before they caught their shuttle bus to jobs at the airport and government offices downtown.

"Hey, *Basrawi*, need some help?"

I looked over my shoulder and saw one of my regulars—a neighborhood boy who sometimes helped me prepare breakfast in exchange for a meal. Nobody knew my real name; I was just "the guy from Basra."

"You'd be a great help, son, if you pulled the tables outside," I said. "The village woman should be here any minute."

The baker came in next, asking me how many loaves of samoon I'd need that day. I'd doubled the bread order since I took over a couple months before, but I was starting to run out again before closing time.

"Give me a thousand."

He cocked an eyebrow and put his hands on his hips.

"I can give you all I've got now, but I'll have to bake more."

"How about if I pay you in advance, for your trouble?" I offered.

Like clockwork, the old woman appeared at four fifteen, carrying a huge bowl of clotted water buffalo cream. My young helper stacked a pyramid of flaky *kahi* pastry next to her *geymar* cream and then fetched a jar of honey and the teapot. My breakfast menu followed one simple rule: give the people what they want. And everybody loves geymar and kahi, the comfort food they grew up eating. The boy barely had time to get the teacups on the table before hands began grabbing breakfast.

I hustled back to the kitchen to brew more tea, and while it was heating, I brought a falafel sandwich to the village woman to thank her for the geymar. She always tried to refuse, but I never let her. She had a beautiful daughter, after all.

After the breakfast rush, I turned on the radio news, just in time for the retirees who were waking up and wanting to find out the latest reports about the Iranian Revolution. There were a lot of hot words flying between Iraq and Iran these days, now that Saddam Hussein and Ayatollah Khomeini were each in charge of their own country. Like all the rulers who came before them, they were arguing about their shared border or, more precisely, over control of the Shatt al-Arab waterway, where the Tigris and the Euphrates came together and flowed as one down to the Persian Gulf. Whoever controlled that joint flow controlled the ships that carried Middle East oil to the rest of the world. And oil was power, and power was money. Now the two lifetime enemies were stirring up ancient ethnic and religious rivalries to try to intimidate the other into giving up claims to that precious waterway.

The war of words consumed my customers, but I tried my best to ignore it. I'd done my time in the military and was trying to enjoy life as an apolitical civilian. When the talk got too political, I took refuge in the kitchen. The Baathists had spies everywhere, and you never knew who was listening. Saddam made this perfectly clear just days after he became president. He called a televised meeting of several hundred of the most senior government people in Iraq, then announced he'd uncovered a plot against his regime. He ordered an informant to take the podium, and the man read aloud the names of the conspirators who were sitting in the audience. One by one, the accused were led, shaking and sweating, out of the room by the secret police, while Saddam chuckled. I don't know if those men are alive or dead, and I don't want to know. But everyone saw the video, and the implication of it was loud enough to silence a culture that used to revel in political debate. Fear was the cement that held people together now. I'd even heard stories of children turning in their own parents for treason.

I was pulling a sack of chickpea flour out of the storage closet when my older sister Samera arrived for her shift.

"Your produce girl is here," she said.

I dropped the sack right where I stood and brushed the dust from my shirt.

"Do I look OK?" I whispered.

She rolled her eyes and went back to chopping cucumbers. I grabbed a falafel sandwich from the counter and smoothed my hair. This time the produce girl had a box of eggplants, and I could tell she chose them carefully. Not one was bruised or wrinkled.

"These were the rejects; my father was just going to throw them away," she said, pushing the box toward me. "Take them."

"I must give you something," I said, brushing my fingertips against hers as I handed her the sandwich.

Her smile faded quickly. Something was wrong.

"I overheard some girls at the marketplace," she whispered. "Are you seeing other girls besides me?"

I had to think quickly. There were several girls who flirted with me, and they were all pretty; it was hard to choose only one. I talked to many girls, and yes, sometimes I held their hands or touched their hair in the privacy of the supply closet. But nothing more. I knew not to ruin their reputations or put them in danger with their male relatives. Women were not allowed to talk to men outside the family, but as a shopkeeper I could get around that somewhat. I was pushing the boundaries, sure, but I had been in the military so long that I had missed out on some things like the scent of a woman. I was doing my best to catch up quickly.

"That sounds like a pretty big story," I said. "I'm perfectly happy talking to you."

"Only me?"

"Only, only," I said. A line was starting to form behind her. I winked at her, and she blushed and scurried out the front door. Crisis averted, I retreated to the safety of the kitchen with the box of eggplants. But it wasn't a true sanctuary—Samera was waiting for me with accusation in her eyes.

"Don't mess this up, Najah," she said, pointing the knife at me. "That girl is our secret ingredient."

The falafel at Bruce Lee Restaurant had a purple hue and a smoky flavor that customers said they couldn't find anywhere else. That's because one day I thought I could stretch the product by chopping the eggplant skins and putting them in the falafel instead of the trash. I wasn't trying for a new culinary twist on falafel, but suddenly I had a secret ingredient that added a dash of mystique to my sandwiches and helped me save a little money. Samera was right; it was good to keep the produce girl happy.

Nobody was more surprised than me that I had a natural talent for business. Of all eight kids, I was the one who didn't walk or talk until age three. I skipped class to go fishing or to play soccer so often that my parents finally gave up and let me drop out after elementary school. Now, to everyone's utter shock, I was supporting the family. I kept two big plastic containers under the counter, one for bills and the other for coins.

After we closed the restaurant at midnight, Samera and I used cups to scoop all the money into two equal piles. We cleared nearly eight hundred dollars a day. It was more money than I'd ever known, and when I looked at it, I had that same sensation of total protection I felt as a child holding my father's hand as we crossed the street, like I had an invisible force field surrounding me. Even after paying for rent and supplies, there was enough to send to my divorced father in Basra to clothe and feed my five younger siblings, to hire four employees, and to buy myself suits and a Rolex watch. Then I did something I'd only dreamed about. I took my first vacation.

Casablanca lived up to its reputation—I walked off the plane and into a swirling bazaar of delicacies, of both the edible and the female kind. I wore a tight suit with wide lapels, just like John Travolta, and bought drinks at the bar for everyone around me. The Moroccan women I met were extremely generous with their time and attention. They didn't cover their heads with hijabs or concern themselves with family honor, which was all right with me. I danced and dined and kissed a different girl each night, like a prophet in paradise.

In fact, I was contemplating extending my vacation by a second month when I turned on the TV news in my rented apartment one morning and discovered that I was suddenly a wanted man. Saddam had ordered all Iraqi men outside the country who were of fighting age to return immediately, which included those born in 1952 like me. The Iraqi government was getting increasingly worried that the Islamic Revolution in Iran would spill over the border and create a similar Shia uprising against the Baathist ruling party. Peace envoys from the United Nations had been trying to calm both sides, but it backfired into a buildup for war. My legs gave out, and I sank back onto the bed. For a fleeting second, I fantasized about staying in Morocco, where no one could find me. But the government could find my family, and I could never live with myself if they were harmed because of me. I had no choice but to defend my country. But I was getting ahead of myself. Being called back to Iraq wasn't the same thing as being conscripted. Maybe I'd get lucky; maybe the military wouldn't call my name for active duty. I packed my dancing shoes and caught an early flight back to Baghdad.

When I returned to the restaurant, there was less laughter inside. It was as if everyone could smell the war coming. There were clues everywhere, in the form of little annoyances, beginning with the shelves emptying in the supply closet. My usual vendors were coming up short, and I'd have to travel to three or four different places to get enough propane or chickpea flour. Then the electricity started cutting out sporadically and we had to keep the restaurant open with candlelight. As more and more men were called to duty, the lines at my counter grew shorter. Every day more military jeeps passed by my restaurant's glass storefront. The final blow was the air raid siren. There I'd be, up to my elbows in falafel paste, and the long wail would sound, spiraling higher and faster in tone, and all my customers would flee to the mosque or one of the public underground bunkers. I turned off the lights and locked the doors and stayed with my restaurant, like a captain with his ship. I sequestered myself in the pantry, where I had a lot of time to think about the future—a future without propane. No flame, no falafel.

I loved this restaurant more than I'd loved any woman. I only left it to catch four hours of sleep a night, yet I never ran out of energy. These walls fed me, clothed me, and gave me the education I never finished, as I listened to my customers hold forth on an encyclopedia of topics. Bruce Lee Restaurant was where I made sense. I had believed this little nothing of a falafel shop was going to take care of my entire family long past the time when we all had grandchildren of our own. Now, if I stayed and watched my restaurant crumble around me, regret would coat me like a second skin. I could get out now with some money saved, or watch everything I'd earned slip from my hands. The choice was obvious. I locked the door, returned the keys to my brother-in-law, and took a bus back to my father's house in Basra. By the time I arrived, I had a migraine from clenching my jaw to keep from crying.

The only solace was that my father truly needed me. Newly divorced, he was exhausting himself working his nine-to-five job overseeing shipments at the port while also raising my five younger siblings. My first errand of each day was to get up before dawn and fetch fresh bread for my brothers and sisters. The two lines outside the bakery window—one for men, one for women—started queuing as early as three thirty in the morning. There was a system. One male would approach the window, hand over coins, and take a package of steaming bread. Then a female took her turn, and so on. It was safer for the women this way; they wouldn't be harassed by the men or be seen talking to them in public.

One morning, a flash of red caught my eye. I snuck a glance over to the women's line, and although it was still dark and all the women were covered, except for their faces, in ankle-length black abayas, I could see one teenage girl had a crimson dress under hers. She had tossed part of her cloak casually over her forearm to reveal a bit of her legs and a peek of that red fabric.

I lit a cigarette and tried to look cool, tilting my head back and blowing a stream of smoke straight into the air. I did this a few times and then snuck another glance. Playfully, she waved imaginary smoke away from her face. Or did she? Maybe it was only a mosquito.

The line was moving, but we stayed in lockstep, thirty feet apart from each other. Curiosity curled around my neck and squeezed; I wanted to see her face. When a car drove past, I waited until its headlights crossed her body then turned all the way to face her. And she let me gaze. Her beauty was suspended in that momentary portal between child and woman; her cheekbones were just beginning to protrude from the round cheeks of a girl. Her olive skin looked untouched, and the ripeness of her held an intoxicating collision of innocence and power that she didn't yet know she had. She gazed back for a brief second and then cast her eyes downward. I shivered, suddenly realizing I was sweating in the cold morning air. Looking at her, all the girls I thought I'd loved fell out of my heart.

"Sir? Sir? Sir! You're next!"

I reached through the window for three loaves of warm bread. When I turned around, she had vanished back into the darkness.

When I spotted her the next morning, she was chatting with her girlfriends and didn't seem the least bit aware of me. I felt like an idiot, mistaking her swatting at mosquitoes for romance. But before I gave up hope, I had to try one last signal to be sure, so I pretended to run my fingers through my hair and gave her a quick wave. As I waited for a response, my left leg started to jiggle uncontrollably. Then, out of the corner of my eye, I saw her adjust her abaya behind her ear to reveal a bit of her dark hair. The movement seemed innocuous, but just before she dropped her hand she quickly waved back.

Salaam, habibi!

We spoke for the next four months in our silent language, through invisible gestures only lovers can see. We both began showing up earlier and earlier to the bakery line so we could extend our sightings. Eventually I was able to distinguish her cloaked form from a distance, to pick her out from a group of women walking to the bakery just by her gait and the way she held her body. Even though we had to keep our distance, it felt like our souls left our bodies and danced together between the bread lines. When one of us was late to the bakery, we'd arrive to find worry lines on the other's brow.

I spent my nights staring at the ceiling, trying to figure out a way to speak to her. There were only two acceptable ways I could initiate a conversation: if she were a member of my family or if her father had granted me her hand in marriage. But I didn't even know her name or where she lived. If she were caught talking with me, it would be a huge stain on her and on her family's honor; the only women who talked to strange men were prostitutes. Approaching her would be considered a crime, the same as if I broke a window in her house and snatched her. There were plenty of men and women in Basra who had inexplicably vanished after breaking these community rules. The risk was simply too high.

So I didn't plan any of what happened next. One morning, I lingered after I got my bread and watched her start walking back toward her house. Just before the morning darkness swallowed my vision of her, I took a step, then another, and without considering the consequences,

I found myself following her. I stayed three blocks behind, my senses heightened like an animal's, listening for the sound of her footsteps and the swish of her abaya to guide me. Just as she rounded a corner, her fingers flashed out of her cloak and beckoned me forward. As I approached the corner, I heard a voice.

"This way."

Did I really hear that? I slowed down, unsure of what to do. A thousand thoughts fired off at once, and now that the moment I'd imagined was truly coming, I was completely unprepared. Should I say hello? Hug her? Kiss her? Turn around and run?

I rounded the corner and nearly knocked her down. She grabbed my arms to stop her fall and backed into the secluded breezeway of an office building. I could only make out the white of her teeth.

"Oh! Sorry. I mean, hello," I stammered.

"You keep looking at me at the bakery," she said. "Are you married?"

"Are you?" I asked.

We heard a noise, and I glanced down the street toward a row of cinder-block houses. A light went on in one of them.

"We can't talk here, it's not safe for you," I said. "Follow me."

I led her to the walled courtyard of my father's home, where we could talk under the enormous date palm, away from public view. Nobody in my family woke up before the sun, so we were safe.

"What do you want from me?" she whispered.

She was direct. I liked that.

"I fell in love with you."

She looked away and thought about this for a moment.

"How do I know you aren't just going to play with me and then deceive me?"

Her eyes were black and piercing. I knew then that I could never gloss over the truth with this one. She'd catch me immediately.

"I've been just looking at you for months now, and I've fallen in love with you," I repeated.

She kept staring, clearly waiting for something more convincing. I was giving her a nonanswer, and she was having none of it.

"Your eyes alone are worth more to me than the whole universe," I said. I know it sounded like a line, like something I'd used on girls at the falafel shop. But I really meant it.

She smiled and reached for my hand. Her fingers were soft, like butterflies landing on my palm. I imagined those fingers tickling the back of my neck, fluttering down my spine, and I felt myself swell with desire for her and it was all I could do not to wrap my arms around her. Instead I plucked a fraying thread from a blanket drying on the clothing line. I tied it around her ring finger.

"This is your wedding band; it's temporary until I bring you a real gold engagement ring."

She twirled the string and turned her hand to look at it from all angles. Then she pulled me down to sit with her at the base of the tree and rested her head on my shoulder.

"Close your eyes."

I obeyed.

"I am in our home, and you just came home from work," she said. "What have I made you for dinner?"

I saw it, too. She and I, sitting on the ground before a low table filled with all our favorite foods.

"Falafel," I said. "Pickled beets, baba ghanoush, dates."

We continued that way, describing all the rooms in the house and the views from those rooms, even imagining what the birds sounded like in the morning. When I felt a light hit my face, I opened my eyes to see that the first of the sun's rays were pushing through the palm fronds. People were stirring in the house, and we could be caught if she didn't leave right away. I took her hand and helped her to stand. She readjusted her abaya, brushed the dirt from it, and smiled at me.

"Are you coming to the bakery tomorrow? Shall I wait for you again?"

"I will come," I whispered.

The only ones who knew about our daily four a.m. strolls were the stray dogs and the pigeons. Each morning after we bought our bread,

Alyaa and I walked with the moonlight casting shadows behind us, and by the time our shadows had circled all the way to the front of us, we parted. I learned that she was nineteen and lived with her mother, who was blind in one eye. Her father had died in the army fighting the Kurds when she was a baby, and she had one brother who had joined the military. Her family had already chosen a husband for her, a thirty-five-year-old civil servant with a hefty family inheritance. But it was me she loved.

Without a father at home, I'd have to negotiate with Alyaa's mother for her hand in marriage. It was a long shot; the family had already promised Alyaa to that other man. When I told my mother that I had found a neighborhood girl I wanted to marry, she was against the idea, saying the war made it a terrible time to get married. What if I was called to duty and then widowed a new bride? Besides, she argued, I had brothers and sisters who needed me to take care of them. Her hypocrisy was not lost on me; Mother was remarried and had started a new family with three more children. Frustrated, I decided to ask my father for help.

But a mother's intuition is spooky. The very next day my father called to say he'd heard on the radio that all men born in 1952 and 1953 were to report to the military recruitment office.

The war had come to get me. And there was no place to run. I would be taken to military court and jailed if I refused, and my family could be hurt if I fled. But if I didn't fight, the Iranians could push into Basra and kill my family anyway. My responsibility was to protect them, to protect my country and help end this war.

The reports on the radio said that Iran's military was a chaotic mess, because one of Khomeini's first orders had been to oust all of the Shah's top military men, and he hadn't had time to reorganize by the time fighting started two months before. Our ground forces had already occupied about ten thousand square miles of Iranian soil along the southern half of the border. We had control of several oil-rich cities in Khuzestan. Saddam Hussein was even offering a ceasefire, in exchange for full control of the Shatt al-Arab waterway. Many were predicting that Iraq would win the war in a matter of weeks. My stomach knotted at the thought of having to go back to the mind-numbing tedium and stink of the army, but I clung to the hope that there would be nothing left to do by the time I finished my training.

I wore my military uniform to the bread line the next morning and chain-smoked to settle my nerves. Worse than having to give my life over to the military again was having to disappoint Alyaa. I was antsy and irritable and didn't want to buy bread. What was the point anymore? I watched her wait in line until she reached the customer window, then lost my nerve and started walking back home. She followed. I reached the courtyard ahead of her and just partially shut the door, only half-hoping she would turn back. When her shadow crossed into the courtyard, I swung open the door and she fell into my arms, sobbing.

"Are you going to leave me?" she cried.

"I have no choice."

I lifted her hand and checked. The string was still there. I held her face in my hands and brought her close.

"Listen. I'm never leaving you. Our love is bigger than whatever our families say, bigger than this war."

She caressed my hands and carefully kissed each of my fingers.

"You can't die," she said.

"We only have to wait a little longer, and when the fighting is over in a month or two, I will come back to marry you."

I tilted her head toward me and kissed her for the first time. I had anticipated tasting something sweet, like berries, but instead her lips were salty, from her tears. But that tang conducted an electrical charge that zinged from our mouths through my whole body. Every one of my follicles sizzled.

"Promise?" she asked.

I kissed the string on her finger.

"Promise."

THREE

CHILD SOLDIER

We listened until we heard Mostafa crank the faucet for his morning shower. Omid went out first, saying he was going to wash the windows of his father's truck. I waited until his mother turned toward the stove again, and then I slipped along the wall like the shadow of a passing cloud, then floated through the washroom and out the door. I ran to Mostafa's truck and found Omid wiping a towel in lazy circles on the windshield. He threw down the towel and jumped off the hood when he saw me.

"Got the letters?" he asked.

I patted my waistband. Omid had always been a better student than me; he was always using big words and trying to sound all high-class, and his handwriting already looked grown-up. Me, I was good at forging signatures. Together we created foolproof permission letters from our parents, allowing us to join the war. We were too young to join the regular military, of course, or Khomeini's new Islamic Revolutionary Guard. But the Basij was the people's militia, welcome to anybody who wanted to volunteer, especially boys like us. I took one last glance toward Omid's house and made sure no one was watching us.

"Don't wimp out now," Omid said.

I slugged him, but not hard, on the shoulder and took off running.

We jogged together toward the mosque. Since the war began eighteen months before, all the mosques had become recruitment centers for the Basij. As we passed by the rubble of what used to be our school, Omid fixed his gaze on the twisted rebar and concrete and roared, "Farideh, this is for you!" I was confused for a second and then I remembered: There was a shy girl in class who always used to peek at Omid through her long eyelashes. I didn't think he cared, but apparently he did. The way his voice rattled with rage, it now seemed quite possible that he loved her; maybe he'd even privately chosen Farideh for his future wife. Normally, I would have teased him about this. But now, it didn't seem right. Out of respect, I stood next to him, silently, until he decided it was time to continue on.

We heard the mosque before we saw it. Now, in addition to the daily calls to prayer, the loudspeakers played revolutionary fight songs. As we got closer, we could make out the lyrics: "If you want the privilege of meeting Imam Husayn, you join the jihad to liberate the holy city of Karbala. You will join the martyrs and ensure your place in paradise."

There was a knot of people pushing to get inside the mosque. Omid and I elbowed our way through the crowd, slipping between legs and dodging other boys doing the same. I guess the Basij took men too old or broken to join the regular army, too, because I saw men with gray hair and hunched backs trying to get through the front door. Everyone was shouting at once about defending Islam, whipped up by the music. All I can say is that I would not want to be an Iraqi and meet these men on the battlefield; they were frothing like hunting dogs.

It wasn't clear to me why we were fighting Iraq, but Ayatollah Khomeini said the war was a "gift from Allah," because it was the chance to give Islam to the whole world. Islam, shmislam. Me, I just wanted to stop being aimless. Mostafa gave me a job out of pity. And I wasn't much help, anyway, because I was too small to do any heavy lifting. I was more like a wife, fixing him meals and listening to his long, boring stories. I needed to do something that mattered, like avenging Farideh from those murderous Arabs. Omid was just copying me, like a puppy, because I was his hero, but I didn't mind. He could come with me if he wanted; war was an adventure big enough for two.

Once inside the mosque, I said a small prayer of thanks—for air-conditioning—and we joined a long line of volunteers snaking down a hallway. I noticed we were some of the youngest in the line, but I did spot some boys who looked to be eight or nine. A chubby recruiter with popping eyeballs like a goldfish approached Omid and me and ordered us to follow him to his office.

"How old are you?" he asked, plopping himself into a swiveling arm-chair that wheezed under his weight.

"Thirteen!" Omid said.

"And a half," I added, standing up taller. I really was thirteen and a half. Omid was twelve.

"Why do you want to join the Basij?"

To get into the Basij, you had to be religious. You had to pray to God in Arabic many times a day like the Muslims do. You had to listen to mullahs and do whatever they said. I knew a little bit about religion from watching Mostafa bow down on his rug, but still I stammered trying to answer the question.

Omid jumped in and saved me, ready with a line he'd picked up from Radio Tehran: "Our religious and national duty demands it of us, the children of Islam, to go fight the devil, or else Islam will be in danger," he said.

The goldfish frown flipped into a wide smile.

"Do your parents approve?"

Omid nudged me with his elbow, and I handed over the letters, damp with my sweat. The man unfolded the papers and glanced at Omid's phony permission letter on top. Then he folded both pages again, not even bothering to look at mine.

"God bless you, worthy children," he said, spiraling his pen across some forms. He stood and shook our hands, then held a cardboard box before us. "Choose one," he said.

The box held headbands, red or green, each with the name of a prophet written on it in Farsi script. They were meant to protect soldiers in battle, and I'd seen Basij soldiers wearing them on TV. Omid chose a red one that read "Ya Husayn!" I chose green, the martyr's color. Mine said "Allahu Akbar."

The goldfish then waved us toward the back of the mosque, where more officers ushered us through a back door and onto a waiting bus filled with loud boys beating their chests and chanting "Long live Khomeini!" The driver put the bus in gear, and as I turned to look at the pandemonium outside the mosque, I couldn't believe our good luck at getting plucked from the crowd for the last two seats on the bus. All the passengers were chattering so fast, it was like we were a rolling birdcage overstuffed with finches. I closed my ears to the churring and dreamed of the adventure ahead. I imagined myself around a campfire, comparing escapades with other soldiers while opening cans of food with my bayonet. At night, I'd sleep in a tent with Iraqi heads hanging across the entrance. I felt hands lifting me up as they carried me through the streets of Masjed Soleyman, singing for their hero who kicked Iraq back across the border with the toe of his massive boot.

"Hey, Omid, you think we'll get pistols?"

"This isn't World War II, dummy; they will give us serious weapons. Machine guns. Rocket launchers."

"What about tanks or fighter jets?"

"You gotta have training for that stuff," he said. "We're the militia— the crazy combat guys on the ground."

After a two-hour drive northwest toward the border, the bus stopped before an enormous rectangular compound ringed by pointy mountains made of layered orange rock, like a giant had smashed birthday cakes together and just left them in a jumbled pile. Tangles of bright green trees knotted with vines sprung from the canyons in the rock, and thin waterfalls spilled to the river below. Armed guards stood at fixed posts all around the encampment, and a line of officers waited at the entrance, ready to greet us. When I got off the bus, the air was wet and thick, and the heat was so intense it felt as if it was massaging the marrow of my bones.

"It's like we're in the jungle," Omid whispered as we walked toward the entrance.

"Do you think Daryoosh is here?"

Until he left me behind to join the Basij, my neighbor Daryoosh and I were the kite-flying champions of Masjed Soleyman, rulers of the airspace above the Zagros Mountains towering over our street. Just the previous summer, we'd ripped all the pages out of my math textbook and made a monster kite that was three feet wide and ten feet long, so big that it took both of us an hour to carry it up to the hiking trail to our flying spot. Dozens of neighborhood kids competed against us, trying to jab holes in our kite or loop their strings around ours and yank it from the sky, but all failed. We had a secret weapon they didn't know about—a special glue that one of my uncles showed me how to make by mixing Styrofoam and gasoline. That glue made paper turn as hard as plastic. We never told anyone how we made our kites, and we never lost a contest. Daryoosh was all thumbs in real life, but he could make a kite look like a ballet dancer in the sky. Ever since he'd left, I hadn't felt inspired to compete.

"We can look for him," Omid said.

I smiled just thinking about having my two best friends with me.

"Soldiers of Muhammad, welcome to the Karkheh battalion," said the first man in the greeting line as he shook my hand, making my arm flap like a rubber band. He must have been the leader, because he was wearing many shiny pins on his shirt, and he was the tallest. As we made our way down the row of handshakes toward the collection of tents and warehouses that made up the compound, my excitement meter hit tilt. All I had with me was a handful of coins and the worn-out clothes on my back, and somewhere in this complex there was a tent and a uniform and a weapon just for me.

Omid and I walked toward the parade grounds in the center of the base to wait for further instructions. We took inventory as we went, noticing the commander's building with thick cement walls and ceiling fans, the camp mosque, the mess tent, a medical clinic, and a repair shop. There were offices for the Islamic Revolutionary Guards, with desks for the morality police who enforced Sharia law and proper religious behavior, and a wing for counterintelligence, and a shooting range. It was like a perfect little city, every little piece snapped in the right place.

At the parade grounds, each of us was given a box containing a tan uniform and boots, blanket, skillet, toothbrush and toothpaste, shoe polish, soap, and fork and spoon. I lifted out a pair of boxers and sized them against myself, but they extended past my knees. I dug through my box again, feeling around for a weapon of some kind. They didn't think I was going to defend myself with a fork, did they?

"Be patient," Omid said as we carried our supplies to the mosque, where all the new boys were going to sleep that night until we got our tent assignments. Omid and I wanted to get to the mosque early and claim a spot on the floor with our blankets. There were so many of us, I didn't know how we were all going to fit inside. "I'm sure they don't pass out guns on the first day," Omid added.

We walked by a cinder-block building we hadn't seen before, and as we got closer, we spotted a small sign painted in sun-blistered paint on the wall: MORGUE. We looked away and picked up our pace.

After dinner in the mess hall, as I settled down on my blanket in the mosque, I was too afraid to go to sleep because I might wake up back at Omid's house and this would all have been a dream. I felt so free, freer than the day I stole Baba's money and went to the movies. That freedom had been a one-shot deal. Now I was truly cut loose from my family, and every decision going forward would be mine, all mine. No more fixing cars, no more making deliveries with Mostafa. I was the boss of me now, and no one could take that away. That fact alone made me feel an inch taller already. The mosque was noisy with so many boys, and every time someone farted, it set off a whole new round of giggling and kicking. Some sort of competition was under way, seeing who could produce the loudest gas. I reached over and poked Omid in the back.

"You can beat them all."

He stayed curled in a ball and ignored me. I poked him again. Nothing.

"Hey," I said, leaning in close to see if he was snoring. I heard a small sniffle and rolled him over to see that he was crying. "What's this?" I asked.

"I miss my mom," he whispered.

I sat up and flicked him hard on the forehead to snap him out of it. "Are you kidding? You're going to wimp out on me?"

He slapped my hand away and cried harder. "I want to go home!"

"Listen," I hissed, "go home if you wanna be a mama's boy. But fuck you if you do."

"Fuck you back," he said.

"Fuck you, period."

"Fuck you, exclamation point."

"Fuck you, infinity!" I squealed.

Then we were wrestling, then we were laughing, then he farted on me for good measure—the ultimate challenge. That left me with just one weapon in my arsenal. I got on all fours and did my donkey impression. I rocked my head back and forth and hee-hawed with ridiculous gusto, and Omid fell into a spasm of giggles. "Hi, I'm Omid. Have you seen my balls?" I said, using my best idiot-donkey voice. I looked left and right and under the blankets. "I seem to have misplaced them."

Once Omid relaxed, I waited until I heard him snoring, then I closed my eyes. Everything was as it should be again, but I'd have to keep an eye on that kid. If Omid went home, I'd be very sad, but I wouldn't follow. He had a happy family to return to, and I didn't. Maybe he was too young for this, and if he needed to go home, I'd understand. But I was going to do my best to toughen him up so he'd stay with me.

I have to say it was a huge disappointment that my first day as a new soldier began at five in the morning with prayers, then an hour of exercising, then a whole day of filling burlap bags with sand for battle shelters. If I thought the heat was bad in my hometown, I take it all back. This was a dryness that peeled off layers of my lips and opened up deep cracks in my heels. Dust mixed with snot and created erasers that plugged my nostrils.

The second day started out as an exact repeat of the first, and they still hadn't assigned us tents yet. This was beginning to be a big problem, as the smell of so many feet in the mosque was making it impossible for me to sleep at night. This was not the war I had signed up for; this was more boring than long drives with Mostafa in his truck. I might as well have joined an orphanage.

I topped off another burlap bag and tied it off with rope. Two boys working with me squatted down, lifted the bag together, and walked it toward a flatbed truck. I was scooping sand into the zillionth bag when I heard a scream. One of the boys had lost his footing when he swung the bag onto the truck, tripped, and sliced his palm open on a barbed wire fence. The cut wasn't too deep, but there was a lot of blood, so much that Omid took one look and fainted, of course. Blood didn't bother me, so I helped the boy wrap his hand in his shirt and offered to walk with him to the clinic.

When we arrived, one of the busy medics handed me some gauze and tape with a pleading look that said "Can you please take care of this?" before he ran back to a waiting ambulance. I washed the boy's hand in a sink and wrapped the white cloth around his wound, winding the strips around his thumb and wrist so the bandage would stay in place. I copied the movements that Omid's mom had made when she wrapped my scalded foot, making sure it was secure but not overly tight.

Just then, the doctor walked by.

"You two. Come here," he barked.

A chill engulfed my body. We had barged into the hospital without permission, and now both of us were going to be punished. We walked softly over to the doctor, keeping our eyes down. He reached for the boy's hand and held it up, examining the bandage from all angles.

"Where'd you learn to do this?"

I looked up from the floor, wondering what the right answer was. I decided it was the truth.

"I've had injuries before, sir. Burns, mostly. And good nurses who took care of me."

The doctor nodded slowly.

"I need another medic. You could be useful to me."

I beamed. Even though medic was considered one of the worst war jobs you could get, like a battlefield janitor who swept up the dead without ever getting a chance to fight, all I cared about was that a real doctor had complimented me. What do you know? I had a skill. I gratefully said yes.

That night, Omid and I were assigned to a tent that already had four boys in it. As we approached, I heard a familiar voice and picked up my step. Omid heard it, too, and we simultaneously broke into a full run.

"Daryoosh!"

His skinny frame appeared in the doorway, and he held his hand up to block the sun so he could see who was calling him. It took him only a second to recognize us, and he let out one of his high-pitched yelps and came running. The three of us clutched one another like we'd just won the World Cup soccer trophy.

"I knew you'd be here!" I sputtered.

"I knew you'd have to copy me," he said, cuffing me on the shoulder.

"Have you seen any action?" Omid asked.

Daryoosh kicked the sand. "Nah. But there's talk we're going to be sent to the front soon."

We nodded like we knew that already.

"Do you have a gun?" Omid asked.

"Not yet. C'mon, let me introduce you to the guys."

I take back what I said about military camp being boring. With each day, I met another boy from my neighborhood or one of the nearby towns. All you had to do was talk to a stranger for five minutes and you'd discover you were related or that you had a friend in common. Omid's spirits lifted, and he found out what his military skill was. He was really good at taking apart a machine gun, cleaning it, and putting it back together. Ever since he got assigned to help the fighters with their equipment, he'd thankfully stopped whining about his mom so much. If he got really fast assembling the weapons and delivering ammunition, he could get a machine gun of his own. Medics didn't get weapons, but he promised he'd show me how to shoot his.

My training began immediately. Or, more precisely, at two a.m. the next day, when the doctor came into the tent I now shared with Omid and four other guys, and shook me awake.

"Follow me. Now."

I stumbled into my boots and lumbered after him, huffing to keep up. He scurried through the hospital front doors, toward a set of stairs that led to a basement. He paused before he went down the stairs and turned to me with an irritated look. "Hurry up, son, this isn't your fucking aunt's house!"

We descended to an underground surgery room, with smooth tiles so shockingly white that I stood transfixed for a second as if I had fallen into a parallel universe, one without dirt and sweat. He led me to a sink and showed me the proper way to scrub my hands and to dry them by spreading my fingers wide and waving them in the air. Then he parted a curtain, and I jumped back. There, on the operating table, was a mangled boy of about fourteen or fifteen. His body had been ripped open from his throat down to his stomach, and I could see his intestines, quivering with his breath. My skin went clammy and my ears started to ring, blotting out all other sound. All the different reds and pinks of the boy's insides swirled in my vision and I doubled over and vomited . . . all over the doctor's shoes.

"For fuck's sake!" he said, hopping out of my puddle.

I grabbed the metal operating table to steady myself, and the doctor slapped me so hard that I spun around.

"Get out!" he roared.

This couldn't be happening. I didn't realize how much I needed to be a medic until he had chosen me. It suited me because I had experience with injuries, and Omid's mom had taught me all I needed to know about healing. If I could be a medic, then I would be saving people instead of killing them. I could serve my country in this clean, safe surgery room out of the line of fire.

"Please . . ."

The doctor couldn't kick me out; he just couldn't. It wasn't my fault I'd never seen someone's guts close-up before. But I could handle it, if he'd just give me another chance.

"*Out!*"

I wouldn't give him the satisfaction of hearing me cry, so I held my breath as I walked toward the stairs, tears streaming down my cheeks. I was two steps up the staircase when I heard him call me back. I quickly wiped my face and turned around.

"This boy has to be stitched up now, and I don't have anyone else," the doctor said. "I need you to hand me the tools. Look away and hand them to me over your shoulder if you want to be a girl about it."

And so I did. I didn't know the names of all the instruments, but he yelled at me until I learned the difference between a scalpel and chisels, forceps and calipers. It was a two-hour crash course in nursing, even if I couldn't see what he was doing with the tools. I told myself it was better that way, to start with basic vocabulary lessons and work my way up to blood and guts. The doctor cussed his way through the operation until finally I felt his hand on my shoulder.

"You can turn around now."

The boy still looked like he was sleeping, but now he had a huge line of stitches like a railroad track running down his chest. I put my finger on his wrist to check for a pulse, and the power of what we had just done surged through me like an electrical current. The awe of it—of being able to give a person his future back—took my words away.

"You did good, Zahed. This one might make it."

Right there, I knew what I was supposed to do with my life. After the war, I wanted to be a doctor, too.

"Will you teach me how to do this?"

"You don't expect me to stitch all these poor bastards by myself, do you? You'll need to learn sutures. And please try not to fucking faint."

There was no time for fainting—or teaching, for that matter. The next day an ambulance raced back from the front line with a boy who looked like he couldn't have been much older than me. Blood was coming out of his nose and mouth, and he had a big gaping wound behind his ear. This time I watched as the doctor sewed his skin together, wincing each time the boy cried out in pain. I handed over fistfuls of gauze, but the boy's head wouldn't stop bleeding. Then the boy started to shake.

"What's happening?"

The doctor threw his scissors down.

"He's going into shock. I can't do anything more for him."

With that, the doctor left me alone in the surgery room with the patient. He'd stopped shaking and was moaning like he was trying to say something.

Carefully, I approached the bedside. The boy's eyes opened halfway, and he squinted at me.

"Brother, what's it going to be like to die?"

He wanted an answer, but I had none. I wanted to say everything was going to be OK, but lying to a dying person was wrong. I couldn't just stand there; I had to answer him. But there was no way I could know what he was asking.

"Close your eyes," I said, taking his hand in mine. "I will sing to you." I began to sing: "Sleep, sleep my future hope, sleep. Hope of the future, sleep."

I sang the lullaby over and over until I felt the life leave his hand. I stayed with him a little longer, crying quietly, so the doctor wouldn't hear and fire me again. I could see now why the doctor had walked away. You couldn't possibly sing to all the patients, or your heart would get so bruised it would die, too.

After two weeks at training camp, our Basij unit was finally sent to war. Omid had his own rifle by then, a Russian Simonov that he'd showed me how to fire a couple times. Me, I had just a medical bag. We packed our stuff and joined a convoy of military trucks carrying about three hundred of us, none older than twenty, south toward Khuzestan Province, where most of the fighting was happening closer to the Gulf. My job was to attend the wounded on the battlefield, but still it would have been nice to have some sort of protection besides my helmet.

Our commanders said we were going to join a big operation called Sacred House, to liberate Khorramshahr, the first city the Iraqis seized when the war began almost two years before. The Arabs had bombed the water tanks and oil refineries, stolen our homes, and taken over the port, and for that, they would pay. They might think Khorramshahr was theirs to keep, but, our commanders said, they didn't know how big our Basij hearts were. The enemy might have more firepower, but our strength came not from bullets but from Allah. We weren't just fighting for Iran; we were fighting to save the revolution, and for Islam. If you killed one of us, ten more would spring up to fight in his place. The Iraqis put land mines all around Khorramshahr, but even that couldn't stop the Basij, we were told, because we had something even more powerful—we weren't afraid to die.

It was an ink-black night when our trucks stopped in the marshy dunes of Shalamcheh, ten miles outside Khorramshahr. Our mission was to block a main road that crossed the Shatt al-Arab river into Basra, to blow up the bridge and cut off the route the Iraqis used to send troop reinforcements into Iran. Our unit was one of many that was quietly cutting off all roads leading into Khorramshahr, encircling the city to trap the Iraqis. Once we had them surrounded, we'd move in and take back what was rightfully ours.

The cold got under our thin uniforms, and the wind tugged at my shirt and made my eyes water. Our feet made sucking noises in the mud as we trudged through a marsh, and I heard some sort of animal hiss and scurry out of the tall reeds as we passed—a fox, or maybe big rats. There were date palms everywhere, but many were singed on top from bombings, and without fronds they looked like abandoned telephone poles. Our commanders wouldn't let us turn on our flashlights, so we stumbled in the muck, trying our best not to fall into the slime. We were making a hell of a lot of noise for a surprise attack, but luckily for us there were no homes for miles. My heart was rattling in my rib cage, but I saw all these boys around me pressing on, so I raised my chin like them and reminded myself that this was the John Wayne mission I'd been waiting for. Although I was terrified, at least I was surrounded by bravery, and that was something like security. We were searching for places to dig foxholes and make blockades when I felt a thunderous blast in my chest and saw a flash of white light up ahead. Then I heard a boy shrieking for his mother. Hundreds of feet stopped at once, and an eerie silence fell down on us.

"There's been an explosion; come on!" another medic shouted as he grabbed my arm and ran toward the screaming. We followed the sound to a boy about eighteen, sprawled on his back with his left leg in shreds just below the knee. His intestines were spilling out of his stomach, and his face was blackened on one side into a grotesque mask.

"My leg! Where's my leg!"

My stomach clenched into a fist and my feet turned to cement. I was too scared to touch him, and I had no idea what to do. The older medic pushed me to one side and told me to call the ambulance on the walkie-talkie. Only then did I look up and see that there were medics attending a handful of boys in a circle around me. It was hard to tell which one of them had triggered the land mine. *Holy shit*, we had walked directly into a minefield.

The medic pulled out the shoelace on the boy's remaining shoe and tied it tight around the stump of his leg to stop the bleeding. He dug in his supply kit and pulled out a thick plastic bag.

"Hold this open over his stomach," he instructed.

I helped him put the boy's intestines in the bag, seal it, and tie it to his body. If the boy was lucky, he'd make it to a hospital in time for a surgeon to put the contents of the plastic bag back into him.

The boy grabbed my arm and tried to sit up. "Did I lose my leg?"

"Yes," I said, gently pushing him back down. "But you still have your other leg. You will be OK."

He closed his eyes, maybe for the last time; I'm not sure. There was nothing else to do until the ambulance arrived. Our battalion by now had gathered into a frightened group of rabbits, afraid to take another step. We sat down together in the sand, safer in a huddle.

The commander stood before us and shouted above the howling wind. "Brothers, your time of martyrdom has come!"

A collective cheer rose from the group: "Long live Khomeini!"

"I need volunteers to clear this minefield. Those who are willing, stand up."

The commander put his hands on his hips. He wanted us to walk in single file, a minute or so apart, to clear a straight path through the minefield to the other side where there was a small river that fed into the Shatt al-Arab. Once we'd detonated all the bombs in that corridor, our professional army could follow through safely and continue about the business of blocking the road to Basra. There was no telling how many of us would die before we set off every explosive in our chosen lane. Although Ayatollah Khomeini said religious devotion would shield us from bullets, the commander was more realistic. "If you get killed in the name of Islam," he told us, "you will join all the prophets in paradise, where rivers run with honey and beautiful women put fruit in your mouth." We would become heroes in our hometowns, the subject of legends and poems and monuments. Our families would get money from the government for our sacrifice, and martyr cards for extra food rations.

To the right of me, to the left of me, boys stood up and shouted the names of the prophets they'd meet in the afterlife: "Ya Hasan! Ya Husayn!" Their fervor was like an airborne disease, and everyone was catching it, as dozens of boys volunteered, then more, then more, until there were nearly one hundred recruits standing, all eager to outdo one another's zeal. I watched in disbelief as they put their weapons on the ground and walked up to the commander, ready to die. I bowed my head, hoping I wouldn't be the only one to say no. I felt the crowd's stare, and the word that was growing larger and larger over my head: *coward*. What was wrong with me? Why wasn't I a true believer like them, feeling lucky for the chance to go to paradise? Why did I have to question everything? My father must have been right; I was weak. I joined the Basij to become a man, and now that it was time to be brave, I was trembling like a ninny. Boys even younger than me were already untying their boots to donate them back rather than waste them in an explosion. I was ashamed of myself, and didn't want my shame to ride on my shoulders for the rest of my life. Then, as if someone else was pulling the strings, I felt my hand rise in the air. Like a puppet, I stood up and walked to join the group of human minesweepers.

Omid watched me and then slowly raised his hand too. As he approached the martyr line, I shook my head and tried to wave him back, but he always did whatever I did, like a younger brother.

"It is time," the commander shouted. "Awake to judgment day!"

Boys secured their headbands tighter on their helmets and jostled to go first. The commander kissed the first boy on the forehead, the boy shouted "Ya, Ali!" and started out into the night like a ghost floating over the dunes. We lined up, and as each boy passed the commander, he kissed him and said a few private words. From the back of the line, I watched boy after boy disappear into the night and thought how strangely orderly it seemed, as one by one we moved up silently and patiently, like we were waiting in line at the school cafeteria. When I reached the commander, he asked if I had any last words.

I thought of my parents, who were probably frantic when I had disappeared. I was probably going to die tonight, without ever getting the chance to make things right with Baba.

"Tell my family that if I've done anything bad, they should forgive me."

He nodded and kissed my forehead. Then I took off running.

My legs pounded the earth, beating out a tempo with my heartbeat as I flung myself forward in the pitch black, squinting to try to make out the shape of the boy in front of me. I pumped my arms and dug my feet into the pitted ground, terrified that each step would be my last. Several times I lost my balance but waved my arms frantically to stay upright. I made it about fifty yards before I heard the first explosion. It burst into an orange flash for an instant, just in time for me to see the silhouette of a body hurtling through the air. It was so unreal; it looked like something in a cartoon, like someone flung from a catapult. My legs trembled and I slowed my pace as the blasts kept coming now from up ahead, some of them yellow, some of them orange and some white. The explosives each had a different power, sometimes throwing the body a few feet, sometimes tossing a boy as high as a building.

My mind unhinged from my body, and all of a sudden I had a bird's-eye view of myself running below. It was a sporting match, and I was cheering myself on. "Go!" I told myself. "Go!"

I kept going.

Only in hell do arms and legs rain down from the sky. Everywhere I looked there were pieces of boys and blood, so much blood, as if it was seeping up from underground like oil. This was worse than any of my nightmares, any of Ghaffor's horror films. The falling bodies detonated more mines, and the blasts were coming faster now. Chaos broke out as boys ran off the path, and others yelled for them to come back. I turned around and shouted Omid's name, but my voice was buried beneath all the screaming.

Something landed ahead of me and as I got closer I could see it was a blackened torso, the boy's face half-peeled away, exposing his skull. I was hysterical now, screaming for my mother, shrieking along with everyone else as death chased us. Tears blinded my vision as I pushed myself forward and thought how stupid I had been to think war was going to be exciting. War is the stench of shit and vomit and burning flesh in your nose, forever. If I was going to die, I only hoped I'd step on one of the big land mines used to destroy tanks, because then I would just be blown into so many little pieces that I wouldn't suffer. "Please, Death," I begged, "come get me. Come get me now so I don't have to see this anymore."

"*Help me, help me, helpme, helpme, helpmehelpmehelpmehelpme!*" I wailed. Or maybe I just thought it. My mouth was open, but I couldn't tell if any sound was coming out. Then I saw a pink hazy light up ahead of me, floating just out of reach, and decided to run to it. As I got closer, the pink light got brighter and I heard the sound of a small girl laughing. Two arms reached out of the light and I reached up and clasped the hands. Dadna, my fairy, emerged from the light.

"Follow," she said, turning and flying in front of me. Pinpricks of pink light pulsated through the veins of her wings. I followed her blinking lights in the dark, until I felt something wet on my shoes and realized

I was standing in water. The river. I'd made it through to the other side. I looked around, but Dadna was gone.

I collapsed into the mud and hugged my knees to my chest. I rocked back and forth, trembling and squeezing my knees so hard I thought they'd break.

Omid.

I staggered back up to look for him and noticed the rest of my unit coming through the secure path, and some were carrying the wounded. I didn't see Omid, but he found me first, and leaped onto my back in relief. We tumbled to the ground, weeping openly and loudly; we didn't care about being men anymore.

"Don't ever do that again!" he shouted.

"But *you* did it," I said.

"Did not."

"What?"

"I started to, but then I just couldn't do it; I freaked out and ran back. Lots of us did."

His confession hung in the air between us.

"How many died?"

Omid put his arm around my shoulders.

"Almost everyone who tried to go all the way through, you crazy idiot."

"Omid, do you believe in God?"

"Do you?"

Mostafa always said that Islam was about peace. But if that's true, why were two Muslim countries fighting each other? Iranians said "Allahu Akbar" and Iraqis said it too. What was the difference between this Allah and that Allah?

"I'm so sorry," I said.

"For?"

"Teasing you about wanting to go home."

FOUR

THE MAGNIFICENT ONE

I used to be a falafel king. Now I was no more than a dog. One whistle, and I leaped out of bed in the morning. Two whistles, and I jogged in formation with the pack, while my master supervised. Run, stop, turn. Good boy. Again. Three whistles, and I got five minutes to lap up some lentil soup before the next command.

But I was a good Iraqi soldier. I obeyed and didn't ask questions.

My second tour in the military had a sharper edge. I thought it was because they were trying to toughen us up for war. We were cussed at, no matter what our education level, no matter what rank we held before, as if all of us were peasants. We were kept in constant motion, going from drill to drill, so there was no time to dwell on the inevitable, that sooner or later we were going to put our lives on the line.

They couldn't have picked a more punishing place to train us, in the middle of a desert outside Az Zubayr on the Kuwaiti border. I'd never seen such nothingness. Haze and sand all the way to the horizon, without a structure or a tree to break up the view. I could see why nobody lived there. It was more than a hundred degrees during the day and teeth-chatteringly cold at night. But it did have one thing going for it: I could practice firing a Kalashnikov in any direction and be assured I would hit nothing.

What I wouldn't do for just a few hours to myself to strategize how to marry Alyaa. At night, adjusting and readjusting my long legs on the floor of the tent I shared with five others, I sometimes could see her face for just a quick flicker before I fell into an exhausted sleep. I was so beaten down I couldn't even muster the energy to dream, and then suddenly it was four in the morning again and I was whistled awake so the whole sadistic cycle could begin anew.

Ten straight days of this monotony, then something out of the ordinary happened. The emergency siren wailed, signaling all of us soldiers to gather. A long caravan of open-air Russian jeeps came rumbling up and out stepped a group of high-ranking officers in dust-free uniforms with gleaming brass buttons. Our basic training was complete, they announced, and now it was time to separate us into different divisions. Some of us would be chosen for artillery, some for administration, some for special forces. I felt dread pool in my gut while the most senior officer circled us slowly, sizing us up like a farmer purchasing cattle. I fixed my gaze on the back of the head of the man in front of me and avoided eye contact. The most senior officer said nothing as he pointed at the soldiers he wanted, and the chosen twenty followed him to the jeeps and were driven who knows where.

The next officer selected fifteen more men and left in the same secretive fashion. Finally, the lowest-ranking officer of the bunch inspected me and the last dozen men left behind. He peered into my face and slid his hands over my arms and stomach to feel my muscles. Then he shoved me to see if I would fall over. I held my ground.

"Are any of you sick or injured?" he demanded.

No one answered.

"Good. All of you are now in my tank division. You have two hours to gather your things."

We were driven another two hours deeper into Az Zubayr, where forty-ton Russian tanks with cannons that could fire up to three miles awaited. Tank duty was one of the better assignments, I guess, because it was more protected than the poor guys who had to fire from the trenches. But tanks were also big, lumbering targets, visible from the air. Before training began, the commanders gave us the rest of the day off to visit our families, as long as we returned by five the next morning. That gave me exactly sixteen hours to find Alyaa.

I took a bus to the nearest town and then a second bus to Basra, willing the wheezing clunker to go faster as it lazily chugged along, stopping to rest in every little outpost along the way. It was so infuriatingly slow that I even pulled the Koran my mother had given me out of my pocket and thumbed through it to distract myself. Religion was always a low-key affair with me, I respected it, but I didn't feel the need to pray, and as usual the verses swirled before me and I gave up, slipping the book back into my shirt pocket. I made a mental note to find a different method of transportation if I ever wanted to make real use of a military leave.

The sun was going down by the time I got to my neighborhood, and I walked the streets and alleys looking for her, passing all the hiding places where we'd embraced during our morning walks. I trekked for an hour, until hunger started kneading my stomach and I turned to go home. As much as I desperately wanted to walk past Alyaa's house, I resisted. It would be too suspicious if a soldier were lurking around an unmarried woman's home. I would have to find another way to let her know I was in town.

I could smell the scented rice cooking as I approached my father's home. My sister Karima dropped the wooden spoon when she saw me.

"Brother! Are you home for good?"

I unwrapped her arms from my neck and told her I had to leave early in the morning. She frowned, then quickly corrected her mood and kissed me on both cheeks.

"What, no smile for me?" she asked.

I slumped against the wall and sighed as if I were deflating. Of all my sisters, Karima was the one who knew me best. She could tell, whenever the crease deepened between my eyebrows, that something was bothering me.

Just then my younger brothers bounded into the kitchen, grimy from chasing each other outdoors.

"Najah! Najah, have dinner with us!" They tugged on my uniform, competing for my attention. They were so unaware of their good fortune to go to school and study the wonders of the world. Their innocence was calming and put my sacrifice in perspective. I was keeping the country safe for them.

"Go wash up," Karima said, shooing them away. Since the divorce, as the eldest girl in the family, she had naturally filled in as mother. It was Karima who cooked the meals, Karima who made sure homework got done and teeth got brushed, and Karima who tonight would wash and iron my uniform.

"Tell me," she said, handing me a cup of tea.

"I love someone," I whispered, and the vault in my heart creaked open.

Karima put down her cup and leaned in. She loved a secret, and she could keep one, too. So she knew lots of things about all of us, while we knew very little about one another.

"Who is she?"

I told her everything, about our sign language in the bread line, about the makeshift ring, about our wish to marry despite the other suitor. That we'd been courting before sunrise for the past year, finding quiet places to be alone. Karima cracked up when I told her I had proposed in the backyard.

"Right under our noses? Sly, my brother!"

I smiled for the first time since being conscripted, and it felt unusual, like my cheeks were irritated by being pushed out of place.

"Who else knows?" she asked.

"Mom wouldn't give her blessing. She said it's not right to turn a young girl into a widow, especially one who is already promised to a rich man."

Karima circled her finger around the rim of her teacup. "She does have a point," she said.

I dropped my head in my hands.

"Hey, hey. Shhhhh," Karima said, rubbing my back.

I looked up at her through my tears. If Karima didn't approve either, I would reluctantly agree I should give up.

"What should I do?" I asked.

"Najah, what you're doing is dangerous. If you get caught, you'll spoil her reputation. But love, *esh*, it doesn't listen." She sat quietly for a few agonizing seconds while I awaited her verdict. "Okay. I need to meet her, then I can say."

Just the fact that Karima would take the matter under consideration gave me renewed hope. Thanks to the snail of a bus, I'd have to leave the next morning at three to get back to the base on time, but even so I was going to stop by the bakery on my way, just in case Alyaa came early for bread.

"Come with me to the bakery tomorrow, and if she's there, I can point her out to you."

Karima's eyes gleamed. The younger ones took their places at the table, and as she retreated to the kitchen to serve us, she grabbed my hand and squeezed it to let me know she was up for an adventure.

The next morning we slipped out before anyone was awake, but when we got to the bakery, I realized my idea was ludicrous. We could see through the closed service window that the bakers were still stirring flour and water. It was only two in the morning, and the first loaves hadn't even been baked. Karima shivered in the cold. I loved her then, for sacrificing warmth and sleep to help me untangle my life.

"She must be really special for you to be acting so crazy," Karima said, kissing me on the cheek. We waited for an hour, until I had no more minutes to spare. I desperately wanted to ask the first women gathering in line if they'd seen Alyaa, but I didn't dare approach. Other soldiers from my unit were already scurrying to get to the bus station.

"I'm sorry I made you get up," I said. "I can't be tardy; they might never let me have another leave."

"Go," she said, straightening my collar. "I'll keep my ears open at the marketplace, and I'll let you know if I see her. Don't worry."

I tried to put Alyaa out of my mind, telling myself she must have been busy taking care of her mother. So I got busy learning all the things I needed to know to drive and shoot a Soviet tank. There were four of us in my tank crew, each seated in a small reservoir with a hatch that lifted to the outside. The driver was in front, the gunner to his right with access to the roof-mounted machine gun, and behind them, two more spaces for the loader, who took care of ammunition, and the commander, who gave orders through our headphones. All of us learned how to load and fire the cannon, shoot the machine gun, and drive the tank. It wasn't that hard to steer, easier than a car. All four limbs were in constant motion in the driver's seat, which I steered with a manual clutch and two steering sticks positioned between my feet. I pushed the sticks forward to drive straight and pulled to slow down, and when I wanted to turn, I moved only one. I had a small viewer to see out of and an infrared periscope for night vision, but if there was a sandstorm, and there usually was, I relied on the directions called out by the commander and the gyroscope compass in my compartment giving me a rough idea of which way was north.

We practiced positioning the cannon to the coordinates relayed over the radio by the commander and sighting targets through the telescope. I listened well, learned fast, and soon the commander was leaving me in charge of the tank crew while he trained some of the slower learners. I guess word of my skill reached the sergeant major, because one day he summoned me. After asking several people for directions, I finally located the blue door to his office inside a two-story headquarters made of cinder blocks. I knocked, and when the door swung open, I recognized an old neighborhood friend of my father's.

"Najah! I heard you were here and I wanted to see for myself. Come, sit," he said. There were only two metal folding chairs, a small table, and a prayer rug in his sparse office. "Look how strong you've become. They tell me you're quite a tank driver."

"I don't know about that . . ."

"I'm sure what I'm hearing is true," he said. "Tea?"

He set a steaming cup before me, not waiting for my answer.

"Tell me. How is your father?" he asked.

"He's OK. He's raising the kids by himself now," I said.

The sergeant major gave me a quizzical look.

"After the divorce," I added.

"Oh?"

My parents never should have married. According to family legend, my father was actually courting my mother's younger sister, but when it came time for the wedding, my mother's parents did a switcheroo, dressing their oldest daughter in the bridal gown because they were concerned she was too ugly and too old for anyone to marry. My father, an orphan whose mother and father had died of some kind of illness, was too polite to argue because he so desperately wanted a family. And my parents have been fighting ever since. Their biggest battle was over how to raise us. My father has a college degree in business administration and an important government job overseeing the cargo that came into the Port of Basra, while my mother never attended school. When my older brother and I skipped class to go fishing, she just shrugged. When my father discovered we'd been playing hooky for months, he was furious, and accused my mother of passing her ignorance on to us. Maybe he was right—my brother and I both went into the military after dropping out of school, and look where that had gotten me. My father threatened to take the rest of the kids away from her, and eventually he made good on his promise, divorced her, and made it his personal mission to make my younger brothers and sisters go to college. Anyway, it was too much to explain, so I gave him the quick version.

"They fought all the time and finally ended it," I said.

"He's still working at the port?"

I nodded.

"Must be rough on him."

Suddenly, I saw my opening.

"It is, sir. My sister Karima helps out, but he's always exhausted. And he's not getting any younger. I wish I could be there for him."

He studied me for a moment and then reached into a drawer, pulled out a form, and scribbled something on it.

"What time does your tank training end each day?" he asked.

"Four, sir."

He signed his name to the form and passed it across the desk to me.

"Listen, as of 4:01 p.m., I don't care what you do, as long as you report for duty at five every morning. This permit allows you off base in the evenings, but screw this up just once and I won't be able to help you."

I jumped to my feet and placed my hand over my heart in gratitude. Now I could find Alyaa. I nearly forgot to thank him as I ran for the door.

"Tell your father I said hello," he called out.

I went directly to the nearest town, where I knew a guy with a clothing shop who had a motorcycle he wanted to sell. It was a German MZ with a big protruding headlight good for driving in the dark. And the next day at one minute past four, I was gone.

Now I could blend into traffic and drive by Alyaa's house without attracting as much attention as I would on foot, as long as I kept my patrols to no more than once an hour. I rode by her home several times that evening, but her lights never came on. I returned at three the next morning, walking so as not to wake the neighbors, and found a doorway where I could hide and wait for her to go to the bakery. I listened to the birds announce the impending day and focused all my energy toward her window, using the power of my mind to summon her. Eventually a light flicked on, and my whole soul lit up with it, like a balloon of warm water bursting inside my chest. I heard footsteps, and could tell by the delicate weight of them that they belonged to her.

She took a few steps, then stopped when she spotted me across the street. I pointed to the alley by her house, but Alyaa just stood there, like a stone. Had she chilled to me? Then I realized she didn't recognize my tank division uniform. I moved closer, and she instinctively clutched her veil over her face, and I knew I was frightening her.

"Alyaa, it's me!" I whispered, and she looked again, breaking into an ecstatic smile. We both sped to the alley and I gathered her in my arms, inhaling the scent of her. I kissed her forehead, her eyes, her nose, and each ear, using the light from her house to guide me. She squirmed, but not with enough force to actually break free. I was kissing her so fast that I forgot to breathe and had to come up for air, panting double-time.

"Take it easy! People can see us," she whispered.

Adrenaline made me brave, and stupid.

"You're my wife, so what if people see!"

She held her hand out to me, so I could see she was still wearing the engagement string.

"I will never remove this as long as I am alive," she said. "And I am alive because of you, so please make sure nothing happens to you."

I kissed her tenderly on the lips. She let me but then pulled away and quickly glanced both ways down the alley to make sure we had not been observed.

"Let's take a walk," she said.

I explained the rules of my curfew and asked if she could start coming to the bakery an hour earlier, so we could have more time together.

"Give me two more days," she said. "My brother is coming to stay with us. I can go to the bakery after he leaves."

I would give her as many days as she wanted. A thousand, a million, an infinity. I could wait forever now that I knew she was still devoted to me. I brushed the side of her face with the back of my hand and kissed her one last time.

"See you in two days," I said.

When I returned to Basra, I waited at the bakery an hour beyond the time she had promised to show up. My mind raced with what-ifs. What if she had forgotten? What if she had given up on me? What if she had met someone else? Had her brother extended his stay? And the biggest one of all: What if I didn't get back to the base by five? When my watch finally confirmed there was no way I'd make curfew, I gave in to outside forces and simply let that worry go. As long as I was going to be late, I might as well be very late and take the whole morning off, plus whatever punishment would come with it. I had to see her. I leaned against the wall, squeezed fistfuls of warm bread into balls, and absentmindedly chewed them. Finally, I spotted her in the distance walking with a friend, and when they came closer, Alyaa pointed at me and whispered something to her companion. I rode up to them on my motorcycle so I could talk to her away from all the ears waiting in line for bread.

"Excuse me," I said, trying my best to sound formal. "I'm going to my father's house and I'd like you to follow me. I have something to discuss with you."

"Of course," she said, lowering her gaze.

I sat under the palm tree in our courtyard and watched the sky lighten from charcoal to steel to indigo and wondered what was taking her so long. She'd wasted so much time already. Normally, Father would be flicking on the lights about then, getting dressed for work, but he had taken a vacation. Whenever he was out of the house, Karima took a little vacation, too, letting the kids sleep in as long as they wanted. Still, something felt off with Alyaa. She should have been here by now. She had decided to leave me; there could be no other explanation. I let myself get so worked up that when she finally arrived, all I had to greet her with was accusation.

"Are you seeing another man?" I pounced.

I reached for her hand and she jolted back, as if she had just touched a hot stove.

"How can you say that to me? Aren't we engaged?"

She burst into tears, and I hated myself for being so insecure. She loved me, she said, but her family was pressuring her to marry the man they had chosen for her, and as the months went by it was getting increasingly difficult for her to stall them. And I couldn't tell her how much longer she needed to wait, because my "quick stint" in the military was turning into an indefinite obligation.

"When are you going to bring me a real gold ring?" she wept. "I'm embarrassed to let anyone see my finger."

And there it was—both of us were starting to lose faith in each other. I felt so ashamed that I couldn't court her properly, in her home, with permission from both our families. I was not an attractive husband, a soldier with a lost falafel fortune and responsibility for a pack of siblings. But when I was with her, all those barriers fell away, and all I felt was an innate sense of possibility.

I held her to me and reminded her how much I loved her, and her sobs subsided into sniffles. Then I pushed open the door to the formal sitting room and led her in. I gathered the floor pillows together and gently lowered her down to rest. She reached for me in the dark and pulled me down to her. I slowly removed each piece of her abaya, letting the cloth flutter to the carpet. We began to rock softly together, the two of us trembling at what we both knew we shouldn't want. But our bodies had taken over where words had failed us, and the urgent need to fuse together grew until neither of us could turn back. I entered her and she gasped one single word—*yes*—and pulled me tighter to her.

For a moment it seemed that the room fell away and a white light arched down to us from the heavens, like an answered prayer. Yes, she loved me. Yes, we had a future. Yes, pleasure was pouring out of me. Yes, it would be that way forever. Yes, there was a higher force looking out for us. We soared together, until our souls slowly shuddered back down into our bodies. She rolled over and brought her knees to her chest, and I curled myself around her.

"You are my wife now, before God," I whispered into her ear. "I will never leave you."

She started to cry, and when I turned her to face me, her skin was so pale, like the color of fog. There was no need to explain the terrible danger we had just put her in. She couldn't marry anyone else now, because he would discover on the wedding night that another man had already taken her virginity. Women like that brought permanent shame on both families, a disgrace that was sometimes rectified by beheading. And if her belly started to show, well, unmarried pregnant women also had a way of disappearing in Basra.

She trembled as she buried her face in my neck. I caressed her hair and assured her that I would talk to my father about marrying her.

"I should get back home to my mother," she said.

"No, stay. Spend the day with me."

"How? Your family will see us."

I crept into my father's room and returned with one of his floor-length dishdasha shirts, a belt, and a kaffiyeh to cover her head.

"Wear this, and I'll take you for a ride on my motorcycle."

"Are you crazy?"

She laughed, and I was elated to see Alyaa come back to herself. She put on the clothes, and the dishdasha was so long I had to roll it several times over the belt to keep it from dragging on the ground.

"Well, if I'm going to be a man, I need a man's name."

"Amjad," I said.

"What kind of name is that?"

"Only the best. It means 'magnificent one.'"

For the next two hours, we felt what it would be like to be man and wife, together in public without anything to hide. She wrapped her arms around my torso and pressed in, turning her head to the side and resting it against my shoulder blade. I felt her thighs squeezing my hips as we leaned into the curves and I pushed back into her to keep our body heat together. I think Alyaa enjoyed being a man. She could laugh out loud, sit with her legs wide apart, and spit freely. We roamed every street and dirt alley in town, even waving when we passed a few of my unsuspecting friends. I finally brought the motorcycle to rest near a grove of trees not far from her house and helped her change back into her clothes.

"Can we do that again?" she asked.

"Once we are married, we can ride every day."

I watched her walk toward her home until she was out of view, then headed home. Karima was watering Dad's beloved white rose bushes when I rumbled up. She set the water bucket down and put her hands on her hips.

"What are you doing home in the middle of the day?" she asked.

"When does Dad get back?"

"Tomorrow, why?"

"Karima, I need you to talk to him. I want his blessing to ask for Alyaa's hand."

"Why don't you talk to him yourself?"

"He listens to you."

"What's the rush?"

My eyes welled up with tears, and I couldn't get out the words. "This morning, I . . . I mean, we . . . we . . . started hugging and kissing and then, dot, dot, dot. You fill in the blanks."

She covered her mouth with her hand. "Oh, Najah, no. What have you done?"

I hung my head. "It's all my fault. I feel like I sucked out her soul."

Karima put a finger under my chin and tilted my head up until she was looking into my eyes. She gave me a pitying look and made a clucking noise, like a pigeon.

"Why couldn't you wait? *Chht.* Now look at you, lovesick. *Chht-chhht.* I will bring it up, when the time is right."

I hugged her tight and told her I'd always remember her kindness. If anyone could make this right, she could.

The route I took through downtown was jammed with more than just the usual traffic, a knot of honking cars and buses and scooters. I cut out of line, steered around the backup, and discovered that the road was blocked by military police, and a parade of some importance was coming through. At the head of the parade were police cars with sirens blaring, and a crowd had gathered to investigate the fuss. As the motorcade got closer, I felt the low rumble of flatbed trailers carrying military tanks, and everyone around me started applauding.

"What's going on?" I asked the man nearest me.

He lifted his fist in triumph and said, "Our men are heading to war, ho!"

When the convoy got closer, I recognized my own tank crew. It was my unit that had been mobilized. I dropped the motorcycle right where it was and jumped on the trailer as it passed, grabbing the outstretched hands of my cheering buddies.

"Where the hell were you, Aboud?"

"Overslept."

"My ass. It was a girl, wasn't it?"

I ignored them, lit a cigarette, and turned to wave back at the crowd, my worries about missing curfew suddenly replaced by the larger fear of what would happen in battle. And that fear was engulfed by the sheer terror of what would happen to Alyaa if I couldn't get back soon to marry her.

"Allahu Akbar!" the crowd roared.

I waved back robotically. Yes, God sure was great.

"Where are we going?" I asked the gunner.

"Khorramshahr."

Our biggest war prize so far, Khorramshahr was on the Shatt al-Arab in Iran's oil-rich Khuzestan Province, and we'd captured it a year ago, within days of the war. The Iranians were making increasingly aggressive pushes here and there to try to take some of the neighborhoods back. They were outgunned by us, of course, but there were so many of them, and they just kept coming, kamikaze-like, with their pistols and shoulder rocket launchers, that they were starting to make inroads. Our mission was to maneuver the tanks into a backup position, to provide a line of defense behind the foot soldiers.

At first, war felt more conceptual than real. I steered the tank where the commander ordered, and we turned the cannon to the requested direction and fired, never knowing if we were hitting anything. The shells sailed for nearly three miles, making it blind warfare, safe from guilt. Technically, I was in combat, but we were really just firing into the abyss. The Iranians didn't fire back, and sometimes weeks would go by until we got another order to fire the tanks. In the downtime, we cleaned the tanks and maintained the engines. The gas needed refilling, the wheels and air filters needed constant cleaning to get the sand out, and the decade-old engines were always in need of a tune-up. We parked the tanks over trenches, so we had an escape route in case we came under fire. This also had the dual benefit of providing a little shade, and a place to have a drink in privacy. As the weeks stretched into months, I worried constantly about Alyaa. My leaves were a thing of the past now that I was deployed, and the only thing that relieved my stress was arak, the clear, eighty-proof kind made from dates; it was a popular escape for soldiers. Officers drank arak, too, and looked the other way when we did, as long as it didn't interfere with our work. I drank it until I felt her arms around me again and the wind in my hair and heard her squeals of joy over the roar of my motorcycle.

For six months, I visited Alyaa in drunken memories, until one day I was sent in a truck with four others to the armory to bring more ammunition to the fighters positioned in the trenches. The road was studded with potholes, and the driver overcorrected after dipping into an especially deep pit and flipped the truck. We were all able to crawl out with only some bruising, nothing serious. But when the field ambulance arrived, we suddenly all complained mightily of broken ribs and ringing ears and torn ankles, so that we were all sent to the hospital. Nurses bandaged my perfectly good ankle and sent me home for four days to recover, exactly as I'd hoped.

When the bus dropped me off in Basra, I kept the bandages and hobbled on crutches to Alyaa's house. I watched from a distance and didn't see anyone inside, so I decided to knock on her door and if anyone answered, I'd pretend I was looking for someone else. My knocks went unanswered. I tried the knob, and it twisted. I pushed it open a little and listened. Nothing. "Hello?"

My call echoed in the empty house. I swiveled around and spotted an old woman across the street and ran to her.

"Excuse me, ma'am, do you know where the family is that lives in that house?"

She studied my uniform, my miraculously recovered foot, and the crutches I held under my armpits and shook her head.

"Dunno," she said, and kept walking.

I was frantic. I stopped a few more people and even checked with a shopkeeper, but no one had any information. Something bad had happened to her, I just knew it. She had given up on me and moved away. Or somebody had found out about us, and God knows what horrible things had happened to her. I ran home and almost crashed into my father, who was just coming in from work.

"What happened to you?" he asked.

I tore off the bandages and threw the crutches on the ground.

"It's fake," I said, not stopping to explain. "Did Karima talk to you about my fiancée?"

He raised one eyebrow and shook his head. He decided not to pry and instead indicated for me to sit next to him on the sofa. His formality was foreboding.

"A woman cannot have a normal life if she only sees her husband two or three times a year," he said. "Son, the timing is not right. It's for the girl's security that I can't agree to this. Your mother feels the same way."

That was it, then. I was boxed in. I couldn't even run away with Alyaa because I couldn't find her.

"Whatever you think is best," I said, and walked out the front door. I went to the liquor store and bought a bottle of arak to help me crawl out of my own skin. I took a few shots and, emboldened, took another stroll past her house. No one was there, so I circled back home. I had another drink, took another walk, and fell into a routine of fifteen-minute checks on her house, becoming more fearless with each pass. My drunken vigil lasted four days. I paced back and forth between her home and mine, crazy with worry that she had been killed by a relative or her mother had moved to escape the humiliation. I didn't sleep, and I couldn't eat despite Karima's pleadings to put something in my mouth. I felt like a walking dead person when I boarded the bus back to Khorramshahr.

My battalion had quadrupled in size during my phony sick leave. I came back to a whirlwind of more than a thousand people shouting and speed-walking this way and that, rushing from meetings and double-checking things on clipboards. Most of the newcomers were special forces types, commandos and snipers. Every day the commander told us to be ready for an attack, that the Iranians were pushing back hard and converging on us. He sent mine specialists into neighboring Shalamcheh

to bury explosives in a protective ring around Khorramshahr and ordered us to move our tanks into position behind the minefields, driving
at night with the lights off so as not to arouse suspicion. We moved into
place and dug a network of new trenches and filled sandbags to build
bunkers. After all that hurry-up, we waited. Then we waited some more.
Out of sheer boredom, we cleaned the tanks and checked the fluids.
When that was done, we cleaned the gears and the air filters. Before we
knew it, a whole winter had gone by.

I had given up on ever getting another leave, and I was certain I'd
never see Alyaa again, when two soldiers approached my tank. I was
underneath it, telling my problems to another bottle of arak.

One of them knocked on the tank to get my attention.

"Hey, Aboud, you're from Basra, right?"

I crawled out, a little clumsily, and confirmed it.

"Captain got a telegram. The electricity went out in his house in
Basra, and he needs you to get your weapon and guard the electrician.
Show the driver how to get there."

I sat in the back of the jeep with the electrician and we chatted about
our families. I told him about my brothers and sisters, and showed him
the camera I got for them at the commissary, one of the new ones where
the photo came out right after you took it. As we crossed the Shatt al-
Arab river into Basra, we had warmed up enough that I felt safe asking
him for a favor.

"All right if the driver drops me off at the bakery and picks me back
up at five in the morning after you've finished the wiring?"

We shook on it, and as soon as the jeep pulled away, I found a spot
on the sidewalk where I could sit and keep vigil over Alyaa's shuttered
house. As the hours passed, I felt my mind melting at the edges. Like a
madman, I started talking to strangers who passed, babbling incoherently about lost love. I considered throwing a rock or piece of wood at
her window but was too afraid. I finally gave up and went home to drink
again until morning pulled me out of night. And by the time the bottle
was empty and the last stars were fading into day, I weaved my way back

to Alyaa's house with a brilliant new plan. I was just going to bang on her door and ask her mother—no, *tell* her mother—that we were getting married. Enough of this hiding like a mouse. I was a man about to go to war, damn it, so why was I wilting before an elderly woman with one eye?

I marched straight for the door, for God and everyone to see, and when I was about to cross the street, Alyaa appeared in the door frame. Her hand flashed out from her abaya and she curled a finger, beckoning me. Something wasn't right, like she knew I was coming. I shook my head no; it was too risky. *Come this way*, I signaled back. We stood at an impasse, furiously signaling each other. She won. I walked over to her, looking over my shoulder, sure this was a trap. What if her brother was waiting for me inside with a knife?

I noticed immediately that she wasn't the same girl. She looked defeated, with the sagging face of a woman twice her age. She couldn't even raise her eyes to look at me.

"What's wrong? Did your brother die?" I asked.

"No, I am the one who died," she wept. "You killed me."

"I would never lay a hand on you," I said. "I'd kill half the Arab nation if necessary to protect you."

I reached out to hold her hand, but she pulled back. My precious Alyaa sensed only danger emanating from me now. I realized she could probably smell the alcohol on my breath, and I stepped back and closed my mouth.

"I can't talk to you here," she said. "Go home. I'll meet you in the courtyard."

I walked backward, stumbling a little, so I could keep her in my sight until she closed the door. Then I swiveled toward home, my vision blurred. Was she going to leave me? Had she already married the other man? Did someone threaten to kill her? I staggered home, dry heaving with dread.

As Alyaa came down my street, it looked like she was carrying something under her abaya. I darted into the secluded alley across from my house and she ducked in behind me, chuffing as if tears were coming out of her heart instead of her eyes. She came so close that her forehead was touching my nose, then pulled aside her abaya to reveal a baby, only a few weeks old, staring directly at me.

Sparks zinged up my spine and my vision and hearing sharpened, like an animal that has just sensed it is being hunted. Of all the possible scenarios I'd been fixating on, I'd forgotten to include this one. I knew the answer, but I asked anyway: "Who is that?"

"Your son."

He gurgled and reached for me with one tiny starfish hand.

"Is this real? Are you telling me the truth?" I asked.

"He is ours," she said.

I felt guilty, broken down. I had destroyed both our lives for one moment of passion.

"Who knows about him?"

"Only my mother."

"But where did you . . . how . . . ?"

She had given birth at an aunt's house, nearly two hundred miles north. The ruse she and her mother had agreed on was that the boy was the aunt's but had breathing problems and needed to be closer to the sea.

"Don't you want to kiss your son?"

My lips were quivering as I bent forward. His skin smelled just like his mother's. I felt his feet wiggling underneath her cloak. He had strong legs, like mine.

"What is his name?"

"Amjad."

He was indeed magnificent. And terrifying. From the miracle of his fingernails that were no bigger than sesame seeds to the way his stare hooked into me, as if he already knew his flesh was mine.

"Do you love him?" she asked.

Her question stirred a latent protective instinct in me.

"He is my son; nobody else will claim him. I will speak to my captain, and I promise, we will be married in two weeks."

"That is my dream."

I kissed them both one more time. Then I remembered the camera was still in my bag.

"Stay where you are," I said.

I stepped back so I could get her face and our baby's in the frame. She turned away, saying, "It's too dangerous for me."

"I won't ever show anyone. It's for me to keep close to my heart."

I pulled the photo out of the camera, waved it in the air until the image appeared, then tucked it safely inside my slim pocket Koran. I squeezed her hand and put my lips to the forehead of our impossibly perfect son.

"Soon," I whispered.

When I got back to Khorramshahr, I bypassed the captain's secretary and barged right into his office. He looked startled and covered some papers he was reading on his desk.

"You can't just come in here, soldier!" Storm clouds gathered on his brow.

"Sir, I'm not going to talk to you like a soldier talking to a captain. I'm going to talk to you man to man. I have no connections, I don't have money, I have no other support; all I have is my honor. I'm facing a big problem."

The captain studied me, then came around the desk and rested his palm on my shoulder.

"Najah, you are a good soldier, and everyone around here likes you. Stop shaking now. Tell me your story."

I confessed all of it, and he murmured supportively, and then I asked him if he would help me marry Alyaa. If he wouldn't help me, I was prepared to desert. In the silence before he responded, I heard the second hand of my watch as loud as a spoon scraping on brick.

"Do you want me to talk to her family or your father?" the captain asked.

"Both."

He snapped his fingers, as if to say this was an easy assignment.

"OK. Give me ten days. You and I will go back to Basra. I will get you married."

FIVE

THE MEDIC

To get Khorramshahr back from the Iraqis, we had to trick them. They had more tanks and rocket launchers than us, because they had lots more countries giving them money, but so what? We didn't let that stop us, because even though the Basij had junkier weapons and never enough ammunition, we had more spirit. Plus, we were creative.

We used water. I was still a few miles away in Shalamcheh, but to hear the commander tell it, it was something straight out of the Koran, like when the Prophet Nuh built an ark and all the pagans who refused to worship Allah were washed away. During the past year while Saddam's troops were busy occupying Khorramshahr, our combat engineers were busy digging a canal to take water from the Shatt al-Arab and shoot it like a fire hose right back at them. It took a really long time to move all that dirt, but eventually all that separated the Iraqi garrison from the waiting deluge was a thin dirt berm packed with explosives. Then one morning during the rainy season, the floodgates were opened on the dams upstream and the new canal filled with water. Our guys waited until just before dawn, and *shazam*! Total water wipeout.

I imagine the unsuspecting Arabs were fast asleep when the flood lifted them from the ground and swallowed them in its thirsty mouth. There probably wasn't even time to scream for help before their tanks sank into the muck and their bunkers turned into watery tombs. By the time my Basij unit arrived, the whole field was a stinky swamp, full of flies and dead bodies.

The medical assistants, because we were always given the grossest jobs, had to bury the dead in mass graves. I slogged through the mud, trying not to breathe through my nose or look down at the graying bodies that were splayed everywhere like zombies. Nearby, bulldozers took big bites out of the soupy earth, digging enormous pits. It was impossible to move a man by myself, so two of us, and sometimes three soldiers, rolled, pulled, and kicked one corpse at a time toward the holes. Sometimes it was easier to pile them up in the front bucket of the bulldozer and drop a bunch in at once. Whenever I started to think about what I was doing, I would bite the inside of my cheek to snap myself out of it. I forced my mind to wander to anything but the task at hand. I'd wonder what the dead man's name was, or where he was from, or imagine him at work or playing with his kids before the war started.

I should have felt victorious while I worked, but I felt sort of sorry for the dead guys. Mostafa had taught me to forgive people, and that everyone deserves a second chance. That sometimes a person isn't bad but his circumstances force him to go against his true self. Maybe some of these Iraqis were in the war because they were running away from something, too. But then again, how could I forgive them for taking a city that didn't belong to them? For blowing up my school and killing my friends? I didn't think Mostafa meant I should forgive people like that. Murderers can't be forgiven, right? My mind felt like a tennis ball, pinging back and forth.

"Hey, are you going to help me or just stare off into space?"

A medic next to me was tugging at the gold rings on a dead man's swollen fingers. He tore his shirt open, looking for a necklace. It was disgraceful, and I didn't want anything to do with it. I took a step away.

"What? You don't think they do the same to us?" he called toward my back.

If they did, they wouldn't find much. Our Supreme Leader said jewelry was showing off and distracted people from worshipping God, so we weren't supposed to wear it. Which was a good thing, because none of the Basij I knew could afford gold anyway, which was probably why this guy wanted so badly to steal it. He was prying open the dead man's mouth now, looking for gold teeth. He must have found what he was looking for, because he stood up and started kicking the corpse in the jaw. I kept walking, so I wouldn't have to hear the crunching of his teeth breaking loose.

The flood helped get us a little closer to Khorramshahr, but about 35,000 Iraqi troops still held the city, protecting it with land mines and tanks positioned behind dirt barriers. Our goal was to take their command post inside an old fertilizer plant on the northern edge of the port. Every once in a while, I got a whiff of burnt matches, and in the distance, I heard shelling, which meant we were getting closer to the front.

According to the latest news, so far our secret Sacred House operation was working, and any day now we'd cut off all the roads leading into Khorramshahr, surround the city with double the number of soldiers the Iraqis had, and then press in on them so they couldn't escape. Until then, we set up camp as thousands of soldiers from the Revolutionary Guard and the regular army joined us over the next few weeks, coming over pontoon bridges and parachuting out of helicopters. They wheeled rocket launchers into position and aimed them at the city. The plan, as usual, was to send the Basij in first, with our rifles and grenades, and the professional soldiers would follow, with their artillery and tanks. I would race from the front to the field hospital in an ambulance, plucking the wounded off the battlefield.

To get ready, we sewed grenades into the backs of our collars, so if caught by the enemy we could pull the pin as we lifted our hands in surrender, killing our captors along with ourselves. To the Basij way of thinking, a captured soldier was worse than a dead one. A prisoner of war was nothing more than a failed martyr, an embarrassment to his family. With these hidden grenades, we would become martyrs-plus, because not only would we have died in battle, we would have gone down killing to the very end. I wasn't sure about all that martyr stuff, but I did know that when I was going to be killed—and after what I had seen so far, I believed my time was coming—I just wanted to go instantly, like in an explosion, and not have to beg for my life or have my teeth kicked in by gold diggers.

Finally, we were given orders to advance into Khorramshahr. As our men moved closer, Iraqi fighter pilots flew overhead and fired with machine guns, and we used surface-to-air missiles to knock them out of the sky. Bullets made snapping noises as I zigzagged the ambulance, driving with the accelerator all the way down as I followed behind the battle searching for wounded soldiers. I could hear the high whine of incoming mortars in the distance as I helped lift soldiers into the ambulance and raced them to the makeshift tent hospital back at camp. We delivered so many wounded soldiers to the hospital that I learned how to tell by sight whether we should drive toward a fallen man or whether he was already dead. If the wild dogs were at the body, that gave me all the information I needed. Our commanders kept saying we were making progress, yet I wondered how that could be when all I could see through the windshield was dying men—so many that I'd lost count.

The battle raged all night, and on the second day, panicked Iraqis began streaming out of the underground bunkers and house basements with their hands up, waving their white undershirts in surrender and shouting "Ya Khomeini!" as if they were our long-lost friends. They would say anything so that we would spare their lives, and sometimes it worked and sometimes it didn't. I saw one man emerge from a hole in the ground, cowering and holding a dinner plate over his head with the face of the Prophet Ali on it. Others dropped their weapons on the ground, ran, and jumped into the Shatt al-Arab to try to swim or float back to their country on makeshift rafts.

"Shoot them," our commander bellowed. "Don't feel sorry for anybody. If you see my mother out there, you kill her. Got me? If someone out there feels bad about it, I will rip his heart out."

Many of the Iraqis who tried to flee were gunned down. The ones who surrendered were forced to sit on the ground in a big group, and sometimes they were killed and sometimes they were spared; I didn't dare ask why. But some Iraqis wouldn't give up and were taking shots at us from rooftops and lobbing grenades from behind courtyard walls. In the downtown area, it was utter chaos as gunfire ripped in all directions, and when an enemy showed his face, it was hard to tell who was giving up and who was charging you. We had no coordinated battle plan, and jumpy Basij were shooting at anything that moved, sometimes one another. In the confusion, arguments broke out between Revolutionary Guards over whether they should execute surrendering Iraqis or take them prisoner.

By nightfall I was ordered to search the bunkers. I was to give medical aid to any wounded Persians I found and a bullet to any Iraqis. I had never killed anyone, and I really, really didn't want to. My only weapon was a flashlight, but abandoned guns were strewn everywhere, so I picked up a rifle as I approached the first bunker on trembling legs. I felt my collar to make sure the grenade was still there. There could be groups of Iraqis inside, waiting for the right chance to make a run for it. They were most certainly armed, and they would most certainly blow my head off the second I walked in. I crouched at the entrance, turned off my flashlight, and waited for courage. This was suicide, the same as walking in the minefield, and again I had no choice. I took one step through the doorway and listened for breathing. It was still as a pond, yet the familiar scent of death—that mixture of shit, blood, and rot—let me know somebody was in there.

"Come out!" I yelled, lowering my voice to sound like an adult.

Nothing.

My hands shook as I turned on my light. The beam cut across several bodies sprawled on the dirt floor, collapsed in a pool of blood that was already starting to form a crust at the edges. These Iraqis had been dead for some time. I tightened my helmet strap, stepped out of the bunker, and continued my patrol.

Up ahead, I thought I saw the dark line of a trench. Safety. I sprinted toward it as gunshots crackled from all directions. If I could just hide in the trench until the gunfire settled, I could continue searching the bunkers later. I jumped down into the trench, landing on top of a dead Iraqi soldier, curled in a fetal position. Helmets and ammunition boxes and combat boots were scattered everywhere. I shined my light toward one end of the trench and saw the door to a bunker. I approached slowly, through an S-shaped entrance that led to a large room with cement walls and floor, obviously built for high-ranking officers, five or six of whom were collapsed in a haystack of bodies. I poked them with the rifle but got no response. Just to be safe, I gathered all their weapons and piled them in the farthest corner, out of their grasp. I turned to go and then I heard a sound, a low "Unhhhh." I whipped back around, and the man at the bottom of the pile was looking at me through half-lidded eyes. Instinctively, the medic in me pulled the corpses off him, and he gasped when the air rushed back into his lungs. I jumped back and hunched down, ready to spring on him if he tried to attack. But he just lay there, moaning and mumbling something. His tan desert fatigues were soaked red from his chest to his waist, and he had an open gash on his forehead and another on his arm. I hoped he would die on me, and those moans he was making were his last.

Then he turned his head and looked directly at me and said something. I didn't understand Arabic, but I think I caught one word of it: "Muslim." It came out like "Moo-zime."

I stood and put my finger on the trigger, but my shaking hands made it impossible to fix on a point. Then he lifted his hand and weakly reached for his shirt pocket. This Arab was going to blow us both up! I dove to reach the grenade first, but my fingers touched paper instead, and I pulled out a pocket-sized Koran. I slumped onto the ground, now the one gasping with relief. Every Basij I knew carried a Koran into battle for protection, and I guess all the Iraqis did, too. I looked back at the wounded man to make sure he wasn't reaching for anything else.

"Muslim, Muslim," he moaned.

There was something hidden in the book. I suspected money, after watching the other soldiers pillage so many dead bodies. I'd learned that the Koran everyone carried doubled as a wallet. I held it open on my palm and the pages fluttered back to reveal a photograph tucked inside. I saw a woman with olive skin and dramatic eyebrows, holding an infant to her chest. The baby's face was in profile, but it was so young that its skin was still bright red. The woman's dark eyes cast a spell, like she could look straight into my secrets. There was something about her gaze, a sadness that made me want to hold her hand and tell her everything was going to be OK.

I knew I was holding his family in my hands. These were the people who loved him, who would die inside if I killed him. She was so beautiful, like the kind of wife I would want someday, and it would be wrong to ruin her life, and even more evil to take away a baby's father. This soldier had a life that wasn't here, that wasn't supposed to end with me shooting him in a bunker. Something had brought him to this war that was out of his control, because why else would he leave such a beautiful family behind?

The Iraqi smiled weakly at me, and that's when I noticed that we were the same. We both had two eyes, a nose, and a mouth. Why was I supposed to hate him? He had never harmed me. I had managed to get this far in the war without killing anyone, and I wasn't going to start now. If I put a bullet in his temple to end his misery, then the guilt would haunt me forever. I could walk away, but letting him suffer was more inhumane than taking his life. Or I could be merciful.

You must be good to people. Zahed, are you listening?

I smelled diesel exhaust, and I was back in the truck with Mostafa, bouncing my hand against the hot wind through the open window. Mostafa was eating pistachios and telling me a story, the same one I'd heard before from my elementary-school teacher, so I was only half-listening. It was the one about a big storm that sent boulders down a mountain and onto some railroad tracks. The next day when the train was coming, a villager who lived nearby ran onto the tracks, took off all his clothes, set them on fire, and waved them in the air to stop the train. The conductor braked, screeching the train to a stop just inches from running him over. The villager became a hero for sacrificing himself to save the passengers, and when the Shah called him to the palace and tried to kiss his hand, the man wouldn't let the king bow down like that. The villager refused to be called a hero, saying he did what any human being would do in the same situation.

Now I was inside my own folktale, facing a big question of wrong and right. I could be killed for helping the enemy. But I could be killed every second of every day in this war. Iraqi, Iranian, so what? We were two human beings who had somehow fallen into the same hell. I put the rifle down.

Blood was trickling from his forehead into his eyes. He was losing a lot of blood and would need more soon. The Iraqi was moaning louder now. I went to his side and reached under his neck to tilt his head back. His lips fell open, and I poured some water from my canteen into his mouth. He drank, and I felt the muscles in his neck slightly relax. I poured slowly, just the way Mostafa's wife had done for me. I knew what it was like to feel helpless, and I felt sorry for this Iraqi. I didn't even have a beard yet, and I was in total control of his fate. But just because I held all the power didn't mean I had to hurt him with it.

From inside my medical bag, I pulled out a syringe and injected him with a painkiller. He mumbled something in Arabic again and half-smiled. Then his eyes rolled back and his head lolled to one side.

"Don't die now," I said.

I could smell gunpowder, and bullets crackled nonstop. From underground, I heard muffled explosions. Iranian soldiers were tossing grenades into other bunkers where they found Iraqis hiding. They were going bunker to bunker, shooting the wounded, even the ones who looked dead, just to be sure. I had to hide him. I got on my knees and pushed the dead bodies into a corner, grunting and groaning as I pulled them into a sloppy pile, to form a low wall. If I stacked them like a log cabin, it would look suspicious. Then I grabbed the soldier's feet and dragged him behind them so that if anyone else found this bunker, they might not see that there was one still alive.

I wadded up a jacket and put it under his head. He seemed unconscious, but then his eyes flicked open in a second of pure clarity and he struggled to slip the watch from his wrist and, with a shaking hand, held it out to me.

I took the gift and put it back in the side pocket of his pants. Then I leaned in close to his ear and put my finger to my lips.

"*Shhhh.*"

SIX

THE PATIENT

Where'd he go? Just a minute ago—or was it hours, days, or never?—an angel came to me. He poured water into my mouth and then gently took my hand to escort me to the other side. But then what happened? Where am I now?

Think, Najah, think.

My skull was being hammered from the inside, and I couldn't move my right arm. It was dark. OK, three facts. That was good. I could make sense of three things. *Keep going. What else?* I was on the ground somewhere. It was smooth, not dirt. There was no wind. *I must be indoors. Am I alone? There's a faint noise that sounds like . . . chewing? That can't be right.*

"Anyone there?" I whispered.

I got no response, except from the flies that kept landing on my face. For some reason, my body didn't move when my brain told it to. I couldn't bat the flies away, so they crawled, crawled, crawled on me with their tickling footsteps. *Am I already dead? Oh God, what if the angel took me to hell?*

There was a metallic taste of blood in my mouth, and no matter how much I swallowed, it wouldn't go away. And it smelled in here, wherever I was. Like a goat that got run over days before. My eyelids were sealed shut with something gooey, and when I finally forced my good arm to move, it felt like broken glass was being pressed into my abdomen. I yowled in pain as I rubbed the sticky blood from my eyes, and when I was able to open them, I could make out something wiggling a few feet away from me in the dark. I waited for my eyes to adjust, and then the grotesque shape registered: several dead men toppled on top of each other, with maggots swarming from their open wounds, coursing in streams, marching their insatiable way toward me. I gagged and tried to smash the insects with my feet, but that short circuit between my brain and body kept me a statue. I was waiting to be devoured. No doubt about it, I was in hell.

Even from all the way down here in purgatory, I heard the whistle. It was a sharp blast, followed by two short ones. A military whistle. The sound slithered into my ear and then I sensed some rustling and shuffling as images started to sort themselves in my brain and line up chronologically. Like with Pavlov's dog, the whistle shook my memory and told it what to do.

Suddenly, I remembered:

I had just come from the captain's office—no, floated from the captain's office—to break the news to the guys in my tent that in ten days' time, Alyaa and I would be husband and wife. But as soon as I set foot inside, I sensed a nervous energy as my tent mates scurried to put gas masks and food rations into their rucksacks.

"What's up?" I asked.

"Someone leaked a telex. The enemy is planning a big attack. Tonight."

Our warplanes roared off the ground as I jogged to my tank, where my crew was already on board, loading up on fuel and ammunition. I crawled into the driver's seat and pumped the purge pump and pressed the air bleeder button to get the air out of the fuel lines. Once they were cleared, I started the engine and then adjusted the throttle by pulling down a lever on the left wall. We stayed rumbling and ready, while more soldiers wheeled multi-rocket launchers into position that had the capacity to fire what looked like an enormous cigarette pack of missiles simultaneously. They fired a few times, a warning to the Iranians that we would not be taken by surprise. Armored trucks swarmed in, taking a defensive line behind hundreds of troops pouring into trenches with their machine guns and automatic rifles.

Then just after midnight, Cobra helicopters roared out of the sky, firing down on us with three-barreled rotating cannons. The Iranian pilots launched missiles that hit with incredible precision, turning our armored trucks and buildings into balls of flame. Our men haphazardly fired back at any light in the sky, trying their best to hit something, but it was a rout as the Iranians circled mercilessly, aided by height and the cover of darkness. I could hear panic over the radio as the call came down from headquarters to move the tanks forward, three at a time, behind one of the massive fortified dirt mounds we'd constructed to camouflage heavy artillery. My hands were sweating as I moved the steering laterals, trying to avoid driving into the deep pits made by mortar blasts. The enemy was coming at us harder than I think anyone expected. Infantrymen were dropping all around us as we got into position behind the berm.

The commander's voice was shaky as it crackled through our headsets: "Tank. Range sixteen hundred. Twelve o'clock."

The gunner looked through the telescope and rotated the range button, looking for the enemy's convoy. "Identified," he said.

The loader shifted the cannon safety switch to the "fire" position. "Up!" he called.

"Ready," the gunner responded.

The commander's voice boomed, "*Fire!*" and the gunner reached for his left handgrip and pressed the trigger button. The sound was like a thunderclap inside the tank, and the force of it shook the walls and knocked me off my seat. We had forty rounds, and the commander instructed us to fire them all. The whole area was raging now, so loud we had to shout to be heard. The gunner lifted his hatch and swung the machine gun turret in a complete circle, firing two thousand rounds like a man possessed.

"They're shooting from behind us!" he screamed, as I fumbled with the radio, trying to contact anyone at our base. But all I got was static, then some faint mumbling and what sounded like people dropping things. Our communication network was severed.

"Radio's out—they must've been hit!" I shrieked, banging the receiver on the wall of the tank. I looked through the infrared periscope and saw our men fleeing their tanks.

"Are we surrendering? What the hell is going on?"

"Keep firing," the commander said. "The captain is in a convoy behind us. I'll run out and ask him what to do."

He's a dead man, I thought, as I watched our leader sprint into the bedlam. *And we're going to just sit here like a bull's-eye and wait to be annihilated.* Out of ammunition now, the gunner, the loader, and I fell silent as we waited for our verdict, listening to the sonic symphony of war, the deep bass of the bombs dancing with the staccato snap of bullets and arias of ambulance sirens. My hands trembled and I wished with every fiber of my being that a cigarette would magically appear between my fingers. Then our radio picked up voices. We jammed our headsets back on and realized we'd somehow picked up an Iranian frequency. Between the three of us, we could make out the important Farsi words: "enemy," "surrendering."

"Are we the only assholes still out here?" the loader asked.

His question hung in the air. The gunner had his nose buried in his pocket Koran, mumbling recitations while chewing on his fingernails.

"We can't be," I said, not very reassuringly.

The commander returned, with big circles of sweat under his arms, and we had to wait for him to catch his breath. His hair, normally slicked back perfectly, looked like it had been through a tornado.

"Uh, Captain doesn't know what's happening," he finally managed to say. The commander then straightened his spine, trying his best to compose himself. "He says to keep resisting until reinforcements arrive."

"What reinforcements?" I heard myself ask. We'd been fighting for three hours now. If there were reinforcements, they should have showed up already.

The gunner cuffed me on the ear with his Koran. "Shuddup, Aboud."

I looked through the periscope again and saw men drop as they ran from their posts, shot down by helicopters or snipers. The air was filled with last screams—in both Arabic and Farsi. I was weighing the options of hiding in the tank or making a run for it—wondering how many days we could last on the food rations we had with us—when a voice cut through the din over a loudspeaker. The voice spoke in Arabic, but with a Persian accent: *"Your army has retreated! Khorramshahr is being recaptured. Surrender now. Whoever plants thorns cannot reap grapes!"*

Our thorny sin was taking Khorramshahr, and now we were paying for it. But the warning could be a trick to make us think we had given up—calling victory before it was true as a tactic to clear out the last of our fighters.

"I'm going out there just to see what's going on," I announced.

"Too dangerous," the commander said.

I ignored him and started lifting the floor hatch, so I could exit underneath the tank. "I'm going with you," the loader said.

"Shit!" the commander said, climbing out of his seat. "Wait here," he told the gunner as he followed us outside. We crawled on our bellies, like three lizards, coughing and trying to decipher landmarks through the smoke. We'd only made it a few hundred yards when out of the corner of my eye, I saw our tank turn and drive toward Iraq, trying to escape. *Motherfucker.*

"He's abandoning us!" I screamed.

The gunner was insane. If he wasn't killed by the Iranians, he'd be killed when Saddam hanged him in the public square with the other deserters. The commander and the loader turned to look, and that's when I felt the ground shudder beneath my belly. Then a massive boom, and I was airborne. Grains of sand needled into my pores, and for the briefest moment, I was suspended above the battlefield. All sound stopped, all the shelling, all the screaming for Allah, all of it silenced, and the orange flashes of mortar fire looked almost pretty in the darkness. Like candles flickering above the desert.

When I crashed back to earth, I had no more faith in anything. I didn't believe in God, in humanity, or in Saddam's war. There was no time for such devotions, as blood seeped from my forehead and chest, and all around me soldiers were being executed as they begged for their lives.

I couldn't feel one of my arms. I ran my other hand over my body, and inventoried the working parts. Legs—still there. Stomach—gaping wound. Head—intact, but blood was running down my forehead. Odd. I didn't feel any pain. Could I stand? I rolled onto all fours and tried to push myself up onto my feet, but the earth spun and I toppled over. I brushed the sand and blood out of my eyes and saw the commander and the loader were rolling on the ground as well. Our tank was listing to one side, and flames were shooting from the auxiliary gas barrels on the back. If I couldn't stand, I could still crawl. I used my good arm and pulled myself to the commander, who was trying to say something through bubbles of blood. I dragged him to a nearby trench and rolled him into it. Then I went back for the loader, and together we stumbled on our knees to the trench while he leaned into me and cried out his mother's name.

"Brother! Help me! Over here!" A third Iraqi soldier called to me in the darkness, and though I knew I was badly wounded, I felt superhuman, as if I were impervious to pain, to danger. It was my duty, so I went to the third man and dragged him off the battlefield, too. When all three men were in the trench, I lowered myself on top of them to protect them, even though I had no idea if they were still alive. Then I heard our tanks being blown up, one by one, rocking the earth and sending small avalanches of dirt onto us. Once the massive explosions subsided, I heard voices— Iranians walking and talking directly above our heads.

The loader heard them, too. He reached out and clasped my shirt, which was now soaked with blood.

"What should we do?" he asked.

I scanned the trench until my gaze settled on a doorway leading to a bunker.

"There." I pointed. "That will be our grave. Let's die in there."

Once I started crawling toward the doorway, I could sense pain. It felt like my intestines had turned to lava, and they were slowly melting me from the inside. I had the sensation that the heat was retreating from my extremities, pulled inward into a molten ball in my stomach, as if the last of my energy was swallowing itself until it would be no more than a tiny pinprick, then blink out forever.

It's true what they say about your whole life flashing by as you wait for death to come sit next to you. It happens fast, like Kodachrome slides snapping into view, all these images of yourself in moments of pure joy. I closed my eyes and saw my brothers and me climbing trees to pick dates. I felt my fingers close around the fur of our big German shepherd as we wrestled in the family courtyard, and heard my mother's voice singing from the kitchen. I tasted the falafel that my sister and I fried in our Bruce Lee Restaurant, and I saw Alyaa's abaya fluttering in the wind as she cradled Amjad in her arms. The last thing I saw was my family together, celebrating the thirtieth birthday I would never have.

Then I felt a hand on my chest. I opened my eyes, but I was momentarily blinded. When I tried to reach for the hand, my limbs were numb and wouldn't move. *It's an angel,* I thought, *tugging on my shirt to take me to the other world.* And, like all nonbelievers who face their moment of death, I found religion instantly.

"Dear Prophet Muhammad," I prayed aloud, "save me."

My vision cleared, and I saw a child soldier pointing a rifle at my temple. He was so small that he had to roll up the sleeves and pant legs of his uniform. This Persian boy had been brainwashed to hate me. I spoke as softly as I could. "Please," I said, "I'm a Muslim, just like you."

He backed up a step and cocked the rifle. He either couldn't understand Arabic or he didn't care to chat before pulling the trigger.

"Muslim! Muslim!" I pleaded.

The boy took aim.

Carefully, I reached into my jacket pocket to show him my Koran, and the boy lunged, grabbing it from me. He rustled through the pages, stopping when he discovered the photo of Alyaa and Amjad. He studied the image, as if he recognized them. He glanced at me and back to the photo again. I think I saw him gently touch her face with his finger.

He snapped the book shut and turned toward me with an expression of utter blankness. I silently said good-bye to everyone I loved. Then the boy slid the Koran back in my pocket. He knelt down and gave me water from his canteen. Then he leaned in close and put his finger to his lips.

"Shhhhhh."

Then he smiled, and all my terror turned to mist and evaporated. We suddenly spoke the same language—the language of humans. I smiled back to let him know I understood that I was safe. I knew I could close my eyes in front of him and give in to my exhaustion. So I did.

I had no idea how long ago that was. Now I was alone, and I could hear the maggots chittering.

Angel, where are you now?

SEVEN

SAVING NAJAH

I needed blood. The Iraqi was going to die if he didn't get a transfusion soon. I waited until the morphine injection took effect and he slipped into a quiet sleep. I needed to keep him sedated, because if he made too much noise, someone would hear him and shoot him for sure. This Iraqi was my secret, and deciding to rescue him was like a rescue for me, too. Just knowing he was there gave me something to feel happy about. I felt less scared, because he needed me. I tiptoed out of the bunker and jogged all the way to the medical tent, where I asked for an IV and a bag of blood.

"And more bandages," I said.

I stuffed it all into my medical bag and headed back. I had never given someone an IV before, but I'd watched it done so many times I was pretty sure I could find the vein myself. The Iraqi's eyes were closed, but I think he knew I was there, because as I got near, he started moaning softly, repeating some words I was pretty sure meant "Help me." I jammed a bayonet into a crack in the concrete wall and attached the bag of blood to it. I squeezed his arm to try to make his veins pop up, but it wasn't working because he was too weak. I forced the needle in and put a piece of tape over it to keep it in place. Working quickly, I cleaned his wounds with water and disinfectant, then wrapped his temple, his arm, and his torso with bandages. It was all I had, but it would have to do. His whole body twitched like he was having a dream, and I put my hand on his chest to try to calm him.

"Muslim," I said.

He let out a long sigh. "Amjad," he said.

He was delirious now, thinking I was someone else. I gave him some more water and snuck back out and continued searching for more wounded soldiers. I walked for a long time but found no one alive, and when I couldn't keep my eyes open any longer, I found an abandoned foxhole and curled up to catch a few hours of sleep.

The following day, the fighting had subsided. I went about my normal duties, trying not to draw attention to myself as I loaded corpses into ambulances and put injured Iranians on top of the dead to be taken to a temporary field hospital. So many Iraqis had surrendered that there were hundreds gathered in groups all over the place, sitting cross-legged in rows with guns pointed at them, waiting to find out their fates. Many were injured, some quite severely, but they were not getting any medical attention. I knew my patient was safer with me than if he was lingering in the hot sun with no medicine and a ticket to prison.

The border was a mere six miles away. If only there was some way I could smuggle him to Iraq, but even if he had the strength to run for it in the middle of the night, he'd probably never make it; there were too many guards at the border. I could take him in an ambulance, hiding him under dead bodies, but I'd be heading in the wrong direction—into Iraq—and would surely be caught. But here he could be found by one of us at any moment. Even if he wasn't discovered, he wasn't going to survive in that bunker. I had to get him into a real hospital.

I waited until there was a lull in the day and then slipped away. The Iraqi was awake, and despite the overpowering stench, he smiled at me as if I came bearing roses. I smiled back, feeling mighty proud of my doctoring skills, until I noticed his arm had swollen to twice the normal size because I hadn't done the needle right. I cursed under my breath and took the IV out and covered the spot where the needle had been with tape. It must have hurt, but the Iraqi didn't even flinch; he just kept smiling at me like he didn't have a care in the world. I gave him some sedative pills to make sure he stayed happy and quiet, and he swallowed them, keeping his gaze fixed on me as I gave him more water. He rested his head back on the ground, then pointed at the IV and then at me. I nodded, to say "Yes, I put that there." I pointed at my chest and then opened my medical bag to show him I was a medic. He didn't respond, so I pointed to the red cross on my sleeve and made hand motions like I was turning a steering wheel, so maybe he'd understand I was with an ambulance. He put his hand over his heart, kind of like he was saying thank you. I did the same.

I was able to get another bag of blood for the Iraqi, and this time I did a better job of getting the needle in his other arm. He seemed to be stabilizing, but if I kept taking bags of blood to the same location, eventually the other medics would notice. Already one of them asked me why I kept going back and forth to the same area, and I wouldn't be able to dodge the questions much longer. I needed a helper.

I found Omid guarding the officers' quarters. He saw me coming toward him and his tough-guy face dissolved.

"Donkey!" he shouted. "How are you?"

"Still alive. You?"

"Alive, too."

We embraced.

"Listen, I need a favor," I said.

I explained that I had a patient and that I needed help taking care of him, and then at the end of my plea I tacked on the fact that he was an Iraqi. Omid stepped back from me, as if I was contagious.

"Are you fucking with me? They'll take you to court and hang you for treason."

"Only if I get caught."

"You *will* get caught. I don't want to be there when you do."

Of all the people I thought would understand, it was him, but I'd forgotten one basic thing about Omid—that deep down he was, and always would be, a mama's boy. He could stand there with a gun and play the part of a guard, but the truth was, he was too much of a scaredy-cat to guard anything, much less a big secret like this.

"You're right. I should've known you couldn't handle it."

Omid glowered at me and spoke through gritted teeth.

"You're insane; get away from me."

"OK, look, I shouldn't have said that. You are not a coward, and I shouldn't have put this big secret in your hands. You just have to swear on the Koran that you won't tell anybody, all right?"

"Fine. I swear. But tell me one thing. Why are you doing this?"

I thought for a second, though I could barely make sense of it myself. "Because he needs help. He's just a regular guy, like you and me," I answered.

Omid rolled his eyes. "I don't understand you. Don't you have enough problems in your life? Why do you always have to go looking for more? You don't know the first thing about that Iraqi."

How could I explain that I had learned everything I needed to know about him by one quick glance at a photograph? Even I realized that sounded crazy. Maybe Omid wasn't that far off; I could be losing my mind.

"I just know," I said weakly.

Omid took hold of my elbow and steered me to a narrow space between two supply trucks, where no one could see us.

"You are a pain in the ass, but you're still my friend," he whispered. "I will help you get blood, but I won't go in that bunker."

I grabbed his shoulders and kissed him on both cheeks. "This is between you, me, and God."

On the third day, the Iraqi was stable, but he needed better care than I could give him. He was sure to get an infection if I didn't get him away from those dead bodies, and there was another wave of our soldiers on their way, and who knows what they would do if they found him? In desperation, I approached the brother of the commander, who was keeping guard over the growing crowd of captives. He was so tall, like a tree, that I had to crane my neck just to get his attention.

"Sir?"

"Mmmm."

"Um, sir, what should we do if we find any Iraqis who need medical attention?"

Two of the tree's massive limbs reached down and grabbed my ears, then lifted me up and slammed me back to the ground.

"This is not a classroom!" he roared. "This is a place of no mercy. See those cowards?" He pointed to several dozen Iraqis running toward us from a grove of date palms, holding their hands above their heads. "They are the enemy. The enemy of you, of me, of our country, and of Khomeini."

Everything around me suddenly moved in slow motion, and I saw him raise his Kalashnikov. I screamed, but by the time the sound left my throat, he was already firing, knocking down every single one of them. I watched in horror as each man fell to the ground.

Then he turned to face me and asked, "That answer your question?"

My knees buckled and I almost fainted, but I picked a spot on the ground near his boots and stared until I found my balance again. I felt guilty, as if I had pulled the trigger myself. When I could focus again, I saw that the commander's brother was peering down at me, waiting for a response. I tried to say "Yes, sir," but it came out as a cough, not words.

I was only making him more furious. "Are you mocking me?" he challenged.

All manner of insults hurled from his mouth. I was a weakling, a disgrace to the Basij, a hairy monkey that should go back to the jungle. I cowered under his wrath, just hoping he wouldn't slam me to the ground again, when one of my former elementary-school teachers, now a high-ranking officer, approached. "Why are two Iranians fighting?" he asked.

"I'm teaching this Basiji a lesson—that we don't kiss the enemy."

"Are we supposed to kill all the prisoners?" I protested. "Why bother taking them prisoner in the first place?"

It was a stalemate. My former teacher sent us in opposite directions and said he'd check with central command for the final word on what was to become of the captured Iraqis.

The following morning, a siren called all soldiers to the downtown mosque. After prayers, there was an announcement. Khorramshahr was officially liberated, and because the city was Persian again, there was no need to fight over it anymore. All the captured Iraqis would be sent to prison camps, and the injured ones would be healed in Iranian hospitals and then incarcerated as well. My heart did a cartwheel in my chest. My patient wasn't going to be killed, at least not on my watch. I can't say what awaited him in captivity, but I'd kept my word and kept him alive.

I went to the field hospital for a stretcher, where I ran into another medical assistant, Ahad-Amin—the same one who had questioned my frequent visits to one bunker in particular.

"What are you doing?" he asked.

"I need a shovel," I said.

He brought me one, the kind with an axe on the opposite end.

"What for?" he asked.

"Don't talk; just come with me. Hurry," I said.

He followed me into the bunker, and when the force of the stink hit him, he started to gag. The bodies by now had putrefied together so they looked more like one big mound than individual people, and a plague of flies rose from them and swarmed us.

"What the hell?" Ahad-Amin came up behind me and held his shirt in front of his mouth to help him breathe. The Iraqi let out a moan, and Ahad-Amin jumped back. I used the shovel to push the dead ones aside and clear a path to the Iraqi. I hooked my hands under his armpits and motioned for Ahad-Amin to grab his feet.

"Is he still alive?"

"Barely. Now, c'mon, let's go."

Ahad-Amin backed up, like he was about to run away.

"Why bother? Just let him die," he said.

I ignored him and hurriedly began taking off the Iraqi's blood-stained shirt so he would look like the other enemy soldiers who'd taken off their shirts to signal surrender. I would get him on the stretcher my-self if I had to. Ahad-Amin was looking at the makeshift IV and the scattering of dirty bandages nearby.

"You were giving him medicine? What if the commander had found out?"

"This man needs to be transferred to the hospital. If you aren't going to help, get out of my way."

Ahad-Amin cussed under his breath and helped me lift the Iraqi onto the stretcher. We guided him through a battlefield littered with burned-out husks of tanks, some of them still smoldering. Off in the distance we spotted another group of Iraqi soldiers without their shirts, walking with their hands in the air, and we headed toward them. It was slow going, and we had to stop often to catch our breath. We were taking a short rest to give the Iraqi water when a young Iranian soldier came running up to us. At first I thought he had an important message, but once he got close, he raised his rifle toward the Iraqi.

"Don't hit him!" I screamed.

Too late. The butt of the gun slammed into the Iraqi's mouth, and he shrieked in pain. My patient's jaw was hideously askew, and his bot-tom and top teeth flapped like they were on hinges as he spat out blood. Without even thinking about it, I leaped through the air and landed on the attacker, knocking the wind out of him. I pushed him into a canal, grabbed the stretcher again, and Ahad-Amin and I hustled toward the medical tent. I wasn't about to lose my patient now, after all I'd risked. The Iraqi was shaking in pain, and every once in a while he looked up at me as if to be assured I was still there, and each time I smiled at him to let him know he was safe with me. Poor guy was so pitiful. He had a streak of blood dribbling from his mouth, down his chin, and all the way to his belly.

It took about an hour, but we finally made it to the medical tent set up for prisoners. It was no more than a canvas roof stretched over some poles sticking out of the sand. There were about forty wounded men there in various states. The healthiest ones sat in groups, telling one another to stay strong, that their military was mighty and would get them out of their situation soon. Some had glassy eyes and amputated limbs, while still others screamed in agony and a few were unconscious. A trio of Iranian military journalists was stepping through the crowd and holding out microphones to the ones who could talk. I heard one interviewee tell his parents that he was still alive and that he'd been captured as a prisoner of war. I steered the Iraqi through the throng to a spot where he had room to lie down. I made sure he rested on his side, so he wouldn't choke on his own blood. About seven hours later, trucks came to transport the prisoners to the hospital in Ahvaz. I helped load all the prisoners into the truck beds, taking note of which vehicle held my patient. I made sure to get into the passenger seat of his truck, and as we drove down the streets, people shook their fists and threw rocks at our criminal cargo: "Saddamis! Sinners!"

Once inside the hospital gates, it was safe to let them out, as armed guards stood watch. I kept my eye on the Iraqi, and as he stepped out, he lost his balance and fell to the ground. I rushed over, pushing aside one of the clumsy medics who should have caught his fall.

"I've got this one," I said, taking his place.

I helped the Iraqi walk through a long hallway as he dripped dirt and blood on the white tiles. I guided him to a hospital bed, and he slumped onto it, exhausted. The doctors were running about with the sudden influx of patients, doing very little to hide their distaste for helping the enemy. When one of the doctors stopped at the Iraqi's bed, he was furious.

"What is this crap you brought me? Can't you see we are busy enough with our own?"

"Please, isn't there anything you can do for him?"

The doctor shrugged dramatically. "If we can get to him. As you can see, there's a long line of people who didn't bomb our cities and rape our women."

I'm pretty sure the Iraqi understood the doctor was abandoning him, because he let out a long, sorrowful moan, as if he knew this was the end of the line. He was losing too much blood again. I walked to the far corner of the room, sank to my knees, and cried.

I remembered what Mostafa had said once, that if you really want something, you should not be ashamed to beg for it. He said you must plead to God from the bottom of your heart. I'd never really prayed before, like *really* meant what I said and really believed anyone could hear me. But now I had nothing to lose. I put my head in my hands, closed my eyes, and asked for help.

God, you've seen how much I've tried to save this Iraqi's life. But if you want him dead, that's your business, not mine.

I knew I was praying only because I wanted something, and you're not supposed to do that. So I struggled a long time trying to figure out how to ask God for help in a way that didn't sound greedy.

But if it's all the same to you, could you please change this doctor's mind?

EIGHT

THE KISS

His feathers were luminescent, a deep green that caught the light and sent it shimmering down his coat when he turned direction in the warm breeze, making his body darken from emerald to black. He had the dangerous confidence of youth, riding the wind like a roller coaster, tilting the tip of one wing slightly to send him plunging downward in a stomach-dropping free fall until his internal speedometer hit the red zone and he arched both wings to catch the updraft and gently float back up to an easy glide. My son pivoted and twirled like an acrobat in the sky, putting on a show but pretending not to, although I could tell he kept one eye on me to make sure I was noticing. He looked over his shoulder and laughed at my clumsy attempts to keep up, as I flapped my stiff arms and banged into clouds, like a befuddled ostrich that had suddenly discovered itself in the air. Why my son had suddenly sprouted feathers was a mystery, but I didn't want to ruin the moment with intrusive realities, so I set that puzzle aside for later.

We settled into a jasmine-scented jet stream, and I blew him a kiss, which he waved off with feigned disgust, flapping his wings harder to force me to chase him. I could hear his feathers fluttering as I pumped my arms harder to stay on his tail, envious of his natural athleticism yet proud at the same time. My boy.

Where we were going was irrelevant, but below us was the sea, its waves curling in unhurried barrel rolls toward the sand. I had laser vision, which I also didn't question, and could see into the deep blue to all the life below. I watched a mother whale put a protective fin over the back of her baby and guide it to the surface to breathe, and thought, *Yes, I know*. I could see manta rays execute slow-motion backflips, and tiny shrimps flex their bodies into miniature bicep curls as they hurried about their errands.

"Amjad! Look down!"

A school of dolphins rocketed out of the surf, wriggling and laughing in the air then plunging underwater, and all was silent again. I could see their dark outlines as they raced under the surface, jockeying for first place, then on some magic cue jumped en masse again, a burst of applause for one another.

"I see it, Dad, I see it!"

The ocean's clowns sent Amjad into peals of laughter. They somersaulted and spiraled to please him.

"Do it again!" he screamed.

And they did.

I closed my eyes and wished this moment would never end. But as soon as I did, I realized my terrible mistake. Everyone knows that as soon as you covet a thing, it gets taken away from you.

When I opened my eyes again, I seemed to have double vision. Two people were standing near my bed, speaking in Farsi. I blinked and then noticed only one of them was wearing a stethoscope around his neck. He leaned toward me and asked me in Arabic to open my mouth. His accent was Saudi.

"Tsk. They're all broken. Have to pull 'em."

My jaw was bandaged up and so sore it ached when I moved my thick, useless tongue.

"Whaa?"

I had to get out of this place. I put my palms on the mattress and tried to stand, but I was groggy, and it required too much effort for my confused limbs. The Saudi doctor sat down next to me and placed a hand on my shoulder.

"You are in a hospital in Iran. You lost a lot of blood and went into shock a few days ago. We were able to stabilize you, fix your broken jaw, and stitch your wounds, but you have been under heavy sedation."

"Am I a prisoner?" I tried to ask, but it came out like: "*Mmmmffffff.*" *No, no, this can't be. I'm supposed to be in Basra, getting married to Alyaa and teaching my son how to say "Baba."* My mouth wouldn't work, so all I could do was plead with my eyes. *Please, please tell me what's going on.*

"Someone is asking to see you," the doctor said, waving someone over. "This boy claims that he saved your life."

My terror evaporated the second I recognized the angel who came to me in the bunker. The boy nodded, and I smiled at him even though it was agony on my jaw. The boy said something to the doctor in Farsi.

"He wants you to know that you are in a safe place now, and that you should take care of your health."

I reached for the boy's small hand, and he gave it to me. The boy said something more to the doctor.

"He says that soon you will be transferred to a military base."

Clearly, then, I was still in the hands of the enemy. And those hands were now fists, wrapped around the promise I'd made to Alyaa, squeezing and crushing it to dust. Whether she would think I lied, forgot her, or was careless and died, it was all the same in the end. I wouldn't be coming back to marry her any time soon. I wondered how long she would wait until she gave up. Worse, how long would her family wait before trying to get her married to someone else? Even worse, what if her secret came out? I couldn't protect her from knives and stones with my hands in handcuffs.

This was supposed to be a quick, winnable war. I was supposed to be back in Basra in a few months, starting my new family and opening another falafel restaurant. My brothers and sisters were all going to work there, fiercely guarding the secret recipe, and we'd bring in even more money than Bruce Lee Restaurant, keeping us all comfortable until Amjad was a grandfather himself. Now, the Iranians would decide my future.

But I wasn't dead. There was no more smell of gunfire or death, and the incessant crack of bullets had stopped. At last, I felt my heartbeat settle to its normal pace. I wasn't in a war zone, at least temporarily, and I was alive. I wanted to ask the boy why he chose me. I wanted to have a long conversation and find out everything about him, but even if my mouth worked, it was too dangerous to reveal our friendship with so many Iranians swirling around the hospital. He could be discovered as a traitor, and maybe even killed for not killing me. I brought the boy's hand to my lips to kiss it, but he pulled back and leaned forward instead to place a light kiss on both of my cheeks.

"Allah yusallmak," I whispered—may God protect and assist you. The boy smiled and stepped back.

"Lean back," the doctor ordered. He poured a liquid in my mouth. "Rinse," he said.

I did as I was told, and soon my gums became numb and I couldn't feel my lips anymore. He reached toward my mouth with what looked like pliers, and I gripped the boy soldier's hand as the doctor pulled out my hanging teeth. I felt a tug and dull pain as I watched the pile of teeth on the metal table beside me grow from two to four to ten to a dozen, and then I stopped counting. My lovely white teeth were sitting there like forgotten beans. The smile that used to be my calling card, the one I had used to greet my customers, the one that had captured Al-yaa's heart—gone forever. Under different circumstances, I would have mourned such a destruction of my face. But as I endured the pain, my mind was wrestling with bigger worries. Similar tortures might be waiting for me in prison, and there they wouldn't use a painkiller first.

When it was all over, I felt my eyelids sliding downward, and I was drifting back to sleep. The last thing I saw was the boy soldier, waving at me with a look of concern etched into his brow.

I opened my eyes again and saw neon orange. Someone was in my hospital room, waving something orange in front of my face. It was a jumpsuit. By his hand gestures, it was clear he wanted me to change my outfit. I took off my bloodstained hospital gown and put on the orange jumpsuit. I slipped my feet into the black plastic sandals the stranger offered. Then he beckoned me to follow. My sandals squeaked on the hallway floor as I wobbled on legs that had been horizontal for I didn't know how long. More escorted men in orange joined us, until we were a small, screaming hazard sign gathered at the hospital's front doors, where a handful of clean buses were parked with engines running. We boarded, and Iranian soldiers carried those who couldn't walk.

"Be strong," one of the seated prisoners whispered as I walked the aisle to an empty seat.

When the bus was full, an armed soldier got in the driver's seat, and two more boarded and systematically walked down the aisle, pushing our heads down out of sight of the windows. Then they took up positions in the front and the back. The engine kicked into gear and we pulled away—a caravan of ghost passengers. After what I think was thirty minutes, the guards tapped us on the shoulder, indicating we could sit upright again. We were on a two-lane road that ribboned through scalloped sand dunes. There was nothing to see and therefore no one to see us. Each time some buildings came into view, the soldiers forced our heads down again so we could drive through undetected. This game of up-down, up-down continued for hours, so that eventually we didn't need to be told anymore; we all automatically ducked as soon as we saw a village in the distance. I didn't understand it. It was no secret that both countries had captured tens of thousands of prisoners of war, so why did we have to remain hidden? Maybe they were trying to protect us from angry mobs, but that seemed much too benevolent. More likely they wanted to stay out of the public eye so they could do whatever they wanted to us. All countries were supposed to register their prisoners of war with the International Committee of the Red Cross so there was some sort of record of each inmate and a neutral third party could inspect prison conditions. But if nobody saw a prisoner, did he even exist? If his holding cell wasn't on any official lists, did he stand a chance of ever getting released?

The sun crossed the highest point in the sky and finally began its downward slide, and my stomach growled, making me wonder if they ever planned to feed us. Mercifully, the bus pulled over a short time later so the driver could get out to pee in a grove of trees, and the other two soldiers passed out hard-boiled eggs and tore pieces of a loaf of bread and handed us each a small section. I bit my egg in small bites so it would last longer, and instead of chewing the bread, I tore it into small bits and let them melt in my mouth to enhance the pleasure of it. The texture reminded me of the samoon bread I used for my falafel sandwiches, and how with a flick of my fingers I had ordered hundreds of loaves a day, and without a second thought I'd thrown leftover crusts into the trash, and now, how I would have given it all back to have just one loaf all to myself.

I brought a morsel of bread to my nose and inhaled, and I was back in the bread line, blowing cigarette smoke in Alyaa's direction to tease her. I felt the warmth of the loaves we carried in our arms as we walked the deserted roads, telling each other our privacies—what scared us most about ourselves and how we wanted our families to remember us when we were gone. Funny thing about bread: it's always there. Bread led me to my livelihood, and to my first love. Now that I'd been stripped of everything, there it was in my hand, still. So much devotion in a tiny crumb.

When we were finished eating, we were allowed to get off the bus one at a time to relieve ourselves in the grove of trees while a guard stood watch. Most of the passengers went, but I stayed in my seat. I was not an animal. Little did I know, we were driving from one side of Iran to the other, a nineteen-hour trip all the way to the eastern border, to a city called Torbat-e Jam, close to Afghanistan. Ultimately, it was more undignified to wet myself than to relieve myself in the open. After several humiliating squats in front of a soldier, and an impossible night trying to sleep sitting up, at two or three in the morning our caravan arrived at an army base surrounded by a chain-link fence topped with coiling razor wire. As we walked single file into the compound, we were each handed a blanket, and on top of the blanket rested a pair of socks, a plate, silverware, and a cup. Then we were divided into large empty rooms that looked like lecture halls, about a busload per room. There were a lot of us, but there was an enclosed bathroom with a sink and a toilet and enough space for all of us to stretch out and sleep.

We were exhausted and said little as we quickly spread out our blankets and rested our weary bodies. The last thing I remember before I slipped into slumber was the click of the door as it was locked from the outside.

A whistle ripped the morning silence into two equal halves—before and after. It took me a second to remember where I was and that my body was no longer my own. In the light of day I could see through the window of our cell that there were a dozen or more identical rooms, and I saw guards whistling other prisoners awake. They were all yelling the same thing: "*Boland sho! Boland sho!*"

And those were the first Farsi words I learned: "Get up!"

Those of us who were able to stand did, and we followed the guards to a central courtyard, where they began to count us and write things down on clipboards. I did a little counting of my own and guesstimated there were ninety or so of us in each room. That's about how many would fit in the dining room of Bruce Lee Restaurant—people from all over the city who liked me and always asked after my family. The guards didn't see that guy, the one with so many friends; to them I was a number in an orange jumpsuit, a bug to be squished like all the rest.

When they were done counting us outside, they went room by room cataloging the injured. I held my breath as I waited for the next thing— my mind racing between me on a chain gang, me before a firing squad, me being locked in a cell—and then . . . nothing happened. The guards ordered us back to our rooms and told us to wait on our blankets. The knot at the base of my skull loosened as my shoulders relaxed on my way back to the room. Collectively, we were starting to allow ourselves to believe they were not intending to harm us. We gathered in small groups, introducing ourselves and asking about hometowns, military divisions, and capture stories. When the guards appeared with large trays of bread and cheese and tea, our room started to feel more like a café as we started to relax a little bit, seeing that the guards were at least taking care of our basic needs. I scanned the room and decided to find out what the animated discussion in the corner was about. When I approached the group, conversation stopped.

"What happened to your teeth?" one of them asked.

"Ajam hit me," I said, using the slur for Persians.

The men nodded gravely and shifted aside so I could join their circle. They were taking bets on how long we would be in this place.

"Three months, tops," said one.

"Months? I say weeks," said the one who had questioned me about my teeth. "Khorramshahr was such a disaster that Saddam is already proposing a ceasefire."

This was news to me. I'd been unconscious so long I'd missed some important developments, apparently.

"What? Saddam is giving up?" I asked.

All eyes swerved to me. The oldest man in the group, somewhere in his forties, with graying temples and bushy eyebrows, cleared his throat and spoke slowly to me, as if I were hard of hearing.

"We lost thirty thousand soldiers," he said.

The group broke into a fusillade of opinions, some cheering the war's end, others insisting we shouldn't back down, and some saying withdrawal was not the same as failure. But what I didn't dare say aloud was, if the war really was ending, why waste all that time and energy driving us one thousand miles away to lock us up? They'd just have to drive us all the way back once they released us. I did not say this, but my expression must have said something similar.

"Would they be bringing us tea and cheese if they were going to kill us?" another older man proposed. He did have a point.

"Don't believe me?" the oldest man continued, getting to his feet. "I'll prove it."

He walked to the locked door and banged on it. When a guard answered, he whispered something and then the Iranian left. Minutes later, the door opened again, and the old man practically pranced back toward us, with a carton of cigarettes and matches in his hand.

"Room service!" he said, laughing and passing out the cigarettes. We inhaled and passed the cigarettes around the room, so that everyone who wanted could have a drag. Emboldened, a few prisoners decided to make similar requests, with similar success. We smoked so much that we asked for permission to open the windows, and got that, too. Even though I'm not carefree by nature, I ignored my doubts and made believe we were on a temporary holiday. To get along with the group, what other choice did I have?

As the weeks passed, it seemed the old man might be right. They fed us so well, thick lamb stews and rice with grilled vegetables, that we actually started getting soft around our middles. We snoozed during the day in our rooms or told stories, waiting for the door to open and an announcement that the war had ended, and after being in a constant state of terror on the battlefield, the stillness felt relaxing rather than confining—almost necessary to restore my mental health.

Finally, after several months, we were told that we had Iraqi visitors. An electric charge coursed through our room as we hustled to smooth our hair and straighten up our blankets in an organized pile, for what we thought was the final time. Three men strode into our room, and our anticipation of being rescued by the Red Cross or some group like it was immediately snuffed out. It was inherently understood by the air of superiority that trailed behind the men that these were not our saviors. They held their heads at a slight upward tilt as they looked down their noses to examine us.

"Sit!"

So many butts hit the floor that it almost sounded like applause. They were teachers, they informed us, and our lessons were about to begin. Now it made sense why we were sleeping in classrooms—we were there to be indoctrinated. Our visitors took a position at one end of our living quarters and lectured us for four to five hours about the virtues of the Islamic Revolution. The words seemed wrong coming out of Iraqi mouths, but they had turned against the Baathist regime. Every day different teachers came, and my renewed hopes to marry Alyaa receded further. Some of the lecturers had turned on Saddam after he exiled them from Iraq because of their politics or family name or association with Shia religious leaders; others were former prisoners of war who had flipped under torture or brainwashing, or both. Whatever brought them to their beliefs, they spoke Arabic, and they were here now to urge their fellow countrymen to come to Khomeini's side.

At first the lectures were a break from the monotony, something to listen to. After a week they became annoying, like a mosquito in my ear, but I could tune them out and pretend to listen. But my brain, I vowed, would never be theirs. No matter what bullshit I had to say or do, my real thoughts would never leave me. But when the weeks turned to months with no end in sight, some of the college-educated in our group began challenging the speakers. Verbal fights broke out, and it became more and more tense as some of the prisoners began siding with the teachers, and allegiances started forming in our room between the converts and the loyalists. We began noticing which prisoners were talking in a friendly way with the teachers, and the teachers were taking note of which of us were asking polite versus antagonistic questions in class. A fog of suspicion took up residence in our room, and now instead of the raucous café chatter that had marked the beginning of our confinement, we spoke in whispers. We never knew which one of us was a spy. The teachers were using politics to divide and conquer us, and one day I just got fed up.

"Islam is a religion of equality and fairness," the speaker was droning on, "so who can tell me, then, in Iraq why is all the power given to the Baath party and not the Muslim people?"

I stood, and the speaker waited, a hopeful look on his face, probably thinking he'd finally turned another one.

"Look, we aren't in Iraq anymore, so if you guys have a beef with the Iraqi government, go back to Iraq and talk to them. We're prisoners because we were defending our country, not Saddam. We're countrymen, not political men."

Some of the prisoners hooted and hollered, but just as many remained loudly silent. The teacher gave me a patronizing look and said there was much I did not understand.

His arrogance was a match and I was the dynamite. I slammed my fist in my palm and exploded: "What's to understand? We are Iraqi soldiers. We were ordered to fight Iranian soldiers. Now the war is *over*! Everyone should just go home, and that should be the end of it!"

Something I said must have been hilarious, because the teacher broke into a cascade of laughs.

"Don't ever believe the war will end as long as Saddam is in power," he said. "Until he's toppled, the war will never end."

I crumpled back to the floor, defeated. All this time that we'd been smoking our free cigarettes and silently celebrating our impending freedom, Khomeini and Saddam had been taking their argument to a higher, more intractable level. I actually learned something in class that day. I learned that in a bid to end the war, Saddam told the United Nations he would withdraw his troops and agree that the shared border should stay as it was. But that wasn't enough for Khomeini. He demanded that Saddam step down and be punished as a war criminal. That the Baath regime become an Islamic Shia republic and give Iran $150 billion as a form of apology. And that was never, ever going to happen.

Once I lost hope, I lost track of time. So I can't say how many weeks had passed after my outburst when armed soldiers entered our room at midnight, flicking on the lights and jarring us awake. They chose one of the prisoners, a Kurd, and told him to read a list of names. Those on the list had to gather their belongings and go to the soccer field outside. In a shaking voice, the Kurd ticked off the names, and only a moron wouldn't have deciphered the pattern. All those on the list were the ones who had argued with the teachers. I clenched my jaw and waited until, inevitably, I heard my name. There were thirty-five from my room, and we joined a couple hundred others on the soccer field, where we sat in rows silently eating and smoking until sunrise. A few tried to whisper, but all the guards had to do was point their weapons at the talkers a few times to express their displeasure at our conversations.

With the morning light came a long line of buses. Muscled guards with torsos like action figures spilled from them and marched toward us like invaders. They shouted and kicked us, then blindfolded us with black strips of cloth. They secured our hands behind our backs with plastic zip handcuffs. Somebody jerked me off the ground by the back of my shirt and pulled me onto the bus and into a seat. He shoved my head down, out of sight of the window. I acquiesced, familiar with the position. A prisoner near me asked where we were being taken.

"*Khafe sho!*" a guard shouted—Shut up.

My Persian vocabulary was growing.

NINE

MINA

Every once in a while I wondered what had happened to the Iraqi, and I didn't imagine it was good. All I knew was that they took him to one of our military bases, and from what I heard, that was just the first stop before prison. When I left him in the hospital, I told him the part about going to a base and left it at that. He looked so pitiful with his banged-up head and the mangled words tumbling out of his mouth. I was sure he already knew he was a POW, yet still he smiled at me with 100 percent trust—as if I was living proof that no harm would come to him. Or his big grin was because of the drugs. Maybe he was so dopey that he didn't sense danger. But he did recognize me; that I'm sure of. He was the only person I'd ever met who saw through my shirt and my skin and inside of me to the person I really was. It gave me a chill just to think about it.

Back in the passenger seat of the ambulance, Ahad-Amin gunned the engine and squealed the tires too fast like he always did. I rolled up the window to block out the huge dust devil he'd kicked up.

"Thanks," I said.

"For what?"

"For helping me with that Iraqi."

Ahad-Amin gripped the steering wheel tighter, and I could see his knuckles turn white. He scanned the horizon, looking for fallen soldiers.

"Don't ever do something that stupid again, unless of course you're trying to get yourself killed," he said.

I didn't bother to argue with him. Anyhow, it didn't matter anymore because things had changed since we'd recaptured Khorramshahr, and we weren't supposed to kill wounded Iraqis anymore. Our orders were to take anyone who needed a doctor to the doctor. Iranian, Iraqi, it made no difference. There was a big red cross painted on the top of our ambulance, and we wore smaller ones on our armbands, and those red crosses meant it didn't matter where you called home.

Ahad-Amin and I made a good team. He was an easygoing road dog with quick reflexes and a repertoire of corny jokes and puns like the kind your grandparents thought were funny, and when he told one he'd throw back his round head and hee-haw like it was the most hilarious thing he'd ever said. I was good at pretending to laugh, but my real skill was spotting things, steering us away from potential hazards such as suspicious wires sticking out of the ground or high walls where snipers could be hiding. I guess you could say that along with Omid and Daryoosh, he was among my closest friends in the Basij, especially now that he'd proven he could keep a secret. What I really wanted to ask was why he hadn't reported me. Did he ever feel like helping the enemy, too? I couldn't be the only one. What I did wasn't special; it was normal, right? Maybe someday when we were old men sitting on a park bench eating pumpkin seeds and reminiscing about our war days, I would ask him. But Ahad-Amin clearly didn't want to discuss it now, and I understood why. If anyone heard us talking about it, we could be killed.

We had a long drive ahead, nearly four hours north to Dehloran, where there was heavy fighting on the border. Our instructions were to clear the dead and the wounded from the battlefield, which meant dragging them from the front line to our waiting ambulance in the back. Diseases could spread to our soldiers if we left the dead in the open; plus if the wild dogs got too accustomed to eating people, they might start hunting us when we were alive.

It was almost dawn by the time we arrived, and the shelling was so intense that at first I thought I was looking at a lightning storm in the sky. Mortars screamed through the dark and shook the ground, and flashes of orange burst from behind dirt embankments where the enemy fired on us with machine guns. We had to shout to be heard, and ended up using hand signals instead, and my sergeant's hands told me to crawl on my stomach through the gunfire and pull fallen soldiers back to the ambulance. I got as close as I could to the fighting and then dropped down like a commando and squirmed my way toward the first corpse I saw, as bullets rained down and kicked up chunks of dirt all around me.

The dead guy was older and heavier than me, and he made me an easy target as I struggled to crawl and drag him at the same time, cursing under my breath. A bullet winged by my head so close that it sounded like someone snapping their fingers behind me and I ducked under him, using his worthless body as a shield. I panted like a rabid animal under-neath him until I heard the volley of gunfire stop, then continued. I was so close; I could see the ambulance in the distance, maybe fifty feet away. I remember looking at the guy's face and thinking how odd it was that he had an open smile and wondering what his last thought must have been. Then I heard a thunderclap so loud that I felt my eardrums rattle and everything clicked off, just like turning off a TV set.

"Are you awake?"

Difficult question. From the looks of things, I was in paradise. There was no heat, no dust, no gunfire, and just inches away from my face was a gorgeous girl about my age with eyebrows that connected in the middle. My eyes were open, but I didn't believe what I was seeing. She asked me the same question again, and this time I detected a slight lisp. I looked closer and could see that one of her upper teeth, one next to her two front teeth, was a little bit behind its neighbor. She was perfectly imper-fect. And she was dressed all in white.

"Dadna?" I whispered.

She smiled at me like a mother whose child just uttered its first word, bursting with pride.

"Don't worry, you are in Masjed Soleyman Hospital." Her words danced, as if her voice had its own soundtrack. "You've been here two weeks. I'm your nurse. My name is Mina Fadaei."

I looked to my left and right and saw soldiers splayed out on cots, filling up the large room.

"They took most of the shrapnel out, but there's still a piece in your brain. Are you in pain?"

It was hard to keep her beautiful face in focus because there was a bandage over my left eye. I reached up and felt the top of my head, which was covered in gauze.

"Not when you're here," I said. Corny, I know. But if this was the reward for getting wounded, I was starting to think it might have been worth it. She rolled her eyes expertly, and I realized I wasn't the only flirt in the building. I tried to laugh but immediately winced in pain. She set a cup of water next to my bed. I reached for it but needed help drinking. She tipped the cup to my lips and waited for my reaction.

"Do you need cooler water? Warmer? Should I bring you juice?"

Her question sent my mind spinning. No one had ever paid that much attention to my needs, so in all my fifteen years, I'd never considered what temperature of water I preferred. It was too strange to have someone trying to kill you one week and someone trying to bring you a perfect cup of water the next. I knew she was just doing her job, but I couldn't help but feel that it was a special question for me alone. I imagined she asked everyone else if they wanted water, but only me what *kind* of water I wanted. I told her I would like whatever she brought me.

"I'll surprise you then," she said.

Over the following days I tried to stay awake so as not to miss her rounds, and when I failed and fell back asleep, I dreamed of her. She became my motivation to recover quickly, but I feigned a slow recovery to stay near her longer. Eventually, though, it was obvious I needed no more nursing, and I had to return to my medic work. But now I had a goal in life. Mina was going to be mine.

After that, every time a patient needed to be driven to Masjed Soleyman Hospital, I was the first to volunteer. I found every excuse possible to make trips to her hospital, and when I didn't have patients, I still sometimes drove there, feigning some need to deliver or pick up supplies. She began looking forward to my visits, which evolved into lunches in the hospital cafeteria. I learned that she was nine months younger than me and had gone to school on the opposite side of my hometown. Over the next year, we talked about our families, describing each relative in exacting detail, and when I told her the horrible things that had happened in my house, she wasn't scared away. She had an understanding heart, so much so that she seemed to understand my parents, too, because she kept encouraging me to make things right with them.

"Maybe one day," I always said.

"You know one day never comes, right?" she would ask.

I became expert at changing the subject. My favorite way to divert her was to start talking about what we wanted to do when the war was over. She had it all planned out. She was going to enroll at Jundishapur University of Medical Sciences in Ahvaz and become a doctor. She was so serious about it, she even pestered the Masjed Soleyman surgeon until he finally agreed to let her watch in the operating room once a week.

"He didn't think I could handle it, but it doesn't bother me at all," she said.

Her eyes lit up the same way mine did when she talked about opening the human body, figuring out its parts, same as like the engine of a car. She laughed when I told her I threw up the first time I saw someone's insides, and how after the boy survived surgery I knew that I wanted to be a doctor. I was envious of her fortune to learn at the elbow of a hospital surgeon, like her own private master class. Maybe I should consider medical school, too.

"We could go together!" she said.

As soon as the words came out of her mouth, my vision of the future opened up to make room for a second person. I imagined walking to class together with our heavy medical textbooks, then I saw us wearing surgical scrubs and working side by side on the same patient, and the most beautiful image of all was us sitting down for dinner inside the home we shared to talk about what happened during our days.

It was this magical future that I envisioned while I worked. I especially needed good thoughts when I was assigned to morgue duty, which all the medics agreed was the grossest task in the grossest job in the Basij. From dawn to dusk, ambulances brought dead bodies that were dry as wood or swollen and smelly, their fixed stares and open mouths twisted in absurd expressions, and we had to search for dog tags to try to figure out who they were. If they were Iranian, we tried to contact their families and send them home. Iraqi—we buried them. But not before first relieving them of their valuables. Iraqis loved gold, and it was a little secret among the medics that any jewelry you came across was finders keepers. Everyone was pocketing wallets and watches and rings, and eventually I gave in to temptation and a few pieces of jewelry made their way into my possession, too. But the worst part of working in the morgue was when the ambulances delivered only parts of dead bodies, and you had to try to match hands and feet and limbs to get a whole person. You had a better chance of success if the soldier had used a Magic Marker to write his name on his forehead and all his limbs, a precaution in case he was torn apart, so you would have clues to put the pieces together again. It was a gruesome puzzle only a psycho killer could love.

I don't know how Ahad-Amin did it, but he always stayed upbeat, as if all this stuff around him was just a video game and he could press "stop" any time he wanted to. Once, he was delivering two wounded Iraqis to the hospital, and he waved me over to the back of his ambulance like he had a big surprise for me. He told me one man's name was Jasem. The other's was Salem, which rhymes with a Persian word for "healthy."

"C'mere, Zahed, watch this."

He flung open the doors and approached Jasem. "Are you healthy?" he asked.

"No, I'm Jasem," he answered.

Ahad-Amin smiled. "I know you are Jasem. But are you healthy?"

The man pointed at the other passenger. "Salem. Salem."

Ahad-Amin made a big show of scratching his head and seeming confused. "You are not healthy?"

"No! No! I'm Jasem!"

The more we laughed, the more flustered the patients got, until they were screaming and pointing at each other trying to clarify, "Jasem! Salem!" which only made things funnier, until Jasem muttered something in Arabic to Salem, which I'd bet all my stolen gold meant "assholes."

I teamed up with Ahad-Amin whenever I could. We spent so much time in the ambulance together, roving and looking for wounded soldiers, that over the months he became like another brother to me. War was making me darker, and I gravitated toward his lightness; it reminded me how ridiculous everything was.

One afternoon we were bumping along yet another pitted, unpaved road when something caught my eye. "Hey, is that somebody waving over there?" I asked, pointing toward the horizon, where I could just make out the shapes of two people on the ground. He yanked the ambulance to the left, and as we got closer we could see they were Iraqi, and one of them was on his knees frantically waving us down for help. The other soldier was crumpled on the ground with a bloodied shoulder.

"Watch out, there's a trench there," I said. Even though he didn't need reminding that one should not drive huge ambulances over deep ditches, Ahad-Amin didn't answer. He parked next to it and I got out to see what was going on. I took only three steps before I felt a sharp poke in my abdomen, almost like a bee sting, followed by a second one an inch away from the first. I clutched my stomach and felt hot blood seeping through my fingers and had the odd sensation that I was looking at someone else's hand, someone else's blood. Just before I toppled, I had a split second to see the barrel of a rifle sticking out of the doorway of a nearby bunker. It was a setup. The man who had waved us down was now on his perfectly good legs running away.

"Sniper!" I screamed.

It felt like flames of propane were bursting from my wounds as I crawled toward the trench. I heard the metal ring of bullets hitting the side of the ambulance and air hissing out of the tires, then the shattering of glass. Ahad-Amin flung himself out of the ambulance and was crouching behind it, using it as a shield, as he frantically called for backup. He saw me struggling toward the trench and started to make his way down the side of the ambulance toward me.

"Don't move!" I yelled. "We'll both be killed." Then I rolled myself into the trench and curled into a ball. My breath sped up, and I started to get cold. The sniper seemed to be enjoying this, taking potshots, then waiting long enough to make us think he'd run out of ammunition, then starting up again. It seemed to take too long, ten or fifteen minutes, until I finally heard jeeps roar up and machine-gun fire answer the sniper. By the time I felt hands lifting me out of the trench, I was shivering. I could still see, but I couldn't speak, as if my brain had a rubber band around it and the words were being squeezed inside. I couldn't thank the men who were carrying me, and I couldn't shout to Ahad-Amin how glad I was that he wasn't dead. But by the terrified look on his face, perhaps I was the one who was dead. *Well,* I thought, *it's a blessing that the sniper only got one of us.* I heard the whir of helicopter blades getting louder and hoped they were airlifting me out. I'd never been in a helicopter before, and felt a sudden thrill at taking a ride in one, just before I passed out.

When I woke up, I was back in Masjed Soleyman Hospital, only this time I had my own room. That's when I knew something really bad must have happened, because only the severely injured were separated from the rest. I heard someone snoring softly at the foot of my bed.

"Mina?"

She bolted upright and came to my side. Her skin looked raw, as if she'd been sleeping in snow.

"Have you been crying?" I asked.

"The doctors said you probably weren't going to wake up."

"How long have I . . . ?"

"Fifty-six days," she said, squeezing my hand.

I looked down at my stomach and saw a forest of rubber tubes.

"What's all this stuff coming out of me?"

"Doctors had to take out a meter of your intestines, your appendix, and your gallbladder because they were damaged. It's OK; you can still function without them."

I almost said, "As long as my heart still works," but I stopped myself from being such a cheeseball.

By my calculations, that made three times that I'd slipped out of death's clutches. The minefield, the mortar, and now this. And that didn't count all the bombs and bullets that had somehow missed me in between. More than a dozen boys from my hometown were now dead, yet for some reason I'd made it all the way to my seventeenth birthday. The odds weren't in my favor, and I knew that pretty soon I'd run out of lives. But as a good Basij soldier, that shouldn't have worried me, because I wasn't supposed to fear death. But having Mina cry over me put things in a new perspective. Four years before, I joined the military because I didn't know what to do with my life. Now I knew.

"Mina, I'd like to ask you something, but I'm too embarrassed."

She quickly looked down at her feet and said something so quietly that I could barely hear her. "I . . . I want to tell you something, too," she said.

We each waited for the other to take control, sitting there in a silence that got more awkward by the second. My embarrassment and her shyness spread out and filled the room like vapor. Then I got an idea.

"Can you bring us some paper? We can each write it down and exchange papers at the same time."

I scribbled, "Mina would you like to marry me?" folded it four times, and placed the note in her palm. She curled her fingers around it, turned, and extended her note to me behind her back and then scurried to the other side of the room to read hers in private. Carefully, I opened her note, and when I saw the words "Will you ask for my hand?" my heart did a somersault. Mina read mine, and all the blood must have rushed to her head because I've never seen her skin turn that shade of red. Then she walked out of the room without looking at me. The needle scratched and the wedding music cut out in my head. Had she changed her mind? Was she afraid? Twenty agonizing minutes passed until I heard her footsteps coming, and I told myself that whatever expression she wore when she walked in the room would tell me immediately what her answer was. I sat up in bed, my whole body a coiled spring. She opened the door with a megawatt smile.

What would happen next, I visualized like this: her saying yes, and me catapulting from my sickbed and tumbling into her arms for our first kiss.

Instead, it went like this:

Mina remained in the door frame and folded her arms.

"Okay, I accept. But on one condition," she said.

My spine slumped a little bit, but then I shook it off. Nothing was asking too much; whatever she wanted, I'd make happen. I waited for her to continue.

"You have to make peace with your parents first. And they must accompany you when you ask my father for my hand."

Except that. The last time I'd seen Baba and Maman, I'd left with a permanent scar on my heel.

"Mina," I pleaded. "It's been four years; there's too much distance now."

"Without their permission, my father will refuse."

I heard myself promising I would try. The war wasn't going to be the death of me—this girl was.

When I returned to my street, I was no longer the scrawny kid with black fingertips stained by engine grease. I had a mustache and the beginnings of a beard, and mean eyes that gave me a look that made people instinctively know not to pry. I leaned forward slightly and hobbled, on account of the soreness in my stomach from surgery. Even so, I was at least a foot taller, and my muscles tugged at the seams of my outgrown uniform. I must have been unrecognizable, because no one approached me, or maybe I just looked too scary; either way, it was all right with me. I did not want to cause a scene; I just wanted to leave the military and marry Mina and start my new life. This home visit was an errand, nothing more. But as I neared my house, my feet kept walking. I found myself knocking instead on Mostafa's door.

"Are my eyes telling lies?" Mostafa gasped, pulling me toward him to plant kisses all over my face. Then he took a step back and braced himself against the door.

"Wait. Where's Omid? Why isn't he with you?"

"Omid is still crazy, but he's fine," I said. "I'm here with good news."

Mostafa waved me inside and poured me tea from a silver samovar on a low glass table. I heard him shuffling for sugar in the kitchen, and when he returned, he placed the steaming cup down along with some walnut-stuffed dates and sat on a cushion across from me.

"You two shouldn't have run off like that. Without telling us," he said, blowing on his tea.

"We were young and stupid. We didn't think you'd let us go. Did you get Omid's note? He said he spotted your delivery truck one time, and he left it under the wiper."

"I got it." Mostafa sighed. "I couldn't have stopped you anyway, but my heart was so heavy." His eyes floated over me. "You look bad."

"Just got out of the hospital. Sniper shot me, but not enough times, apparently."

"Have you finally come home?"

Mostafa listened intently as, for once, I told him a story. I started with the morning Omid and I fled. I told him everything, making sure he knew his words had guided me when I decided to save the Iraqi soldier. We drained the samovar as I told him about my life as a medic, walking through the minefield, and getting shot by a sniper. Then I told him about Mina, and that I was ready to end my voluntary service in the Basij for her.

"You know how you told me once to give my heart to the one I love, and don't ever doubt?" I asked.

Mostafa put his calloused hand over mine.

"Soldier and nurse fall in love. Oldest story in the book," he said.

I explained Mina's requirement, that I somehow smooth things over with my wicked parents and get them to go with me to ask her father for her hand. I asked Mostafa if he had any words of wisdom for that sort of situation.

"Not really," he said, getting to his feet and putting on his sandals. "But I do think we should start by inviting your parents over for tea."

"Now?" I protested, but before I could say anything more he was out the door.

I heard my father's voice and stood when he came through the door. He had a lot more gray hair than I remembered, and seemed smaller to me, but maybe that's because I had grown. He froze, like a photograph, and only his eyes moved, like lasers, scanning me up and down. His voice was a dry blade of grass, rasping in the wind. He was nothing to be afraid of, and the sight of his weak body infuriated me because nobody so insignificant should hold a child in such terror. He'd duped me into thinking he was all-powerful.

"Son . . ."

He reached for me, but I ducked out of his embrace. Partly I was protecting my surgical wounds, but the truth was, I still shook when his hands got too close to me.

"Are you OK?" he asked.

"What kind of question is that?" I hollered. "After the way you've treated me, now you suddenly want to know if I'm OK? You have no idea what I've been through!"

Maman put her head scarf over her mouth and tried to muffle her sobs, and Mostafa, ever the peacemaker, coerced us all to sit down, murmuring assurances that everything was going to be all right and plying us with more tea.

"Zahed is here for a reason. He wants to get married," Mostafa began.

"Married!" Baba snorted. "He can't even pull up his own socks."

My anger flashed and I stood, ready to stomp out the door, but Mostafa grabbed my wrist and gently guided me back down.

"This is no longer a boy you are talking to," he said, locking eyes with Baba. "This is a person who has been through a lot, more than you can ever know."

Baba waved his hand as if he were getting rid of an annoying fly. Then he rolled his tongue over his teeth and said, "No. I do not accept this marriage."

I leaped to my feet. By now I'd seen all the various ways you could kill a man with your bare hands. And I probably would have done it, too, if Mostafa and Maman hadn't dragged me to another room and shut the door. And so the negotiations began. For the next three hours, while I was sequestered out of harm's way, Mostafa and his wife, Fatemah, Maman, and a growing crowd of neighbors and friends who wanted in on the action wheedled and cajoled my donkey of a father into changing his mind. I listened by the door and gathered that his major objection was that he might have to take care of Mina, to feed and protect her from other men, if I died on the battlefield. When Mostafa explained that I intended to leave the Basij, he just swerved into a different lane, insisting I could die any old way, like crossing the street, and then he'd be stuck with another mouth to feed. There it was, that same old line again—as if by our very existence as his children we were draining him of his rightful happiness. To my father, everything could be measured by a cost-benefit analysis, even true love.

Eventually, the old man got hungry. At least, that's how I would place my bet. Say all you want about the arguments before him: that times were changing and more young people were choosing their own spouses now, that marriage should be for love and not family prestige, or that he could mend our troubled past by granting me his blessing. He never was one to let himself be swayed by talk. To tell the truth, I think it was his internal clock that seized. The deliberations were pushing past his dinner hour, and at one point he just clapped his hands once, said "Fine," then left for home, where the kitchen was.

To my utter shock, Baba kept his word. He arranged for the initial *khaseghari* meeting between parents at Mina's father's home to discuss a possible engagement. Before my parents left for the meeting, Maman took me aside and assured me she wouldn't leave Mina's house without a yes.

"Don't worry," she whispered, "I'll make sure he doesn't say anything stupid."

I paced a circle into the fibers of the rug waiting for them to return. Maman blew through the door, and I could tell she had done her job and done it well. Mina's father had agreed to host the engagement party at his house and invited his whole family, more than one hundred people. Mina's sisters were already planning a feast: *khoresht gheymeh,* stew with lamb, yellow split peas, tomatoes and dried lime, and my favorite— *ghormeh sabzi*—a green herb stew with dried fenugreek and red kidney beans. There would be music, we'd link arms and dance in circles, and the tables would be decorated with coins and candies. Her sisters even insisted on the old-timey tradition of grinding sugar on our heads to guarantee our marriage would be sweet. And the best part: her father would stand up and formally announce our engagement, and I would put a ring on Mina's finger before the clapping crowd.

My whole family of twelve—plus Mostafa, Fatemah, and my uncle—rented a minivan to get to the party. My hair was smoothed and plastered in place with some of Mostafa's hair oil, and I put on cologne. Maman put on lipstick and sprayed herself with rose oil. There was so much perfume colliding inside the sweltering van that I had to roll down the windows just to keep from getting nauseous. I had a cream roll cake that Mina liked on my lap and a bouquet for her mother, but the real prize was in a hinged velvet box inside my pocket. When I'd gone to the Basij office to inform them I was leaving, they'd congratulated me on my years of service, thanked me for my dedicated work as a medic, and slipped an envelope in my hands with the monthly military benefits I'd never collected, a little more than ten thousand dollars. I went straight to the jewelry store and picked out a gold ring, shaped like two hands holding a ruby heart. There was enough left in the envelope for a matching necklace and earrings.

I looked out the window, and for the first time in my life, Masjed

Soleyman sparkled. I saw the light filter through the trees like a stained glass window, and when we passed the marketplace, I saw Bakhtiari nomad women weaving carpets in neon colors that screamed with joy. Birdsong mixed with the laughter of children playing soccer, and I laughed to myself that I'd never seen my city all dressed up before.

Two blocks from Mina's house, the long wail of an air raid siren sliced through the conversation in the van, and everyone started shouting at once, directing my uncle where to drive the van to a safer spot. Some pointed left, others right, and my youngest siblings demanded a U-turn.

This can't be happening, I thought.

And then it did. Less than a minute after the siren, I felt the road drop out beneath our tires and we hung in the air for a moment, and then a thunderous blast tipped the van on its side and sent our heads knocking into each other. Someone was able to kick a door open, and we pulled one another out, one by one, our best clothes now rumpled and stained with the food we'd been carrying on our laps. Mostafa's coat had split clear down the back. Baba had injured his hand, and Maman was holding her head but insisted she was fine.

"Everyone's OK," Mostafa said. "Go, go see what's going on."

As I ran toward Mina's house, I smelled fire. Then I heard a motorcycle gaining speed on me and recognized the driver as he pulled up and stopped before me. It was another Basij soldier from Masjed Soleyman who had shared a tent with Omid and me at training camp. He now delivered coded messages on his bike for the war effort.

"Do you know where Mostafa is?" he asked.

I pointed in the direction of the minivan, where a group was now pushing it, trying to get it right way up again. He stomped on his kickstart, and I grabbed his handlebars.

"Why?"

"Unfortunately, Omid is a martyr now," he replied.

Omid had been on the front lines in Dehloran when his machine gun ran out of bullets. The enemy got him with five or six shots to the chest, puncturing his lungs. I felt each one of those bullets in my own chest as the news knocked the wind out of me. I sank to the ground and punched the earth with my fists, damning God for taking everything away from me all at once. When I couldn't sob anymore, I slowly rose to my feet and continued toward Mina's house, dazed and shocked, as if I'd been struck by lightning. When I got to her block, the buildings were gone, reduced to smoking piles of rubble. The air was so thick with dust that it was like trying to see underwater in a murky lake, and shadows of people stumbled in the cloud, screaming and hitting themselves in the head with grief. I tripped over bodies as I pushed forward toward her house, shouting her name over and over.

As I knew it would be but chose not to believe, her house was a heap of dirt, bricks, and mangled steel. And when I saw the huge crater where her courtyard used to be, I knew the bomb had fallen right on our feast, the bowls of stew probably still steaming from the stove. All down the block, survivors were lifting bodies from the wreckage and laying them in rows on the street. Women were on their knees ululating and weeping over their broken babies.

I tilted my head back and aimed my voice at the universe. "May there be an ocean of eternal misery upon these Arab killers who bring God's name to their filthy lips!"

I flung away chunks of cinder blocks and torn pieces of corrugated tin, cutting and burning my hands in my frenzy to find her. She was underneath a tangle of bricks, her olive skin burned to an unrecognizable shade of orange. A piece of rebar had pierced her through her back and come out through her breast, and one of her legs was twisted so that her foot was up by her hip. Still, she was beautiful. I cleared away the dirt and removed the rebar stake, and as I covered her with my shirt, I felt the ring in my pocket. I opened the box and slid the ring on her finger.

Then I leaned in and put my lips to hers for our first kiss.

• • •

Over the next days, as I helped wrap the bodies of my would-be in-laws into funeral shrouds and dig their graves, steel walls slammed around my heart, trapping my soul inside a tight, dark prison. Life was short, and it was shit. So I returned to the Basij office inside the mosque and asked to be reenlisted. This time, the recruiter was more respectful and told me I was a veteran now and could work in any division I wanted.

"Give me the most dangerous one," I said.

"You'll have to be more specific," the recruiter said. "War is all kinds of dangerous."

There was no more mercy left in me.

"I want to kill as many Arabs as possible."

My answer received a crocodile smile.

"How's your aim?"

"The best," I lied.

So despite the fact that I'd never fired a gun directly at someone, I became a sniper. Sure, I'd fired Omid's gun in the direction of incoming gunfire, but I'd never known if I hit anyone. I mean, I'd never selected a victim, then aimed. I didn't know what it was like to intentionally kill another human being.

My first mission was to spy on an Iraqi garrison in Basra. I disguised myself in an Iraqi uniform taken from a prisoner, and tried to look nonchalant as I obscured myself in the shade of a cluster of palm trees and peered through binoculars and the scope on my rifle to count their tanks, locate their trenches, and report the size of their battalions back to command. I was getting some good intel when, out of nowhere, someone turned on a radio, and the Sadoun Jaber pop song "My Mother" wafted through the air:

Oh Mom, Mom, you are a rainbow from heaven, the air that I need
   to breathe,
You are the most valuable creature to me.

I peered through my scope and saw an Iraqi officer about six hundred yards away, snapping his fingers to the beat as he made his way to one of those makeshift toilets, which was nothing more than a hole in the ground with a tire over it, enclosed by walls of corrugated metal panels for privacy. In his left hand he carried a small plastic pitcher of water for washing his privates. I raised my semiautomatic Simonov, kissed my trigger finger for good luck, and squeezed. The bullet pierced his temple and he spun in a circle. I fired again, hitting him in the shoulder. I cracked my knuckles as he dropped to the ground.

One down, a zillion more to go.

TEN

DUNGEON

When the bus sighed to a stop, I instinctively turned to look out the window even though I was still blindfolded. Freedom is a stubborn habit, I guess. I had a stabbing pain between my shoulders from several hours in zip-tie handcuffs but didn't dare adjust my position or surreptitiously try to stretch because I might draw attention. I needed to be a mote of dust, unnoticed and insignificant.

Dread collected like bile in the back of my throat as I waited for something, something terrible. I could hear the lumbering feet of Iraqi prisoners getting off the buses ahead of me, which meant I only had a few minutes until it was my turn. These very well could have been my last minutes, and if so, I wanted to die while having pleasant thoughts. So I went inside myself, and back in time, and saw my older brother Jasem wink at me as he detoured from our route to school and slipped through the brush to a secret shortcut to the river, where he dropped his schoolbooks, stripped down to his underwear, and plunged in. I remembered the time we made fishing poles out of branches, and I felt the mud between my toes as I braced against the tug of a fishing line, battling a gasping yellow carp and making a little bit of a bigger show of it than necessary to impress Jasem. Cooking it later over a fire on the shore, I asked my big brother with 90 percent seriousness if we could live outside forever, just him and me.

He opened his mouth to answer and screamed like a rat in the talons of a hawk. My bones froze when I realized the sound was real, coming from outside the bus. As if on cue, each prisoner shrieked one after another, like they were being electrocuted, wailing with equal parts pain, shock, and outrage.

The bus door opened with a sucking sound and a hand grasped the back of my collar and yanked me out of my seat. Outside, I stumbled blindly toward whatever despicable horror was happening to the others, trembling with each step. When my blindfold was removed, I was standing at the entrance to a dark hallway lined with a gauntlet of Iranian soldiers, each brandishing some sort of beating tool: batons, leather belts, thick electrical cables. Pools of hot blood and piss marked the path between them.

My strategy was to lower my head and run past them like a soccer champion. I made it halfway through the two lines of men without getting hit when a soldier kicked me from behind and I toppled onto my face, my hands still tied behind my back. Groaning, I struggled to my knees while the sadistic bastards waited until I started to crawl to beat me. The first blow landed across my spine with a dull thud, spreading out ripples of hot pain. At first I could feel the individual lashes, but then they came so fast and from so many directions that I couldn't distinguish them. My entire back ignited. I heard a sickening crack behind me and a prisoner protest that his ribs had been broken. There was nothing I could do for him, so I kept going.

I stumbled to the end, where the hallway emptied into a dungeon of some kind—a musty, dark cave with walls of hand-cut basalt blocks, a high arched ceiling, and no windows. There were Persian words crudely scratched into the walls and the air was fetid, like hope itself had decayed there long ago. The floor had been tiled at one point in history, but it had since crumbled underfoot into a powdery gravel. I crammed inside with all the moaning prisoners, so many of us pressed together that not even a pin would fit between our bleeding bodies. Some were coughing blood; some had eyes that had swollen shut. I was one of the lucky ones, with only welts on my back and arms. Dizzy and stunned, we leaned on one another for support, propping each other up as we shivered together, listening to the echoes of torture until each and every one of us had been properly welcomed to our new quarters.

Eventually, a handful of soldiers appeared and cut off our handcuffs. One could speak Arabic, and I sensed a touch of pride as he told us that we were deep inside a mountain, in an ancient caravansary, where five hundred years before traders traveling on the Silk Road would rest with their pack animals. But the tea service and carpets were long gone, and the warren of caves hadn't been occupied since the 1930s, when Reza Shah had locked up Iran's most notorious criminals. On the map, we were in a village of less than one hundred people called Sang Bast, which translated into "closed rock."

"This is the end of the line, Saddamis," the guard chirped. "Prepare to die here."

It was like being entombed in a sewer, or a subway tunnel or abandoned mine, with three hundred others. We'd been removed from the living but were not yet dead. The guards stood silent. I imagined they enjoyed watching us as the realization sank in. They could do whatever they wanted to us underground. So this was our punishment for arguing with the lecturers back at the military base, for defending our country—a country that would have punished us had we refused to defend it, I might add. I lived in a foul pit of constant night, where the hours and days bled into one never-ending moment. Maybe they were going to kill us immediately or leave us to starve underground. I closed my eyes and thought about the Iranian boy who had saved me a year before. *Buddy, you went to all that effort for this.* The irony of it made me laugh out loud, which drew menacing stares from several prisoners. They were right; I needed to pull myself together.

The guards ordered us to follow them. Our footsteps echoed as we marched through a maze of hallways that were covered in black mold, and we made so many lefts and rights that I was completely disoriented. They divided us into five caves of about sixty men each, the only light coming from a three-foot-by-three-foot square cut in the ceiling covered by a thick piece of clear plastic, so guards could monitor our movements from aboveground. The caves were large, like the entire bottom floor of my father's house including the courtyard, with enough space for all of us to lie down, and we could move freely from room to room. The ceiling was so high that if three of us stood foot to shoulder we still couldn't reach that square hole.

Before leaving us, the guard demanded to know if any of us could speak Farsi, and a few men raised their hands.

"You!" a guard said, pointing a long finger at a quiet prisoner named Rasoul, whose creased forehead gave him a perpetually worried look. Rasoul took a step back, like maybe if he walked away from the fingertip they'd choose someone else. But that only made the guard come closer and raise Rasoul's hand and bark something. Rasoul translated: "He says I'm in charge of the food and sleeping arrangements. Anyone who disobeys will be beaten."

My ears perked up at the word "food," because that was a sign that they didn't intend to kill us. Even more proof: we were each given two wool military blankets, rubber slippers, a plastic plate and cup, and a spoon. I found a spot next to my friend Sharshab and sat against the wall next to him. He was staring up at the small square of faint light in the ceiling and twisting the corners of his mustache.

"Think they ever open that thing?" he asked.

"They have to," I said. "How will we get any fresh air?"

"You're assuming they give a shit."

I unfurled my blanket and carefully placed everything I owned on it in a neat row. Plate next to cup next to spoon, and I bookended the set with my new slippers. Sharshab was the even-keeled one who kept everybody else from falling apart. We couldn't have him fade on us; morale would plummet.

"You're an engineer. Can't you build a ladder or something out of all these spoons?" I asked.

"Agricultural. Agricultural engineer."

Something with an exoskeleton and six legs skittered over my foot, and Sharshab lifted a slipper and annihilated it. He flipped the slipper over and examined the heel with intense interest. Beetle, cockroach, spider—hard to tell in the dim light.

"Get the manager on the phone," he said. "This hotel has bugs."

I smiled, relieved to hear a joke. The bruising on my back made it hurt to laugh, but laughter was the only thing that made my mind feel better.

"How badly were you beaten?" I asked.

"Not too bad," he said. Already it was getting steamy in our room, with so many of us inhaling and exhaling the same air. Sharshab wadded his second blanket into a pillow, trying not to wince as he stretched out carefully on his side. I did the same.

"Tell me one of your stories," he said.

I made sure Sharshab's eyes were closed, then asked him to imagine a mysterious island off the coast of Hong Kong, belonging to a former Shaolin monk gone rogue. His name was Mr. Han, and he lived there inside a huge walled compound with servants and concubines, and he only emerged once every three years to host an international karate competition.

"Trouble is," I said, pausing for dramatic effect, "strange things keep happening. White ladies keep washing up on shore. But they didn't drown; they died of drug overdoses."

Sharshab opened one eye at me.

"British Intelligence Agency did autopsies," I added.

He lowered his eyelid.

"So Bruce Lee gets a coveted invitation to Mr. Han's martial arts competition. When the Brits find out, they recruit Bruce Lee to spy. They suspect Mr. Han is trafficking in opium and slaves, but they can't get access to his lair."

I explained that Bruce Lee was dubious, and didn't want to accept the dangerous mission.

"But then, one day, Mr. Han's henchmen come ashore to Bruce Lee's village and try to gang-rape his sister!"

By now, several more prisoners had gathered around.

"They chase her through the alleys and across rickety bamboo bridges, clawing after her with their lusty fingers, but she fights valiantly, karate-chopping and helicopter-kicking them to the ground, knocking several into the canals."

I pantomimed her flashing arms as they sliced through the air and felled her pursuers, one by one.

"But then . . ."

Most of the room was now sitting near Sharshab and me, cross-legged on the floor.

"She makes a bad decision. She runs into a wooden warehouse, crammed to the ceiling with broken furniture and other junk. The three thugs crash through the windows, backing her into a corner."

I got on my knees and acted out the rest of it, pretending to lift a dagger-shaped shard of glass from the ground, turning it toward my stomach and clasping it with both hands.

"She has nowhere to go. So she stares them right in the eye and plunges the pointed glass into herself, dying before they have the chance to violate her!"

I toppled on my side in slow motion, acting out my best dead stare.

"Where's Bruce Lee?" one of the listeners called out.

I sat back up.

"Not there. But he finds out later that Mr. Han's men were responsible for the death of his sister. He's furious for revenge and tells the British he will accept their spy mission."

I stretched back out on my blanket and let the anticipation build. Finally, someone asked what happened next.

"Find out tomorrow," I said, staring up at the hole in the ceiling and willing a rope ladder to drop down from it. "We have plenty of time."

That night I dreamed that I was in a new grave and someone was shoveling fresh dirt on me. I coughed and sputtered, and tried to claw my way to the surface to let them know I was still alive, but there was too much earth in my mouth and I couldn't make any sound. I couldn't die, I kept trying to say, because I had a family now. I had promised Alyaa that she wouldn't become a widow, and I had never broken my word to her. The dirt got heavier and heavier, pressing on my chest, and I was losing my energy to fight back. Finally I let my body go slack, and just when I accepted death, I heard someone aboveground shouting for me to get up.

"Boland sho!"

I awoke at the wrong end of a gun. The guards were back, and this time they were demanding that we pray on our blankets. We were so turned around inside the mountain that even the religious ones who did pray daily had no idea which way Mecca was. There were Kurds and Christians among us, and agnostics, but it didn't matter; all of us had to follow Islam now. We blinked in the dark, confused with fear and sleep and afraid to get punished for facing the wrong way. A guard rolled his eyes and pointed to his left, and we all shuffled in unison and placed our blankets in that direction. We kneeled down, bowing forward and lowering our foreheads to the ground. The ones who knew the positions lined up in front so the rest could copy their movements. We murmured and prostrated ourselves through a complete round of prayers, and sat back up.

"Again!" barked the guard. "You unbelievers owe God more prayers for all the past years that you didn't pray."

As I went through the motions, I tuned out my surroundings and played a mental game. I challenged myself to find one good thing about my life right now. I was being forced at gunpoint to pray, and it was demeaning, but it was . . . it was . . . it was stretching. Morning stretches were good for your health, and I pretended I was warming up for a soccer game like I used to when I was a teenager in Basra. Each time I bent forward and sat back up, I chose a different muscle in my body and squeezed it. I relived my best plays, the fakes and passes and goals that stayed with me all these years. This way, I stole praying away from them. I started with my toes and worked my way up my entire body, clenching and releasing each muscle to build my stamina.

A whistle pierced the air, signaling prayers were over. Now it was time to chant slogans against our government. The guards taught us three sentences and made us repeat them over and over until we could pronounce them in Farsi singsong:

Death, death to Saddam!
Go and tell Saddam we'll never be oppressed by him again!
Oh God, God, give Khomeini long life!

Our voices fell into a dull rhythm, and I felt my temples knock to the beat and realized it had been a full day since I'd eaten anything. Because the guard had put Rasoul in charge of food, I was hopeful that meant a meal was in our future, but the more I imagined what they might give us to eat, the more my stomach twisted with want. I felt anger coming on, and returned to my search for one good thing to chase it back. I was chanting, I didn't want to chant, but . . . what? But I was expanding my Persian vocabulary: *life, oppress, him, never, give, we.* I tucked the words that might be useful into the folds of my brain. To conquer your enemy, you must first understand him.

After we'd chanted, the guards finally left us alone and I repeated the vocabulary words in my head: *life, oppress, him, never, give, we. We never oppress him, give life. We give him life, never oppress.* I was still making sentences when I heard a scraping sound and looked up to see the lid slide off the hole in the roof. An angled column of sunlight shot into our cave, making a hot, white circle on the ground so bright I had to squint until my pupils were ready for it. Men jostled to the light, turning their faces up to feel sunlight on their skin. Slowly, a large black net like the kind fishermen use was lowered through the hole, and as it got closer we could see it contained an enormous bowl. Rasoul, already taking charge, ordered everyone to back up as the cargo dropped to the floor. He approached cautiously, peered over the rim, and raised his palms upward in thanks. Bread and hard-boiled eggs. We lined up, and when it was my turn, Rasoul solemnly placed one slice of bread and one egg in my hand. This time I ate the shell, too. There weren't enough eggs to go around, and when they brought us a big pot of sugary tea, I refused it because I didn't feel right taking my share when others needed the calories.

The meal shortage was not an accident. As the weeks went by, we came to expect that there would never be enough food in the net. Dinner was often rice and lentils, and by lentils I mean you could count them on your plate. Sometimes I gave my meals to the ones who were elderly or ill, because I was younger and could bear the hunger better than they could. My skin started to turn yellow from lack of vitamins and sunlight, and I started to feel the curves of my hip bones. Some days it was all I could do to fake pray between naps, all the power seemingly sucked out of my body. The guards avoided the foul air of our caves by keeping a twenty-four-hour watch over us through the clear plastic manhole cover, opening it for just five or six hours a day to air out our rooms and feed us like zoo animals. But that one small vent was no match against the olfactory power of so many armpits and so much stale breath, and the odors from the communal bathroom of squatty toilets down the hall. It was a combined aroma so assaultive that I taught myself to breathe through my mouth. But still, the letting in of the light each day was an exciting event, like a dinner bell calling us together for a common reprieve. That column of light was our gathering spot, where we could see one another fully and remind one another that we were real. We had a few former doctors in our group, and we went to the light to have the experts examine our toothaches and itchy rashes.

I began etching tick marks into the wall to record the passage of time. And that's how I figured out that the meal with meat came every other week. This "special meal" became an obsession in the cave. Days beforehand, we would start fantasizing about the ingredients. Instead of our regular stewed onions or prunes with rice, would we get chicken? Lamb? Beef? We talked incessantly about how much meat there might be, how our mothers used to prepare stews, which dishes were our favorites, which restaurants in which cities made the best shawarma or kebabs. I was asked over and over to tell the story of how I made falafel at Bruce Lee Restaurant. No description of cucumber slices or parsley was too insignificant. The special meal wasn't delivered like clockwork, but I knew by my rough calendar when it was close. And I knew for sure when they opened the manhole cover and I smelled grease.

The first time the scent of meat wafted into our cave, all conversation stopped. I stood up with the crowd, looking heavenward with sunken cheeks. But the bowl just hung there, as our mouths filled with saliva below. Finally, a voice called down to us, and Rasoul translated.

"Hungry?"

"Yes, yes, yes!" we hollered.

"Then give thanks. Chant for your food."

We knew exactly what our captors wanted to hear, and we collectively sang: "Death, death, death to Saddam! Long live Khomeini!"

The bowl lowered halfway, then stopped again. Whoever held the strings above wanted more enthusiastic chanting, accusing us of just mouthing the words. I yelled louder this time, and the chorus reverberated off the walls and pounded the ceiling: "*Death, death to Saddam!*"

I was hoarse by the time that bowl made it all the way down, and by then the chicken had gone cold. Rasoul doled out a cupful to each of us, trying his best to give everyone at least a thin shred of meat. But I wasn't lucky; I just got a taste of where the meat had once been. But it was better than no food at all.

If only our former lecturers could have seen us then, chanting down our own government and praying to Mecca daily. We had been sent to this cave because we were the bad students, which was funny to me, because we had our own secret school in Sang Bast. We figured out who among us had special skills or knowledge, and during our free time, we collected into classes. There were groups to learn mathematics, others that liked to discuss history or debate politics, and even poetry lessons. Some groups were more like therapy sessions, where people would give one another courage and inspiration to help steer themselves away from depression. Our curriculum was our method of counteracting the fakery we had to do each day to get fed and avoid beatings; it was our own little camouflaged insurrection. I had an aptitude for languages, so I chose to go with the group that spent three or four hours a day learning English.

Our instructor was self-taught, a former middle-school math teacher before the war. Both his parents were teachers, so he had a natural talent for understanding how people learn, in my opinion. He even gave the equivalent of an entrance exam, quizzing our skills and dividing us into beginner, intermediate, and advanced levels. I was a beginner.

"Sorry I'm late," I said one day, running up to the group. When one of us was missing, the whole class went looking until we found him.

"What did you say? We speak English only here," the teacher said.

"Oh, soorree I wath late."

He looked at the other pupils. "Who can correct Najah's verb?"

"Was!" they rang out.

My teacher nodded at me. "Say it one more time."

"Wath."

He raised an eyebrow and drew *W-A-S* in the dirt. "Wuzzzzzzz," he said, pointing at the word. I felt my tongue slip on my barren gums and knew that I'd never be able to pronounce an *s* properly again. And suddenly, I found this hilarious. I grinned to remind my teacher that I had no teeth, then belted the word out like an opera tenor: "Waaaaaaaaaaaaaaaath."

One of the students, a former sergeant named Abu Amad, laughed himself into a coughing fit. When it lasted longer than seemed normal, I clapped him on the back, and he finally gained his composure, but his breathing was still labored. We were approaching a year in the mountain, and we had become skeletons of our former selves; there was no position to sleep in that wasn't agonizing on our bones. Without enough circulation, disease and germs hung in the air, and it was impossible to avoid getting the same head cold or intestinal flu that everyone else had. Men died of illness, of malnutrition, and of lack of spirit. More than a dozen had been buried outside already, and it seemed like now we couldn't go two weeks without adding another grave. We cut the lesson short and went back to our room so that Abu Amad could rest and we could tell Rasoul that he needed to see a doctor.

Rasoul stood under the hole in the ceiling and shouted to the guards. "Hello! We have a sick man down here!"

Nothing.

"Can you hear me? We need a doctor!"

Silence gripped our room as we waited for an answer. We heard footfalls above, but no words. Rasoul cursed them in Arabic, calling their mothers whores, and returned to Abu Amad's side and began massaging his chest in small circles to increase circulation. A group of us joined in, rubbing his temples, his arms, his legs—anything to help him relax and fall asleep.

"I have two baby girls," he said, his voice wet and raspy. "If I don't make it, promise to tell them about me; tell them what I was like."

Abu Amad slept fitfully that night, talking in his sleep about needing to return money he'd borrowed. The acoustics in our dungeon were so sharp that every murmur, every scratch, every digestive growl could be heard from all points in the room. We rubbed his arms and shushed him, telling him that his debts were good, that he was not in trouble with anyone.

That morning, Abu Amad was done. We lowered his eyelids and put a blanket over him, and this time, when Rasoul shouted to the guards that we had a corpse in the room, he got a response. Five hours later, a prison doctor arrived with a clipboard. He inspected Abu Amad and then asked us a lot of questions, writing the answers down on his paper. What were we eating? How often were we eating? Were we washing our hands regularly? Was there soap in the bathrooms? I don't know why we needed a medical professional to convince the guards of this, but the doctor determined our quarters were unsanitary and a breeding ground for communicable diseases. He recommended that we be relocated immediately. Two prisoners were chosen to go outside and bury Abu Amad.

Lucky bastards, I thought. And by that I meant all three of them. The gravediggers got the chance to see the outside world again, but really Abu Amad was the luckiest of all. He got out.

Although the doctor said we needed to leave Sang Bast "immediately," that word had a different definition in prison. Another five months went by, and during that time, every week or so someone else would get the same far-off stare as Abu Amad, and that's when you could almost count the hours until he'd stop blinking. The burials continued until we'd lost twenty-five or so. While we never had an exact diagnosis, I can tell you this: people died of heart attacks, malnutrition, and the flu. But they also died of fear, anger, and depression. But on paper, I'm sure, everyone died of "natural causes."

I somehow did not get sick. Maybe it was because I spent each day looking for one good thing. Maybe because I secretly exercised during prayers. Or maybe it was because despite the disaster of my life, I found something to laugh about, whether it was my lisp or an old story I told from Bruce Lee Restaurant or someone making kissing noises in the middle of a dream. Because let's face it, our situation was utterly ridiculous.

Then one day, mercy came. Guards entered our room and blindfolded us. We walked in single file, with our hands on the shoulders of the man in front of us, out of the mountain. The clean air settled like silk around my forehead, and I gulped mouthfuls of it as if I were drinking spring water. I could only see glints of sunlight at the edges of my blindfold, but those slivers signaled hope. A wake-up call accompanied by a blindfold meant we were going to a new prison.

By now I knew enough Farsi to ask a guard where we were being sent. "To a special prison," he answered.

I shuddered to think what could be more special than Sang Bast.

ELEVEN

YADOLLAH'S RAM

One supremely annoying thing about the Basij was that they were very strict about daily prayers. We were expected to pray three times a day, and the only exception was when we were in the middle of battle, of course. Other than that, hundreds of us would routinely form a perfect line, bow down at the same time, and come up at the same time, all singing the same sound together. But if I was going to talk to God, I wanted to do it in my own language. Why did I have to just repeat stuff in Arabic that the minister of ideology and politics ordered me to say? That wasn't really praying; that was being a parrot. If I was going to talk to Allah, it should be in my own language, and what I would say in Persian was, "You are an asshole." Every time I asked him why he killed Mina, all I got was silence.

I had no use for religion, so I found every excuse to skip prayers. Sometimes I had a stomachache. Sometimes I pretended to be off spying on the enemy, when actually I was hiding in one of the caves not far from the base, overlooking the bombed-out city of Dehloran. I'd been given a warning—several of them, actually—that I'd be kicked out of the Basij if I continued to miss prayers. I nodded like I was sorry, but I truly didn't give a shit. They were empty threats, anyway. In the year since Mina was killed, I had honed my skills as a sharpshooter to the point that I could shatter the telescope lens on an armored tank. The driver would be forced to come up through the hatch to get his bearings, and I'd wait for it . . . then kiss my trigger finger and nail him in the head. When I got a direct hit like that, for a brief moment I felt one or two of my heartbeats, just before I went back to being numb again.

Since Mina had died, my tongue had stopped tasting food and my eyes had stopped sleeping at night. There was something wrong with my ears, so when anyone spoke to me, all I heard was a voice clogged by a ball of cotton. I didn't have the energy for conversation, and I muttered so many one-word answers that people stopped talking to me altogether. Killing was my only accomplishment. Yeah, I was an excellent sniper, and I was pretty sure the commanders couldn't afford to get rid of me. So I wasn't going to join the performing parrots every day. *Go choke on your prayers for all I care*, I thought.

So that's why I was standing outside my tent alone just before sundown while the rest of my unit was off bowing to God, when I heard the soft tinkle of bells approaching. I turned and saw a gray-haired shepherd herding a flock of sheep, with a young girl in bright red robes by his side. He raised his wooden staff toward me and said hello in the Lori tribal dialect that my grandmother used to speak, and when I said hello back, they gasped in surprise that a soldier knew the right words. I watched them crest a small hill and then stood for a moment, staring at the rams and ewes trotting behind. One of the rams at the back of the pack wandered near our battalion's garbage pit and began rooting in it. I sidestepped closer. I took another step, then another. A few sheep snorted to let me know I was too close. The ram stomped its foot and tossed its head a few times, and I felt my pulse pick up, knowing we had chosen each other. It lowered its brown head and showed me its spiraling horns, and I drew out my bayonet. The landscape narrowed to a pinpoint, with only that ram in my crosshairs. And before I could stop myself, I grabbed one of those horns and twisted the animal to the ground. I clamped one hand around its mouth as it thrashed, and ran the edge of the bayonet across its throat.

The animal made no noise as it stilled. When its rectangular irises no

longer registered me, I let go and rose to my knees. The earth spun and I
fell to all fours and waited for the dizziness to pass, but it just kept going,
and waves of panic amplified inside me. I could justify killing the enemy,
but the ram was an innocent, and I can't tell you why I killed it. It was
like my brain disappeared for a second, and when I snapped out of it, I
couldn't believe this was the work of my hands. Whatever evil was inside
me was growing and starting to take control.

There was nothing to do but get rid of the carcass. Luck was on my
side, and the shepherd didn't return as I hurried to skin it. I was almost
done butchering it when the guys returned from prayers. We hadn't had
meat in months, and when they saw what I had, I was their hero, a king
of kebab, and I went along with their assumption that I'd hunted on
purpose. We buried the intestines and the head, hid the meat in our tent
with some ice, and then later that night a bunch of us hiked up a trail to
one of the caves, where we could roast the mutton over a fire. Word had
spread to several of my military buddies from Masjed Soleyman, and by
now we were a good-sized dinner party. I was the guest of honor, but I
didn't feel like celebrating. Every time someone clapped me on the back
or shook my hand for the feast, I saw the betrayal in the ram's yellow
eyes again, and the blood that seeped from its tear ducts as I squeezed
its mouth closed. The men ate the entire beast, even after their bellies
swelled in agony, never knowing when they'd have roasted meat again. I
took a few bites, felt sick to my stomach, and put the kebab down.

The next morning, we were called together for an announcement.

"Brothers, we have a friend," our commander said. "Maybe you have
seen Yadollah the shepherd; he walks by our base to bring his animals to
a spring not far from here."

The commander explained that the old man was born and raised
in Dehloran, had never left Dehloran, and refused to leave his beloved
hometown even after the Iraqis bombed it. Like many of his displaced
neighbors, he'd moved his family and livestock to a big tent in the mountains near our base, where it was safer. We'd given him a radio and he
helped patrol our perimeter as he moved his flocks.

"He came to me this morning. He is missing a ram, and his livelihood depends on that animal. I want you boys to keep an eye out and let
me know if you see it."

I wished the earth would open up and swallow me, leaving no trace
of my sinful existence. I heard snickering behind me, and another soldier
whispered, "We've got all these boys dying, and they are worried about a
ram?" A few dinner-party guests quickly looked my way, but I kept my
gaze straight ahead. There was no way they would rat on me, because
then they would have to confess they ate the ram as well.

All this time I'd been telling myself I was a good person because I'd
saved that Iraqi, and I used that one event to ignore all the bad things I'd
done since then. But I was no better than anyone; I was a ruthless killer,
and all the denial in the world wouldn't change that. As I thought of the
displaced shepherd and what now would become of his family without
a breeding ram, I wished everyone on the planet could spit on my face. I
deserved no less. My stomach heaved, as if it were trying to expel that bite
of the ram still in there. I slumped forward, silently looking at the ground,
but in my mind, I screamed so hard that my vocal cords were ripped out.

That night, the ram chased me in my dreams. He pawed at the
ground and gnashed his teeth, and I felt his hot breath on my face. His
eyes were pools of blood and the light glinted off the sharp points of his
horns as he roared at me in a voice of rolling boulders.

"For each of your blows against my body, I will kill you a hundred
times over!"

Flames shot out of his nostrils as he chased me down, and I ran for
my life, apologizing for killing him, but my voice was lost in the land-
slide of his hooves getting closer, until I could feel his hooves smack into
my back. He knocked me down and stomped on me until I was flat as a
leaf in a puddle of my own blood. He had fangs like a tiger and picked
me up in his mouth, whipping me from side to side so that little pieces
of me tore and flew everywhere, until I was nothing more than a shred of
flesh dangling from his jaws. He spit me out, laughed, and trotted away
with a little bounce in his step.

"Zip it, Haftlang; you're keeping everybody awake!"

There's no way to hide a nightmare in a military tent. My sweat had turned ice cold in the winter night air, and my teeth were chattering. I bit my blanket to keep from crying, to hold on to something real. I was too frightened to close my eyes for the rest of the night.

Night after night, the ram came back. He gored me. He butted me off a cliff. He sat on me. He kicked me into outer space. Each time he demanded to know what right I had to kill him. My troubled sleep was starting to exhaust me to the point that I was delirious all the time, walking around half awake and half asleep in a dream state that allowed the ram to visit whenever he liked. I started seeing him in the daytime, around corners, behind trees, or on the horizon, making me a constant, jumpy nervous wreck. Rumors started that I was losing my mind, probably started by my sleep-deprived tent mates, who were forced awake by my cries. When sleeping pills had no effect, one guy in the battalion offered to put me under a spell and chanted something at me in Arabic in a gravelly voice as I lay very still.

I did sleep, but the ram came after me again, this time from the air with eagle wings that were as big as an airplane's. The sky parted and he flew at me with outstretched talons as I tried to sprint out of his shadow, but no matter which way I ran, the silhouette of his body grew larger and larger around me like a spreading stain. I closed my eyes in terror, and when his hooves landed on my back, his wings shrank back down to the size of a crow's. He knocked the wind out of me, and the weight of him pressed on my bowels and forced my lungs up into my throat. I gagged for air as he picked me up with his teeth, and we flew so high that the earth looked like a stone. I was crying and my teardrops stayed suspended in the air like stars. I could feel his fire breath singe the back of my neck, and I begged for him to let me fall to my death. But he only laughed.

"You are contaminated with sin, from head to toe," the ram roared. "You think you are so brave; you think you are a man. Do you know how many people you have killed with your ignorance?"

"Forgive me," I sputtered.

"Your hands reek of blood, your breath spreads blasphemy in the air! Your veins flow with poisons, your skin is made of slime."

He was right. But if he only knew the whole story. It wasn't my fault. I wasn't always this way. Maybe if I could convince the ram that part of me used to be good, he'd leave me alone.

"It's war. What else can I do? Why don't you go speak to the person who started the war? I had no choice."

As soon as the words came out of my mouth, I realized how pathetic I sounded. None of my leaders ever said anything about killing animals.

"Still a sniveling boy. You want to be a man? Go tell Yadollah what you've done."

Then the ram dropped me, and I fell to the earth, exploding like an egg on impact.

When I awoke to the frowns of my tentmates, I knew what I had to do. I went to the supply room on the base and liberated a couple of wool blankets and a kerosene lamp and made my way up the mountain, 1,500 feet up to Yadollah's tent. It was one of those large tents like the nomads used, held up by wooden poles and covered with black canvas, with an open square for a door. Yadollah was outside milking a goat, and as I approached, he stood up and casually walked into his tent. He returned holding an antique Brno rifle across his chest, the kind used by the Iranian Army in the 1930s and '40s, and stood with his legs slightly apart, determined-like.

"Who goes there?" he asked.

I stopped a few feet from him, put my bag on the ground, and stood with my hands clasped in front of me. It was so cold that I could see my breath.

"I'm Zahed. I'm with the battalion."

He studied my uniform and glanced at my bag.

"What are you doing here?"

"It's cold; I've brought you wool blankets and a kerosene lamp."

He lowered the rifle and came toward me, reaching for my hands.

"You're freezing. Please, come in where it's warm."

The inside of his tent was the exact opposite of the drab exterior. The dirt floor and the walls were covered in colorful woven kilim rugs, and the perimeter was lined with pillows for sitting and sleeping. A wall of bedding and storage trunks made a dividing line down the center of the large tent—one side for Yadollah, his wife, and their six children, and the other for the herd of sixty sheep and goats, plus a horse, two mules, and a cow. There was a fire pit for cooking off to one side, and a flat rock for kneading bread. The children were huddled around one kerosene lamp for warmth, with lambs and baby goats in their laps. All eyes, animal and human, followed me as I entered their sanctuary, not ready to decide if I was friend or foe. I presented Yadollah's wife with a loaf of bread I'd squirreled from the army kitchen, and she hugged me in thanks.

"I just made some butter," she said, handing me a glass of carbonated yogurt doogh just like the kind Maman made for me every night.

Yadollah lit the kerosene lamp I'd brought and set it down next to the children, and they squealed with delight. Half of them separated from the original circle and closed around the second lamp, sharing the heat. They'd need several more lamps to beat back the subzero nights. The smallest boy reached up for my hand, pulling me down to the group. I sat cross-legged on the floor and he wiggled into my lap, hiding his chubby hands in his legs. I felt like an uncle, returned from a long trip, and I didn't want to leave. *I took food out of this boy's mouth.* I pushed the shame away and tried to be a comfortable throne for him.

Yadollah brought out a silver tray heaping with steaming flatbread and a cup of fresh butter, and set it on the ground.

"Our guest goes first!" he ordered, and the kids drew their hands back from the tray and stared at me. Yadollah and I each took a piece, then sat on some pillows while the feeding frenzy commenced.

"We aren't starving, you know," he said. "Don't let them fool you."

I nodded politely, to protect his pride.

We talked late into the night about where we came from and what we wanted out of life. Now that I was right next to him, I could see he wasn't the hunched-over old man I'd thought. He was fifty-five, with a plain wisdom and a broad chest and the energy of someone half his age. He'd been born in Dehloran, grew up there, earned his living, married a cousin, and had kids in Dehloran, and when the bombs started falling, he lost his home, but he wasn't about to lose his birthplace. It was no longer safe for his animals to roam free, and if they couldn't graze, he couldn't make a living. So he packed up his family and the whole herd and moved them to the mountains, close to our battalion for protection.

"And the herd was happy here, and then pooft!—my ram, he vanishes."

I was planning to tell Yadollah the truth in my own way, but he brought up the ram first and caught me off guard. I choked on a crumb and erupted into a coughing fit. Yadollah's wife ran to me with a hot cup of tea.

"Thank you," I croaked.

Yadollah picked up a ney cane flute and began blowing a sad tune on it, and it gave me the feeling he was talking directly to me through the sound, saying he knew what I'd done and this was what my betrayal felt like in his heart. Then he paused, as if he'd suddenly forgotten the next note.

"None of the soldiers saw him?" he asked.

"Everyone's still searching."

As soon as the lie fell out of my mouth, I wanted to run out of the tent.

"That was the finest beast I've ever had," he said, setting the flute down. "I was going to slaughter him when the war ended. To celebrate."

Now more than ever, I needed to come clean, but it would've been too much of a sucker punch to confess right after he told me that. It was getting dark, but not dark enough that I couldn't see the disappointment on his children's faces. I left the warmth of his tent with an invitation to return the next night for dinner but without a clear conscience. I vowed to tell him when I returned.

Five more kerosene lamps later, and I still hadn't said a word. I returned to Yadollah's tent several times a week for months, on the pretense that I needed walks to clear my head and to help me sleep at night, which everyone was only too happy to oblige. I exchanged stolen jewelry with a kitchen cook for fish and sometimes chicken to bring to Yadollah, and the more I became a part of his family, the further the ram receded from my thoughts. He was still there, but it was more like he was a dot far off on the horizon and too tired to come all the way over here and chase me. I had a secret family now, and I didn't tell anyone in my battalion about it. Yadollah's tent became my church, where I went to get away from the violence all around me as well as the violence inside myself. Like Mostafa before him, Yadollah became my guide, listening to my story of how I joined the war and about Mina, and giving advice when I asked. Now the children ran to me when they saw me coming, their hands grasping up to see what delicacies were in my bag. I had become their Uncle Zahed, and the oldest daughter now blushed when I came over, maybe because she wanted a husband.

Yadollah was hungry for any news I heard on the base about the war coming to an end. It was 1988, and even our own commanders were saying the war was on its last legs, that UN peace negotiators were drafting a resolution to end the war and both Saddam and Khomeini were going to sign it.

"So, my friend, are we going to win this war soon?"

I was stretched out on some pillows, and Yadollah was in his favorite position, sitting on a stool and polishing the wood handle of his rifle with animal fat, even though it was already so shiny you could see your reflection in it. A wild dog came sniffing by the tent and Yadollah's wife grabbed a rock and threw it, sending the thief away.

"I don't think we'll win, Yadollah. There are thirty-plus countries supporting Iraq, and we only have Libya and Korea on our side. We need more tanks, and nobody is selling us equipment or ammunition anymore."

"Hmpf."

I knew Yadollah didn't want to hear it, but I tried to explain that the Iraqis had sophisticated stuff. Machine guns that had electronic ears that

could pick up sounds and aim themselves. They had night-vision goggles
with heat sensors. We were a joke with our pistols that kept jamming.

"Listen, Yadollah, I have to tell you a secret, and I beg you to consider forgiving me."

"My son, you've always been good to us. What is it?"

I started sweating profusely, and wiped my forehead with the back
of my hand.

"I killed your ram."

A heavy silence descended on the tent and I felt seven pairs of eyes
turn toward me, everyone's except those of Yadollah, who stared out the
door of the tent with his jaw clenched and every muscle in his face shaking. Then he picked up his gun and pointed it at me.

"Get out."

I rose carefully, keeping my eyes on Yadollah as I backed toward the
door. He pivoted in place, keeping a bead on me. I lowered my head, then
ran like hell. I sprinted all the way down the mountain, stumbling and
springing right back up. I didn't really think Yadollah would shoot me
in the back, but you never know. And wouldn't that be just too perfect—
soldiers dying all around me year after year, and somehow I escaped
mortars and snipers and land mines, only to be shot in the back over
a beast. Served me right. I somehow still hadn't learned my lesson that
stealing has consequences. Liars and thieves can't expect things to turn
out for them, and now I'd just lost my third family; I thought that must
be some sort of sorry-ass record. My own, then Mina's, and now Yadollah's. Clearly, I was put on this earth to be alone.

By the time I reached my tent, my failure felt total and complete.
I'd tried to make up for what I'd done by bringing gifts to Yadollah, but
somehow I'd doubled down and made it worse: not only had I taken
his ram, I'd taken his trust by building a friendship before I confessed.
I was rotting from the inside. Outside of me was a shell that I could
fool people with, but only for so long; inevitably they realized I was
made of garbage. I would have killed myself if I wasn't such a coward,
but I couldn't even manage that. Without the sanctuary of Yadollah's

friendship, the ram was going to come back for me and finally finish me off. The only thing I could do was stay in bed and wait to feel the heat of his breath on my neck, just before he gored me. Only this time, I wasn't afraid, because I didn't see the point of living. The ram was coming to do me a favor, to do the one thing I didn't have the guts to do. So I waited, immobile, hiding under the covers. I certainly didn't want to see Yadollah again as he herded his animals to the spring. But by the third day of my self-imposed bed rest, someone must have reported me to the commander, because he popped his head in the tent and scowled at me.

"You gonna get up, soldier?"

I sat up, hoping he would think I was just sick.

"Haftlang, you used to be a medic, yes?" he asked.

I confirmed.

"Then get up; you're going to Halabja, in Iraq. Need you to help with the corpses."

I nodded and followed him outside, happy for the chance to get away from Yadollah's orbit. I didn't know what had happened in Halabja, but a soldier filled me in along the drive. Just that week, our military, along with Kurdish guerrillas, had captured Halabja and a bunch of rural mountain villages just inside the eastern border of Iraq. It must have been one hell of a battle, because more than one hundred of us left the battalion for the eight-hour drive to help with the cleanup. Our convoy stopped on the border just a few miles short of town, and we were directed to a tent and each of us was given a gray hazmat suit and a gas mask. Three days before, Iraqi planes had flown over the town and dropped bombs that contained some kind of chemical gas, and thousands of civilians had choked to death within a matter of minutes. We didn't have to take the assignment if we feared for our health, but for a lowlife like me who deserved to be dead, this was the perfect duty. At nineteen, with six years of death under my belt, I was what you might call a death professional. I zipped up my suit, tightened the straps of the gas mask, and marched into Halabja.

Everywhere I looked, people were frozen in time, like photographs of themselves. Little children who had been playing in the street were now sprawled on the ground, their tiny fingers still clutching dolls. Parents had taken their last breaths as they crouched over their babies, trying to protect them from the gas. And the creepiest thing about it was that there was no mutilation or gore, just ordinary people toppled over like they were sleeping, yet with gray slime trailing from their mouths. A dog lay on its side with food still in its mouth, its tongue hanging out. Birds littered the ground, and frogs and fish bobbed on the river's surface. Lizards were frozen mid-crouch.

I shuddered. Whatever had happened, had happened in a flash, and the calculated evil of it stopped me cold. Even the silence was violent— streets stripped of birdsong, conversation, running engines, shutting doors, or babbling televisions.

I went from building to building, writing down addresses and counting the dead, making notes of how many bodies were on each floor. But after three days, my sergeant told me not to bother with the paperwork. There were so many corpses that there was no point in cataloging them all; it was just slowing down the more pressing need to get them buried. Bulldozers dug large graves, and we lined the pits with a limestone powder that was supposed to absorb the poisons in the bodies and prevent toxins from leaching into the soil. I put the bodies neatly into the graves, careful to keep family members together and all facing the same way. I stacked fifty to sixty bodies at a time, and tried to close my mind to what I was doing, but still I couldn't stop myself from smoothing down tangled hair or a wrinkled shirt, looking for any small dignity I could give them before lowering them into the hole. At this point in the war I had become so accustomed to corpses that they no longer shocked me, but this kind of death was different. Even as I was burying these villagers, I knew their faces would haunt my dreams. There were thousands, too many to count, and even more victims who were wounded and disfigured in the makeshift clinics on the border. The poison gas was indiscriminate; it was hard to distinguish the doctors from the patients because everyone was burned.

In one house I found a dead couple in a sexual position in their bed. I untangled them and carried the wife out first in a sheet. I returned and wrapped the man in a blanket, but he was heavy, and as I dragged him through a doorway, the back of my right sleeve caught on a nail sticking out of the door frame, exposing my arm to the poisonous air. I dropped the body and frantically searched my pockets, pulled out the emergency syringe of atropine, and plunged it into my thigh. It contained enough nerve agent antidote to hopefully protect me until I could get the secondary shot at the medical tent, about two miles away.

By the time I stumbled out of the building, my arm was already blistering, and it itched something awful. Nobody was sure what sorts of poisons were still in the air, but everyone thought it was some combination of mustard gas and hydrogen cyanide. I was dizzy and sweaty, and held onto the wall to ride out a full-blown coughing fit when another soldier found me and helped me run to the medical tent, where the doctor gave me the secondary injection, which didn't seem to do much. The doctor led me to a water truck with high-pressure hoses, all the while assuring me that I'd be OK. I didn't believe him. I stripped off my suit and stood in the pounding spray, wondering if I was going to have the same death as the bodies I'd been clearing away, just a slower version, my throat taking days instead of minutes to close up. When I was clean, the doctor put an antibacterial ointment on my arm, gave me painkillers, and ordered three days of bed rest.

My arm still hurt, but I went back to work. After a month, we didn't have to wear gas masks anymore. The wind had blown away the chemicals, and we could allow relatives from other villages into Halabja to hold funeral ceremonies for their loved ones. Every day, mourning Kurdish families recited poetry and sang songs as we lowered their family members into the ground. By the third month, we had finished burying the dead, and residents who had fled were living in their homes again. By the time I left, a huge boil had developed on my arm, and it oozed so much that I had to change the bandages several times a day.

When I returned to my unit, I volunteered to go with a group being relocated to Sumar in Iran, a mountainous crossing point on the border a couple hours south in a desolate region dominated by Kurdish tribes that had joined forces with several Iranian rebel groups fighting Khomeini's revolutionary government. We had a military camp in Sumar, but it was basically undefended, because the knuckleheads stationed there were so stoned on hash that they were letting the enemy guerrillas slip freely across the border. My job was to help get the place back in order.

We had to rely on mules to get our supplies up the steep mountain passes, as howling winds threatened to send us tumbling down the narrow dirt paths. When we arrived, the camp was completely disorganized. The commanders had been killed in a rebel ambush. The generators were out of gasoline, ammunition was dangerously low, and there was only enough canned food, bread, and dates to last a few days. Water was scarce because the mules could only carry a few gallons and had to make several treks a day up and down the mountain. Excavation equipment couldn't reach the rugged terrain, so our guys were fighting from aboveground bunkers, easily visible from higher elevations. Our army lacked intelligence, unable to keep track of the ever-shifting alliances between the different militias and clans that regularly attacked our frontier posts, killing our soldiers and making off with our weapons.

I walked into a beleaguered platoon that didn't see any reason to fight anymore. It was disgraceful, and I was determined to stop them from getting picked off one by one. When I arrived, I found soldiers sleeping off opium or hash binges, and when I confronted them, they complained that they couldn't aim their weapons properly because the mechanism that calculated coordinates was in Russian. I had to show the lazy bastards how to aim with their own eyes, sighting off the barrels and using plain common sense. Every day, another guy deserted, and reinforcements never came; few dared to travel on the rural transport lines, exposed to sharpshooters who hid behind tall shrubs and in caves. No one wanted to take that risk, especially now that the United Nations had put Resolution 589 on the table, a promise on paper that both Iraq and Iran would lay down their weapons. The word was that after eight years of war, in which neither side had gained anything, both sides were going to sign the document. Any day now. But that didn't mean we should give up early and let our country down. We still had to be men and fight until the very end.

One night, when there was the smallest of fingernail moons in the sky, I heard somebody yelling nearby. I looked over and saw one of my men being dragged, kicking, on the ground, by someone with a gun. I took aim, shot the intruder in the head, and then jogged over to my soldier. He'd been shot in the upper thigh, and I tied my jacket around his leg above the wound to stop the bleeding. His breath came out fast, and he told me there was a major ambush on the mountain pass and the enemy was heading this way. I heard the ting of a bullet fly by us, and I dropped to the ground. I had to get him behind some cover before the sniper got us.

"Can you walk?" I asked.

I helped him rise and lean into me for support, and we hobbled together back to camp, where I sat him down behind a tent near the bottom of a trail that led up the mountains. I wanted to get to the peak so I could look for orange flashes in the night and determine where the shooters were. I was nearly to the crest when I heard panicked screams and spotted Iranian soldiers retreating from the west, racing through our encampment, rousting everyone out of their tents. Our men were surrendering, but there was nowhere to run, as machine-gun fire erupted in a ring around camp, and men ran in every direction, firing their last bullets randomly, hoping to at least take one down before their own slaughter. It was over. We were being annihilated. I ran back down the path and flopped down next to the injured soldier. I turned my rifle over in my hands and then rested the barrel under my chin. He reached over and pulled the gun out of my hands.

"Hey, what are you doing? It's not over yet! Climb back up and use your last bullets to kill a few more!"

His voice snapped me out of it, and I started back up the mountain. The gunfire had stopped for the moment, and when I looked over the ridge to the valley below, I saw dozens of my men, pressed in together with their hands on their heads, guns pointed at them. I didn't wait to see what was going to happen next. I ran, stumbling in the dark, down the path and away from camp. And right into the barrel of a gun.

I dropped my rifle and lifted my hands ever so slowly. My captor pushed my own weapon into my back, and I could hear explosions now as he guided me toward the other prisoners. I put my hands on my head and looked at my feet, blending into the crowd. I should have killed myself when I had the chance. Figures, I was too cowardly and the price I paid for it was getting caught at the very last minute of the war. But I did have one tiny piece of luck. There was the barest of moonlight, and I just might be able to slip away in the pandemonium. I looked at the prisoner next to me and tapped him on the shoulder. I nodded toward the mountains, indicating that I was going to make a run for it, and he nodded yes. I counted to three, and we peeled off into the night, running like two men with nothing left to lose. The explosions and shouting covered the sound of our footsteps as we huffed up the trails and ducked into a cave.

At daybreak, the firefight was still crackling. My companion wanted to run north, higher into the mountains. That was rebel territory, and I argued that it would be safer to run east, deeper into Iran, but he was adamant, so we went our separate ways. I scurried through the bushes, in what I thought was the best route, but then the gunfire got louder. I spotted a small depression at the bottom of a hill and hopped into it, crouching into the smallest ball I could make with my body. Then I felt grains of sand fall into the collar of my shirt. I looked up and saw two shadows. Then I felt a gun barrel rest on the crown of my head. One of the shadows knew Persian.

"Don't move, motherfucker."

TWELVE

SPECIAL PRISON

If the calendar I'd scratched into the cave wall was accurate, it had been almost two years since I'd seen the sun. After marching us blindfolded out of the mountain, we were driven eleven hours back across Iran to the western border. During the ride, I could only catch glimpses of shapes where light leaked into my blindfold, but my body responded to the warmth of the sun like a stooped-over plant that had suddenly been moved into the light, my muscles injected with instant strength and my skeleton stretched taller, photosynthesis restored. When the bus finally stopped and my blindfold was removed, I had to squeeze my eyes shut against the harsh light and wait for the white circles to stop swimming behind my eyelids before I could try again.

When I finally found my equilibrium, I was standing in a dirt courtyard with ten-foot tan walls on all sides, topped with coiled razor wire. We were at a military base in a city called Arak. Even though we were still imprisoned, above the walls there was so, so much to see. My gaze rolled over the jagged rust-colored mountaintops, lingering on the clouds as they scudded across the summits, shape-shifting into white mushrooms, then spaceships, then steam. There was a date palm in the courtyard, with its outstretched fronds like a mother's protective arms, welcoming us to rest in her shade, and I noticed the diamond-shaped pattern in the bark of her trunk, which reminded me of the net that was lowered into our cave at Sang Bast. The colorful roar of the outside world was enthralling, and for a second I felt so happy that if roots had suddenly shot down from my feet and anchored me in place, I would have been pleased to live in that one spot forever, just noticing everything.

When the guards at Sang Bast told us we were being sent to a "special prison," they said it with a sneer. The Iranians had converted a section of their Arak military base into three adjoining prisons, one for regular enlisted men like me, another for the volunteer militia members, and a third one for the high-ranking Iraqi officers. The barracks were reserved for POWs culled from prison camps all over Iran who were deemed the "unteachable" inmates who stubbornly stayed loyal to Saddam. So I expected to walk into a torture chamber, but Arak might as well have been a hookah bar compared to where I'd come from.

Our cells were unlocked from six in the morning until six in the evening, so we could go outside to the courtyard, spending our free time any way we pleased. There were no forced prayers or chants, and they fed us more stew, bread, and rice, sometimes even giving us fruit, so that we were no longer so hungry and sick. Our rooms were in a low-slung, U-shaped building facing the warden's office, and guard towers marked all four corners of the compound. The cells were ten feet by ten feet, with windows, and contained about twenty or twenty-five men each, so tight we had to sleep on the floor head to toe like spoons. But compared to the caves, this was a mild complaint. Twice a week, inmates from all three prisons could mingle at mealtimes.

Even the guards, low-ranking grunts in their early twenties who were sent to Arak for prison duty as punishment, went easy on us, some even confiding that they had a low opinion of the Islamic Revolution. Many were dirt poor, from Baluchistan Province, which shares a border with Pakistan, and because of their mixed Iranian-Pakistani blood, they were considered second-class ethnic minorities in Iran. They complained of discrimination by "pure" Persians who singled them out for the lowliest job in the military—babysitting enemy prisoners. In this way, the guards felt imprisoned, too, and sympathized with us, some even sharing their cigarettes and teaching us Farsi words. They worked at less than half-speed, coming by only sporadically to check on us, just to make sure we weren't digging holes to escape. I enlisted one of the guards to tutor me in Farsi in exchange for Arabic lessons, and within a year I could understand most of what he was saying. I couldn't hold a debate about world affairs, but I could converse about the need for soap or a blanket or an aspirin.

Even the warden was a pretty decent guy, giving us a couple hours notice before he'd inspect our rooms. He let us call him by the Farsi word for "colonel," *Sarhang*, and often called on me to translate between him and the prisoners. Within eighteen months, when the inmates held an election and chose me as their spokesman and prison translator, Sarhang gave me my own cell next to his office, where he could easily summon me to interpret when prisoners needed to see a doctor or he needed to make announcements to the inmates. Besides privacy, my new quarters had a few upgrades: a small wooden desk and chair, an electric teapot, a cup, and a spoon. I hadn't felt this rich since my restaurant days, when I wore a Rolex watch and vacationed in Morocco.

We found many ways to pass the time. Some of the prisoners became excellent craftsmen, using spoons or their fingernails to carve date pits into miniature roses and faces and animals, then stringing the beads into rosaries and necklaces, using thread they'd pulled from their blankets. They found rocks in the yard and carved and polished them into tigers and squirrels and soaring birds. Some men spent a long time shaving with sharpened stones, and one guy even used tweezers to make his grooming ritual last longer. The way we read books was by telling long stories, and I continued recounting all five Bruce Lee movies in an episodic fashion, embellishing the storyline here, twisting the plot there, and blending scenes from different films so the movies never sounded the same twice, or like any Bruce Lee movie they had already seen. Something about Lee's personality, his attention to physical and mental strength, appealed to the prisoners' need to make something useful out of their rage and helplessness. Often I demonstrated Lee's moves while telling my stories, and the men became interested in martial arts and wanted to learn it for themselves. So I started giving lessons.

"Your side kick is your longest weapon," I said, leaning all my body weight on my right leg and flicking my left leg high into the air like I was going to kick someone in the chin. "But you must be fast. If you think about it, you've already lost too much time."

We paired off and performed imaginary duels, stopping our punches just inches away from each other as I critiqued everyone's form. We put moves together into katas, sidestepping and thrusting our arms left and right into a sequence of ferocity, turning, shouting, and stomping like warriors. The guards were amused by us, at first gathering on the sidelines to snicker and point, but eventually the novelty wore off and they let us be.

I'd never taken a class in karate or kung fu or tae kwon do, but I was a star pupil in the Bruce Lee Film School. I had one of those memories that wrapped itself around words and fused itself to song lyrics and movie dialogue. I remembered what Bruce Lee said, and all his fight scenes were cataloged in my head, so I just brought them to life, with a confident voice. My pupils began calling me Arshad, which means "wise one." Generally it's a word meant for seniors, but I have to admit it was a little flattering even at the ripe old age of thirty-four.

"Empty your mind," I instructed one afternoon, crouching and holding one fist close to my chest and the other straight out like an arrow. "Be formless, shapeless, like water." I switched my fist positions, throwing a lightning punch and expelling all my air in a loud "*Hunh!*"

Normally, this would be the moment when my students would copy my movement. But they stood still, fixed on something behind me. I looked over my shoulder and saw the prison commander accompanied by a mullah wearing robes and a turban. The clergyman was there to inspect conditions, Sarhang said. He wanted to address the whole prison population, and Sarhang asked me to translate for our visitor.

When we were all gathered in the courtyard, the mullah smiled at me and in Farsi said he had an offer for the men. If they would disown their Iraqi government and join the Iranians, they would be treated nicely and fast-tracked to the top of the list of prisoners to be exchanged with Iranian POWs.

"When the time comes," he added.

It was the worst non-offer I'd ever heard, and I thanked Bruce Lee for all the lessons in mental strength that kept me from bursting into laughter. Just the previous week some new prisoners had joined us and told us that our government was aware of where we were imprisoned, had mentioned Arak by name on the news, and promised to support us 100 percent. They were already working to get us out.

The mullah was waiting.

"Tell them," he said. "Tell them to be smart about this."

I faced the crowd and repeated the mullah's offer in Arabic, which landed like a slap. The men clicked their teeth and curled their lips in disgust. They'd been through brainwashing countless times before at other prisons, and were outraged at the audacity of this stranger to think he could rip our nationality from us in a matter of seconds, just by being *friendly*.

I asked the crowd, "Can I answer this clergyman on your behalf?"

"*Yes!*" they roared.

The mullah's eyes became worried, as he flicked them between the prisoners and me, likely sensing the deal was souring on him.

"I'm going to tell you a fable," I said to him. "A poor man wearing flip-flops approaches a prostitute and tells her he would like to take her out on the town. He has no money, no car, and no place of his own where he can take her, but he tells her he's a really nice guy. She says, 'Why would I go with you when you have nothing for me? Even customers who pay haven't been good to me overall, and now you want me to join you simply because you are being nice and courteous?'"

The mullah's lips flattened into a thin line.

"Is this what you are saying, or what the captives are saying?" he asked.

"They gave me permission to speak on their behalf."

The last of his politeness flew out of his finger as he shook it at me.

"Tell them exactly what you just said to me," he fumed. "Maybe they don't agree with you."

When I repeated my homemade parable, the prisoners stood up and cheered. I glanced at the guards and saw them holding back smiles. Even Sarhang stood off to the side, suddenly very interested in his shoes, letting the mullah fend for himself. Our "guest" sputtered through the rest of his prepared religious speech while the prisoners talked among themselves, then he stomped off to wherever he had come from.

That night, long after everyone had fallen asleep, Sarhang summoned me to his office. He was sitting with his elbows on his desk, holding his fingertips together in a triangle in front of his nose with a look like he had just swallowed milk that had gone sour. I rubbed the sleep out of my eyes, took a seat, and waited for the bad news. His triangled fingers closed into a two-palmed prayer.

"Son, I thank you for what you said to the mullah today. I don't like them coming here and meddling with my prisoners, and what you said will discourage them from coming back."

My shoulders lowered an inch. This wasn't so bad. But couldn't he have waited to tell me this in the morning? Then he cleared his throat, and I could tell he wasn't finished. The worst was yet to come, and I gripped the armrests. Reflexively, my shoulders clenched again.

"The mullah gave me orders to punish you. He is going to write a report to the government about his visit, including that you were tortured for what you said to him."

I wasn't sure if Sarhang was conspiring with me or warning me. I bored my eyes into his mouth, waiting for his lips to move again.

"Stay firm."

"Thank you" was all I said.

New guards I hadn't seen before, four agents from Iranian military intelligence in dark green uniforms, were waiting for me outside Sarhang's office, and guided me toward a bank of empty solitary-confinement rooms down the hall. I felt no fear but a surge of courage as I walked, proud to be taking a beating for my men. Their support was the solid ground under my feet as I walked, and I would gladly suffer pain to spare them the same. The agents steered me into one of the rooms and locked the door. I noticed they were all wearing name badges and told myself I would memorize each name before this was over. One was chubby and short, one had a long neck with a protruding Adam's apple, and the one in glasses kept staring at the floor. The fourth had a small frying pan in his hand. All had beards.

"Go face the corner," the short one said.

I imagined they were going to hit me with the pan, and I tensed my muscles to prepare. I heard them rustling and banging the pan on something, and then silence. Five minutes passed, and still they weren't doing anything. It was like they had sent the amateurs, and maybe they'd lost their nerve. It was almost comical. Then I smelled cooking oil. The short one grabbed my shoulder and flipped me around. Behind him, the frying pan sat atop a portable kerosene burner, smoking with hot oil.

"You son of a bitch," he hissed. He reached up with his cigar fingers and slapped me, or at least he tried to. He wasn't that strong, and I was able to silently make fun of him by standing so still that I didn't even blink each time he slapped me. The other three men got a big kick out of this, laughing at his flailing attempts to hurt me. Adam's Apple stopped chortling and picked the pan of hot oil off the flame. He pushed the fat guy aside and stood facing me.

"How do you like this, donkey?"

He looked directly into my eyes as he tilted the pan and the sizzling oil fell in a molten stream through my socks and singed the tops of my feet. I could feel my skin peel back and blisters rising, but I didn't give him the satisfaction of grimacing. I held his gaze, bent it, and aimed it right back at him.

The torturers then looked at one another, as if to ask themselves what they were supposed to do next. They set the pan back down and filed out. As soon as they were gone, I allowed myself to look down. My feet were swelling up like potatoes, and the socks had melted into my skin where the oil had landed. It still felt like I was standing in a pot of boiling water. I didn't dare move, in case they were coming back. About ten minutes later, I heard footsteps and stopped myself from trembling. I stood at attention and braced myself for more.

One of my tormentors entered—the quiet one in glasses. He came so close I could smell his stale breath, then he reached into his pocket and held out . . . a cigarette.

"Here," he said. "Don't hate us; we're just doing our job. We had orders to torture you."

He lit the cigarette for me, while Tubby came in with a chair and offered it to me.

"Sit, rest," Eyeglasses said. "When you see the other prisoners, exaggerate how much you were tortured, OK? Same with the warden; if he asks, tell him it was a lot worse."

I nodded and eased myself down slowly onto the chair.

Tubby sighed heavily.

"We love Iran, but we don't like our government," he explained.

If only he knew how much I understood.

"Forgive us?" Eyeglasses said.

I drew the cigarette smoke into my lungs and held my breath as long as I could before I let it out in a blue-gray stream toward the ceiling, contemplating my answer. I was starting to believe that nobody, no matter which side of the border he lived on, had free will anymore.

"If I were in your position, I would have done the same," I said.

And I meant it.

The Arak guards became even more sympathetic toward us after I was tortured. If the men asked for extra soap or sugar packets, they got them. If the guards saw a prisoner who seemed gloomy, they'd take a walk with him in the yard to try to cheer him up. After taking me to a doctor, they made sure I had enough burn cream and bandages for my feet. The guards liked the necklaces and bracelets the inmates carved, and began trading things for them, such as pens and nail clippers and multivitamins. It seemed important for the guards to show they respected us. But their generosity came with an implied price: that they could loaf around and listen to music and smoke cigarettes. But it was a little unsettling, because nothing is ever truly free, especially in a prison. I needed to keep my eyes open.

One day a guard put a small aluminum packet in my hand, and inside I found a small plug of green-brown opium, a sticky roll about the size of my pinkie that looked a lot like tamarind paste. I had never tried the drug before, and I quickly squirreled the gift in my slippers, and shared the news with a handful of my closest friends. We met by the palm tree in the courtyard and cut the roll into tiny pieces, held a match under the aluminum foil, and smoked the opium through the tube of an empty Bic pen. I leaned back into the sturdy trunk, and within a few minutes my body felt buoyed, like I was on an inflatable raft in the sun, and I could hear Alyaa laughing at something I'd said. I floated on the tide of her tinkling voice and thanked her for loving me. She rested her head on my shoulder and placed Amjad on my lap, his pudgy hands pressing into my chest as he tried to crawl up to me. He had a full head of hair now, and a fierce gaze, like mine. She whispered something in my ear, but I didn't catch it. Didn't matter, just feeling her skin again I knew that everything was going to be all right. The opium smoke curled around my cells and for the first time since I'd been captured, I thought of Alyaa and Amjad without becoming sad. They were waiting for me, and all I had to do was stay calm like this, and one day we'd be together again. I felt so certain of this now, now that the opium had given me permission to believe it. I was giddy with the sudden realization that I had free will to assume the worst, or the best, outcome for my life. I rested my head against the tree for the next six hours and meditated on faith.

I was thankful for the opium because it gave me a way to check out, but it was a rare experience because the guards never brought enough drugs into the compound for addictions to form. But the drug hazes caught the attention of some of the older, more educated prisoners, who were becoming increasingly concerned about the sharing between captors and captives. They warned such openness could only lead to trouble. I told them not to worry, that it was innocent enough.

But I should have listened, because not long after, things went from chummy to alarming.

Some of the Iranian guards began providing the prisoners with tools to dig holes. They brought steel spoons, shaving razors, and scraps of metal, and the prisoners hid them around the yard. Soon after, rumors swirled around that some of the high-ranking POWs in the neighboring prison were planning to escape through the sewer pipes and some of the guards were going to help them. I wanted no part of it. There must have been a reason that the Iranian boy snatched me out of death's clutches, and it wasn't so I could get gunned down in a sewer tunnel underneath a prison. Eventually, when I returned to my homeland, I thought, it would be as a hero, not as a war casualty.

I was trying to fall asleep, wondering what I should do about all this, when whistles and sirens blared from all directions. Floodlights clicked on and special forces soldiers, dressed all in black like commandos, tore through the prison, unlocking all the doors and ordering everybody into the courtyard, where they had us lie facedown with our hands on our heads. They demanded to know which one of us was the interpreter, and then I felt a boot press down on the back of my head.

"If you don't tell the truth, you will be the first one executed! Give me the names of the guards who were collaborating with you!"

I could hear similar shouting from outside the compound walls and knew that identical interrogations were happening at all three prisons. I rolled to my side so I could free my mouth to speak, then told the boot that I didn't know. He pressed harder on my head, and I prayed that he wouldn't snap my neck.

"Boland sho!" he said, kicking me in the side.

They ordered us to stand and strip so they could search our bodies and clothes for weapons. Meanwhile, they took everything out of our cells and dumped it on the ground, separating all the contraband into a small hill of razor blades, rope, metal shanks, and pieces of heavy wire with filed points. The search took about four hours, during which time we had to stand there without water or a bathroom break, until finally they put us back in our cells sometime after midnight. We huddled close together without our blankets, and one of the older prisoners in his sixties approached me. His face was red and his eyes were watery, like he had been holding his breath too long.

"Arshad, they took our bucket."

I looked in the corner, where the bucket we used as a toilet during the night was gone. The man tugged on my arm.

"Please, I need to go outside to the washroom."

I banged on our door, and a guard came. One of the new ones clad in black.

"Sir, we have an elderly man here who really has to use the bathroom."

"He can piss himself," the guard said, slamming and locking the door.

I banged again, harder this time. The guard returned, whipped open the door, and put his nose an inch from mine, so close that I could feel his breath on my face. Spit flew as he cursed me. "Listen, you fucking Arab, nobody's leaving until we find out who the traitors are. Bother me once more, and you'll wish you hadn't."

When the old man saw the door close a second time, he clutched his stomach and groaned. He bent forward, and his legs jiggled uncontrollably. The indignity of it seized my hand and I slammed my fist over and over into the door and the windows. Now a few of the men in the cell were shouting with me.

"Animals, have you no decency? Let this man out!"

This time three commandos came to our cell, each one carrying an inch-thick cable sheathed in rubber, like a section of telephone wire.

"Who has to go to the bathroom?" one demanded.

Nobody answered, but nobody needed to. They stomped in lockstep toward the man with white hair cowering in a puddle of his own urine, grabbed the back of his shirt, and dragged him into the courtyard. It took only one blow to the head to knock him down. He writhed in the dirt as they pummeled him and we screamed in horror, begging them to stop. That man could have been my father; he was gentle and had barely the strength to hold his arms in front of his face to try to block the blows. When he gave up and let his arms fall to his sides, I felt a rage like nothing I'd ever experienced, not even during my own beatings. This man was nothing to these guards but a prop to remind us that we were powerless.

"Hey! Beat me, beat me instead!" I shouted. "For the love of God, beat me in his place!"

My heart rate rocketed as I realized I was running out of time to solve this. I screamed louder, reminding the guards that they had grandfathers, that this man deserved mercy. Blood spattered their uniforms and they kept going, stopping only when they were sure he wasn't twitching anymore. Then they left him there for the buzzards to eat his eyes.

They left his corpse there for two days as a reminder that Arak was under new management. We were on lockdown, but we could see his crumpled body from our cell, and whispered prayers to him, asking forgiveness and blessing his soul. I was in a stupor, for once at a loss for words, unable to stop blaming myself for his death. I didn't want the men to call me Arshad anymore—I wasn't wise; I was a failure. If I had been a more capable translator, I could have said the right thing to get those guards to back down. I could have saved his life, if only I'd known how to negotiate. Now I was too afraid to open my mouth, for fear I would cause more trouble. I sat with my back against the wall and refused to eat, punishing myself.

Meanwhile, the search for the escape plotters continued. The investigators weren't getting the information they wanted, so they called us all back to the courtyard. One commando pulled a piece of paper from his shirt pocket and read off three names, including mine.

"Come with me," he said.

As we followed him toward the warden's office, the rest of the prisoners went berserk, yelling and screaming and shaking the doors to their cells. I found myself in the same room where I'd been tortured. This time I faced the wall before they had to tell me to. For the next half hour, several interrogators whaled on me with the same whips made from

high-voltage cables that they had used to beat the old man to death. This
time I wasn't stoic; I covered my head and screamed as my shirt ripped
open and my back swelled into a topography of red and purple welts. In
the brief moments when the tormentors stopped to catch their breath,
I could hear men being beaten in the adjoining rooms. The prisoners
outside were still roaring in outrage, pounding on walls.

"Confess," the commandos demanded. "Tell us which prisoners and
guards were working together."

I was on all fours now, heaving and gasping for air. The men stopped
hitting me and waited for my answer.

"I don't know anything," I said.

If only I knew something, anything, to make them stop. I could have
told them which guards brought in opium, or more sugar cubes, but that
didn't necessarily mean they were the same ones who were involved in
the escape plan. If there even was one. People flapped their mouths all
the time in prison. I could see how a wish to escape through the sewers
could become a boast, then a faint idea, then an unfettered rumor that
solidified into almighty truth. I could have given a name, any name, just
to stop the pain. But the prisoners trusted me as their leader, and I had
promised never to let them down. Only I had failed, and an old man was
beaten to death. Now I accepted each whip to my body as payment for
each strike to his.

Four times they asked me. Four times I answered the same. Dis-
gusted, they dispatched me and I hobbled back to the courtyard and
collapsed. The men rushed forward and carried me back to our room.

"There are more of us than them, Arshad," whispered the prisoner
who was pouring cold water on my wounds. I looked up at the gun
towers.

"We are unarmed," I said. "Think of the frail and elderly among us.
For their sake, we will not riot."

THIRTEEN

CAPTIVITY

Days after I was captured, the war ended. I heard the news over public loudspeakers while I was riding in the back of an Iraqi army truck,
squeezed in with a dozen other prisoners of war. We had to sit there
quietly, our hands tied together with our shoelaces, as the two armed soldiers guarding us waved to cheering Iraqi crowds, as if their country had
won the war or something and we were the spoils. But that was bullshit,
and the whole world knew it. After eight years of fighting, neither side
had gained a thing: no borders had changed, Saddam had not stepped
down, and nobody grabbed anyone's oil fields.

I was more lost now than when I ran away to the join the Basij
almost seven years before. I'd tried my best to avenge Mina, but I had
failed. The war was over but not for me. Iran and Iraq had signed the
ceasefire, but they were going to keep fighting with politics, using POWs
as human bargaining chips.

I bounced in the bed of the truck, choking on dirt and exhaust, ex-
changing glances with my fellow prisoners, trying to get a sense of what
this meant for us. If the war was over, they couldn't keep us in Iraq, could
they? What would be the point?

The soldiers kicked us out of the truck and I landed ass-first in a desert, where the view was beige in every direction, a blank sand canvas for
the wind to sculpt into shapes. I had envisioned a hulking fortress of a

prison, with a spiked iron fence all around it, floodlights and gun turrets, tanks parked all around. But instead the soldiers herded us into what I swear must have been an abandoned cattle pasture, an area about the size of ten soccer fields surrounded by a crude barbed-wire fence. In the distance, I saw a collection of one-story cinder-block buildings with broken windows that seemed to be listing in the sand. To the left of them, about fifty shipping containers, some red, some blue, scattered around like a child's toys left on the floor. I stepped over bricks and broken glass and garbage and came up with a new theory—maybe this place used to be a dump. I figured they had selected us for slave labor, and we were going to have to unload whatever was in those shipping containers. I felt faint just at the thought of it, standing under a punishing sun with only bread and water for the last three days.

A tree of a man emerged from the one building, growing taller with each step as he approached. He moved as if he had an invisible entourage, almost high-stepping with thighs that were bigger than both of mine put together. His perfect nose came to an arrowhead point over a thick mustache that hid his upper lip. If God made man in his image, he must have used this guy for the mold. The man drilled his eyes into us from beneath his red beret, glaring down from more than six and a half feet. He said nothing as he paced before us. What frightened me even more than his size was his personality. This man was so . . . *still*.

One of the prisoners couldn't stand the silence any longer. In a trembling voice, he shouted, "Where are we? What are you going to do to us?"

Red Beret's eyes snapped. An interpreter translated into Arabic, and in one fluid movement, the silent man removed his gun from his holster, pressed it to the questioner's temple, and squeezed the trigger. The prisoner fell like a sack of rocks. Nobody moved while his blood spread toward our feet.

"I am your commander, Mira Sahib," the tall man said, letting us know that he expected us to use the respectful term "Master" when addressing him. His voice was toneless, preprogrammed. "If you obey me and don't give me any problems, you will all go back to your homeland—alive."

Then he gave his first command.

"State your names. And your skills."

When it was my turn to answer, I left out some stuff. "I am a medic. I can also make tea," I said.

I thought I saw one edge of that mustache lift, as if he was smirking under there, like my answer amused him. Good. He didn't need to know about my talent aiming a rifle from very, very far away.

Once we were all recorded and categorized by abilities, the guards passed out black-and-white-striped pants and shirts. Sewn into the back of the shirt was a brown cloth patch with the letters PW drawn in black ink. An officer dug into a box of plastic slippers and handed us two apiece. I noticed my left slipper was a size forty-four and my right a forty-three. The boots they confiscated from my feet were size forty-one. Next they separated us into groups of about thirty and led us toward the cargo containers. The guards opened the creaking double doors on one end of the long steel box, and it was empty inside, except for two buckets. There were two jagged holes about the size of shoeboxes that had been cut with a blowtorch at the roofline on either end of the forty-foot container. They had welded rebar over the holes. With a sudden horror, I realized those cutouts were for ventilation. I hadn't seen our barracks because they were hiding in plain sight. They were going to lock us in these airless cages.

I could already feel waves of heat floating out of the container. We were going to be cooked alive in there, and I opened my mouth to say this and then remembered what had happened to the other guy who spoke his mind. I shuffled in with everyone else like dejected sheep. One of the guards picked up one of the buckets and pointed to a red line that was painted on the inside, a few inches from the rim.

"Do not let your piss rise above this line," he said. Then he stepped outside and slammed the doors with a dull clank, plunging us into darkness. I found a small bit of space on the floor and sat, resting my head against a hot wall, not caring if it left a burn. To survive I would have to become a stone at the bottom of a river, without sensation and of no worth to any living thing. I passed the hours by concentrating on the temperature of the metal wall behind my head, feeling the heat slowly leave it as day turned into night. I tried to stay awake, but at some point exhaustion won the battle.

The wake-up whistle came at six in the morning, but it was unnecessary. The sun was already out and the heated stench of infection and blood and our two "toilets" had assaulted all of us out of sleep. There was also a smell of death. Agha-ye Ahmadi, a former doctor who had been captured with me in Sumar, knelt over the bodies of two of the most severely wounded in our container and felt their necks for a pulse. He dropped his head and sighed.

When the guards opened our container and we showed them the two bodies, they dragged the dead men out by their feet. Agha-ye Ahmadi and I followed at a safe distance to see what would happen. The guards pulled the corpses outside the fence and walked a ways into the desert, then just dropped them out in the open, for the wild dogs to find.

Agha-ye Ahmadi spat on the ground. "Barbarians," he hissed.

Behind us, a group of prisoners had gathered in one corner of the yard. In the light of day, I could see a sea of yellow jumpsuits—prisoners from the other buildings. We walked closer and saw guards dragging an industrial-sized stew pot toward the crowd, sloshing and spilling a brown liquid inside. The emaciated prisoners stood quivering, staring at the pot. On a whistle, they all ran for it, like horses out of a starting gate. They elbowed to get to the food, pushing and kicking and shouting. The ones who made it to the pot thrust their hands into the slop and scooped as much as they could in their mouths before being knocked out of the way by other prisoners. As hungry as I was, all I could do was watch men morph into animals, while the guards cackled and looked at their watches. When a minute passed, a guard blew a second whistle and held up one finger. The prisoners pressed on, some pairs even peeling out of the melee to throw punches at each other. A third whistle, and the guard raised two fingers. Now the jostling was more desperate, and then men tore clothing and bit each other to clear a path to the food. After

whistle four, the guards yanked the pot away and ran it back to the officers' building, where the kitchen was. The prisoners dispersed, not even
wiping themselves off, and went back to normal, talking to one another
like nothing had just happened. I glanced over at the doctor, who looked
aghast.

"Agha-ye Ahmadi, they make us fight to eat?"

"We're going to have to design a system," he said under his breath.

That first day, trucks arrived with construction materials and tools.
Mira Sahib gathered us together and gave us an insincere apology for
the uncomfortable sleeping quarters but promised our accommodations
would be changing. As soon as we built our own cells. We should be
grateful for the opportunity to expand Ramadi prison camp, Mira Sahib
said, because productivity would give us purpose and keep away boredom. But first we had to build living quarters for our captors. And, of
course, their rooms were large and comfortable, with tiled floors and
flushing toilets, lighting, and lots of windows. We worked from first light
until we couldn't see anymore. I was assigned to do electrical. And I'd be
lying if I said I did not forget to ground a wire here and there so that
someone might get a shock when he flipped a switch.

Meanwhile Agha-ye Ahmadi came up with a way we could all eat
during our three-minute meals. We were fed a rancid mystery stew made
from the leftovers of whatever the officers ate, twice daily, at six in the
morning and six in the evening. Dr. Ahmadi divided us by height. The
shortest among us crouched shoulder to shoulder around the slop pot.
The tallest men stood in a circle around them and reached over their
heads into the stew. These two rings of men were the food servers. They
grabbed fistfuls of food with bare hands or sopped it up with chunks of
bread, and handed it back to the rest of us. They fed others this way for
the first two minutes. For the final minute, the servers fed themselves,
cramming food into their front pockets and their mouths. When the pot
was taken away, they walked the camp looking for the frail and ill who
couldn't rise for the meal and fed them what was in their pockets. The
food was a step above compost, a revolting mess of rotting vegetables,

moldy rice, and gristle that looked like it was mixed with snot and vomit, but I forced it down to stay alive. I once found bits of a shoe in it and simply picked them out and kept eating.

One afternoon I was making cinder blocks, pressing them into shape by hand, when a prisoner next to me clucked his tongue to get my attention. I looked up and Mira Sahib was coming directly for me—smiling. Never a good sign. When he was grinning, that meant he had come up with another game. When he was in a mood, he devised amusements such as making us stand in two parallel rows and slap each other until he grew tired of it. He leered at me when I stood to face him.

"So. Today's your twentieth birthday."

The Iraqis had stripped us of our dog tags when we arrived. He must have read the date on my ID. For a brief moment, I felt flattered. It's amazing how birthdays are special, no matter where you are. Everyone has one, and everyone can relate when it's your day. I looked up, making sure to deferentially avoid his gaze, hoping he might give me the day off from work.

"It is, Mira Sahib."

He snapped his fingers, and four burly guards appeared like out of a genie's lamp. They encircled me, and I nearly wet myself when I saw they were carrying green bamboo switches, flexing them with both hands so that I could see they had been softened in saltwater to make them better whips. One held a three-foot section of copper telephone wire. They took off their berets and handed them to Mira Sahib, who stepped aside as the thugs lifted their weapons.

"Why?" was the only word I had time for before their whips whistled through the air and struck me from all sides, and I toppled right there in front of the construction site, while the rest of the prisoners pretended not to see. The guards kicked me with their boots, and I curled into a ball and tightened all my muscles to try to blunt their blows, but it was no use. I heard one of my ribs crack. As I rolled on the ground, shielding my head with my arms, I vowed revenge. I didn't expect to make it out of Ramadi alive, but in the days I had left, I had only one goal: to get back at Mira Sahib. It didn't matter if I died trying because I had no reason to live anymore—the love of my life had been killed. I had no one waiting for me if I survived prison, so in a sense I was already dead, which meant I'd risk nothing if I were to attack Mira Sahib. So before I was smote from this earth, I vowed to complete one last errand: kill that man.

My cries pierced the sky as they dragged me across the courtyard to the flagpole, where they looped a length of copper telephone cable through an eyehook sticking out of it. Someone wrapped the ends of the wire many times around my thumbs, until just the tips of my thumbnails were exposed. Then they hoisted. Daggers of pain shot through my thumbs all the way down to my shoulders as the devils lifted me until I was a foot above the ground, dangling there like a fish caught on a hook. I didn't know pain could be like that, worse than being scalded with a skewer, beaten with fists, or shot in the leg. It felt like a million knives were slicing me from top to bottom, in slow motion.

"Let me down, I beg you!"

I felt my joints stretching beyond where they should, and my mind unhinged. A fusillade of curses roared from my throat; everything I'd ever been angry about in my entire life poured out in a bitter vomit of hate. I swore at the sun and the earth and Allah and my parents as the men kept whipping me with the bamboo switches.

"Fuck you!" I roared, trying to spit on their heads. "Baba! Fuck you too! Fuck me! Fuuuuuuuuuuuuuuuck!"

My torturers called me trash and a traitor, and blamed me for something that I only caught a snippet of, something about faulty wiring that had injured Mira Sahib's nephew. My eyes rolled back in my head and their voices were lost to the ringing in my ears. I didn't know how long it would be before my body weight would tear me from my thumbs. I just hoped it would be soon.

"Just kill me!"

Then I passed out. I floated in and out of consciousness for several hours, and each time I awoke I let out another torrent of curses that went ignored. The guards had moved on, and the prisoners were still laboring a few hundred feet from me, slathering mortar on cinder blocks to make a wall. But one, the old prisoner we called Uncle, sixty-eight-year-old Amu Safar, moved a wheelbarrow closer to me and put his fingers to his lips. Amu was the only prisoner who had the guts to approach Mira Sahib, and had some sort of magic touch because Mira Sahib never hurt him. Old man Safar was planning something. I shushed, and waited.

Amu Safar scurried away from the construction site and, not long after, returned with Agha-ye Ahmadi and Daryoosh to cut me down. I shook uncontrollably as they carried me to the shipping container and removed the wire from my thumbs. My tendons had been sliced, and I couldn't move my thumbs, my right index finger, or the first two fingers on my left hand. My remaining fingers had curled into claws.

"Drink," said Agha-ye Ahmadi, pouring water between my lips.

"It's over now," Daryoosh said, wiping my forehead with his sleeve.

I stayed in that shipping container and out of Mira Sahib's sight for nearly two months, as the doctor nursed me back to health by bringing me food and water and making a cast for my wrists from plaster stolen from the construction supplies. I learned that Amu Safar had saved my life by telling Mira Sahib that I was almost dead and not worth the commander's important time to cut down, convincing him that the prisoners could do the errand for him.

When the casts were removed, my hands refused to unclench. And there was nothing Agha-ye Ahmadi could do to stop my trembling, which had developed into a permanent tremor that made me slur and drool when I tried to talk, and stumble when I walked. I'd been kicked too hard in the head, Agha-ye said.

"Sometimes these tics correct themselves. Other times, not."

I became a source of great amusement to my captors. I could no longer work construction, but they still put me in service, pouring them tea in the officers' dining room. My slippers squeaked as I dragged my wooden feet across the tiles, and the saucers rattled as I set teacups before the officers with my crippled hands. Each time I spilled tea, they sent me back to the kitchen, demanding I do it right. They laughed cruelly each and every time.

"Are you belly dancing for us, Zahed?"

"Hey, Zahed, need a napkin? You've got some drool on your chin!"

Go ahead, laugh. Don't mind me while I do this shaky dance to pull a dead mouse out of my pocket, lift the lid of the samovar, and drop it in. They played their games with me, and I played mine. I came up with all sorts of additives for the tea. I drooled into the teapot, peed in it, and even shook my hair over it to share some of my lice. I'll never know if it was me that did it, but whenever one of the tea guests fell ill, I rejoiced.

Within a year, we were moved out of the containers and into the new cells. Our two-story cinder-block dormitories were designed like American roadside motels, with long rows of ten-foot-by-twelve-foot rooms, and a single covered corridor running past the front doors. Each cell had one window covered by iron bars, and contained two bunk beds shared by twelve men. We had to double and triple up in the beds, and rotate turns on the floor, to keep things fair. The rooms were unlocked, and we could come and go during the day. But at night if you went outside you were likely to be shot, so no one dared. The prisoners had constructed an auditorium, a kitchen, bathrooms, and a storage room. We dug a large well in the yard and built four watchtowers and an iron gate for the camp. We painted the command building and paved the road leading into camp with asphalt. We even built solitary-confinement rooms, each no bigger than a broom closet, with the spike ends of nails protruding inward from all four walls, so that a prisoner would be forced to stand totally still inside. The space was so tight that you could barely bring your hand to your mouth, and falling asleep or leaning on a wall could be deadly, or at least extremely painful. Imagine standing in an upright coffin made of cactus leaves.

One afternoon as I was clearing the teacups, an officer's hand flashed out and grabbed me by the wrist. "Leave the dishes. We have something better for you."

A group of soldiers led me outside, behind the dormitories, until we were standing at the edge of a massive dirt pit, a hundred feet across and ten feet deep, where all the sewage pipes emptied. Mira Sahib had ordered us to put a plastic tarp over it, but still the smell permeated the entire camp. Now the guards rolled back the cover, and inside, the sludge had risen to a height of about three feet. The pit wasn't lined or anything, so the liquid sewage had seeped into the dirt, and the shit had risen to the top and baked in the sun, forming a fetid crust.

Even though I garbled most of my words these days, there was one word I could still say with perfect clarity.

"No. No, no, no, no!"

I tried to backpedal, but someone kicked me over the edge anyway. I felt the crust briefly bend under my weight and then give way, sucking me into a putrid muck that oozed up my pant legs and down my collar and into my ears, and I clamped my hand over my mouth and held my breath until I could thrash my way back onto my feet. I did my best to stand at attention like a soldier despite my involuntary jerking. I dripped in filth while they threw bottles and stones at me, refusing to grovel because that's what they wanted. I remained a statue, letting the objects bounce off my body, but this only made them try harder to break me. When they failed to get the reaction they wanted, Mira Sahib approached the edge of the pit and unzipped his pants. I didn't move as his hot yellow stream arced through the air and splattered on my chest.

When the novelty of their new game finally wore off, they left me in the shithole. Maybe if I was my whole self with working hands and no shakes, I could have crawled out of the pit, but in my current condition I was trapped. I waded to one side of the pit so I could at least lean against the dirt wall if I fell asleep. Night came and I watched the stars come out and thanked them for reminding me what beauty was. I looked up and imagined the white pinpoints in the sky were part of a big lace curtain, and behind that was some force watching me.

"OK, God, you have my attention," I shouted to the stars. "What have I done to deserve this? What can I do to make it right?"

As I waited for an answer, I tried to go back and figure out where my life had gone wrong. Was it when my parents first met? When I was born? Was it when I stole Baba's money? When I ran away? When I saved the enemy soldier? When Mina died? When I stole gold from a corpse? When I killed my first man? My life seemed like a series of bad luck, bad juju, and bad decisions, so many wrong turns that it was beyond impossible to find my way again. God still hadn't answered me by the time the sun began to show itself, but I wasn't surprised. I would have given up on me, too.

Not long after sunrise, I heard footsteps. I pushed myself up off the side of the pit and my tremors kicked into high gear, anticipating that Mira Sahib and his cronies were back for more. I blinked into the sun at the outline of two silhouettes and saw that it was Agha-ye Ahmadi and Amu Safar, lowering down a ladder. Maybe God had been listening. I crawled up a few steps on the ladder and they hoisted me up while I clung there, blubbering like a baby.

"Barbarians," Agha-ye Ahmadi said as he helped me to my feet.

My saviors walked me to the showers, but Mira Sahib blocked the washroom entrance with his hulk.

"Oh, no, you don't," he said. "Back to your cell."

Just when I thought I'd mastered the art of turning myself into a stone without feelings, Mira Sahib discovered one little nerve I'd overlooked and bit down on it. He had found a way to make me the Ramadi untouchable, a shaking, drooling, retch-inducing turd disgusting even to myself. My clothes were so soiled that I couldn't distinguish stripes anymore, and I smelled like the inside of a squatty. I had to walk down the corridor like that, as the other prisoners hurled shoes and whatever else they could find at me, pelting me until I tripped and fell onto all fours. It took everything I had left to stand back up, because all I wanted to do was curl into a ball and howl. But amidst all the hollering directed my way, I could still hear Mira Sahib laughing at me, clear as a bell, and I have to tell you, that supremely pissed me off.

Sometimes, when Mira Sahib was feeling generous, he would wave me over to a high-pressure hose, the kind that firefighters use. He'd open the valve and aim the water at me, knocking me to the ground. He'd hose me off as I rolled like a log, taking off what felt like two layers of my skin.

I'd return to my cell dripping and dejected. No one wanted to sleep near me anymore, so my rotation in the beds came to an end.

This became my new routine. The guards continued to toss me in the pit whenever they felt like it, which was like every week. And it always depended on Mira Sahib's mood whether I could wash afterward or not. Sometimes I had to keep the layer of slime on me overnight. One time he waited a whole week before granting a shower. I developed skin infections and an uncontrollable itch. One day I looked down and saw worms crawling under my skin. Agha-ye Ahmadi tried to treat the worms and sores with salt water, which was all we had for medicine, but it didn't do too much. I repelled everyone in prison, except for the three prisoners who tried valiantly to stick up for me and remind the others that I was an Iranian just like them: Dr. Ahmadi, old man Safar, and Daryoosh.

Daryoosh knew what it was like to be hated in prison. People were envious of him because lately he had been getting special treatment. He was taken off work duty and for the last month he was allowed in the officers' kitchen to eat anything he wanted. He came back describing kebabs and fresh vegetables and yogurt, and even though we all asked for reports, at the same time we didn't want to hear the answers. It turned out Daryoosh had a rare blood type, one that matched the blood of one of the Iraqi officers who needed a kidney. A while back the guards had come by with syringes and taken blood samples from all of us. Daryoosh was the lucky winner. In my nearly two years as a prisoner, I'd never seen a doctor at Ramadi or heard of a prisoner being taken to a hospital, but one night Daryoosh was whisked away for surgery.

A few days later, two guards deposited Daryoosh back in our room. It was the middle of the day, and everyone was out doing construction while I was passing the time alone until I had to pour tea. His skin was ashy, and he was stooped over like an old man with sunken eyes that focused on nothing in particular. He shuffled his feet as I helped him to one of the bunks.

"What happened?"

Weakly, he lifted his shirt. His belly was so bloated that the skin was stretched like a drum, and a jagged five-inch vertical line of stitches on the side of his belly-button was infected and oozing. His skin was hot to the touch, and his sweat was already soaking the blanket. Then he pointed to his other side. I rolled Daryoosh toward me and saw a second line of stitches.

"They took both," he said faintly.

"Barbarian" was too kind a word for Mira Sahib. He'd had Daryoosh butchered, then brought him back on purpose so that we'd have to watch him die a slow, painful death as the unfiltered blood inside him collected and turned toxic. Daryoosh's eyes fluttered closed and he groaned in agony.

"Brother, make sure I get a proper Muslim funeral," he said.

I promised, and put his head in my lap so that he would know that he was loved. There was nothing I could do but try to make him comfortable, so I hugged and kissed him and brought him water, and then four days later he died in my arms. The cries of grief from our cell drew Mira Sahib like a vulture.

"Get away from him," he barked, and we scattered like mice.

Mira Sahib walked up to Daryoosh and when he was satisfied that our friend was dead, the commander raised his foot and stomped on his distended belly, then walked out, leaving a bloody footprint in his wake. We rushed to Daryoosh, caressed his limbs, and began to pray. Each man poured a bit of his daily water ration from his canteen into a cup, and I ripped the lining from my jacket pocket, wet it, and wiped up the blood from his stomach. Then, following his last wish, we went through the traditional funeral rites. I took the wet cloth and wiped the top of Daryoosh's head, then his face, and then the right side of his body from top to bottom before moving on to the left, all the while whispering the first *surah* of the Koran:

In the name of Allah, the Beneficent, the Merciful.
Praise be to Allah, Lord of worlds,
The Beneficent, the Merciful.

Master of the Day of Judgment,

Thee alone we worship; Thee alone we ask for help.

Show us the straight path,

The path of those whom Thou has favored; not the path of

those who earn Thine anger nor those who go astray.

We carried Daryoosh outside, behind the buildings, and buried him. I sat next to the mound of new dirt for a long time, and came to a decision. *Okay, Mira Sahib, you win.* I was done. I didn't want to live with cruelty like this anymore. I walked back to the camp and waited until Mira Sahib crossed my path, then I waved him over.

"Mira Sahib! Come here."

He stopped, stunned that I was ordering him to do something.

"You motherfucker; you don't tell me what to do!" he thundered.

Still, the surprise tactic worked. He stomped over to me with his pile-driver gait.

I fell to my knees and bowed my head.

"Just kill me."

That laugh—again. In the chess match between Mira Sahib and me, he had just cornered my queen. I heard him spit and felt saliva land on my head.

"Don't be silly. Why would I kill you when I can slowly torture you to death?"

FOURTEEN

RADIO

The welts on my back healed. The commandos left Arak prison, assigned to torture Iraqi POWs elsewhere, I guess. Our regular guards resumed their halfhearted watch over us, but with one major change: they stopped bringing sharp objects in from the outside. They still brought us gifts, cigarettes and candies and whatnot, but thankfully no more digging tools. Escaping through the sewers—come on, who came up with that? Someone was watching too many James Bond movies. The only way we were going to escape prison was to keep our heads down, stay calm, and ride it out. This war couldn't go on forever.

But 1985 became 1986, and marinated into 1987, and still the war dragged on. I fell into a routine designed to cut the days into smaller, predictable segments. Basra and Baghdad were so far away from me now that they were like dreams I had had once. With each passing year, the edges around them grew fuzzier.

My days began with a whistle blast, then the morning lineup to be counted. This was followed by breakfast, which was always one of three things: boiled eggs and bread, cheese with bread, or lentil soup with bread. Then we went to the yard and separated into three tribes: those who exercised, those who made handicrafts, or those, like me, who sat around and told stories. I was a bit more fortunate than the others because I had a prison job to distract me. I was called on almost daily to translate for the commander, and my Farsi became almost fluent. Every afternoon, during the hottest part of the day, we escaped indoors for a nap. This was followed by the evening meal, which was indistinguishable from the morning one, then a second body count and the locking of our doors at six p.m. We only veered from routine every two weeks, when we were given a bucket of cold water and soap to wash ourselves, and on the rare rainy days, when we gratefully hung our jumpsuits outside to wash them.

When I wasn't translating, I was a storyteller-slash-actor. Eventually I ran out of Bruce Lee material and had to make my own movie. I decided on a murder mystery and set it during the American Civil War with Christians fighting Christians over power and borders and the right to own slaves. I gave it the title *A Trip to the Gypsies*, which will become clear in a minute. I had no paper or pencil to write my script, so I memorized the whole plot, creating seven episodes that each took an entire day to tell. I wrapped the inmates in its spell like a soap opera, giving them something to debate and anticipate. When everyone assembled in the courtyard to hear the latest episode, all I had to do was lift two fingers and a cigarette would appear there, a gift to the artist. Even the guards found reasons to linger on the sidelines, eager to watch even if they couldn't understand the words.

The movie opens in Texas, with two American cowboys, professional criminals, sitting under a tree. The one with the face of a fox tells the chubby one he's going to give up crime. After a lifetime of victimizing almost everyone in town, they have become targets of a growing vigilante movement and have decided to skedaddle.

Foxface marries and has a son who becomes a high-ranking police officer, lauded in the newspapers for his exceptional crime-fighting skills. This son marries a rich girl and they have a boy. One day the baby is found dead at the bottom of the staircase, and no one ever figures out what happened. The couple has a second child, also short-lived, found choked to death. When a third child is born, the father goes on high alert. He locks all the windows, loads his gun, and paces the house at night waiting for the murderer. He falls asleep and is awoken by a cry, rushes to the baby's crib, and finds his wife with her hands around the child's neck. He lunges to slap her hand away but accidentally hits the baby instead, killing him. Both parents are arrested, each accusing the other of murder.

I left my audience there, the perfect cliffhanger, and when we gathered the next day, it was time for opening arguments in the courtroom. The wife hires the biggest attorney in town, who argues that no woman in history has ever killed her three children. He says the real killer is a former victim of the accused man's father, back for revenge. The jury begins to turn on the father, until the mother, who has stayed silent through the entire trial, asks the judge for permission to speak.

At this point, I feigned having to go to the bathroom, to build dramatic tension. Also, I wanted to sit quietly and remember her dialogue, to make sure I hadn't forgotten anything. When I returned, the men fell silent, their looks expectant.

"Okay, where was I?"

"She's on the stand!"

"Yes, the mother tells the judge, 'I was the one who killed my babies intentionally, and if I had more babies, I would have done the same.'"

The prisoners gasped, waiting for an explanation. I straightened my spine and took on an air of righteousness, to get in character.

"'I am a woman who loves her children more than any mother in the world. I wanted to send my babies clean without corruption to God. Today's young American men are depraved criminals who fight wars, they have become corrupted and dirty and addicted to drugs, so I wanted to do a favor to my babies and send them with total innocence to heaven. If you believe in Jesus Christ and God, you should do the same.'"

The mother's theory was so dangerous that the judge ordered all the courtroom doors locked and made everyone inside take an oath that they would never mention what she said to anyone. The grief-stricken father falls into a lifelong depression. The mother escapes prison with her attorney, and they flee the country to go live with the penniless gypsies.

A good storyteller knows who's listening, and I made sure the prisoners would identify with every character. The inmates were Foxface and Chubby, men who had killed other men, wishing they could exchange their pasts for a fresh start. They were the mother, desperately needing to believe that God would take care of them. They felt compassion for the babies, knowing intimately what it was like to be a pawn in the middle of a war. Yet they also empathized with the accused father, born into a history of violence and vendetta, destined to pay for the sins of previous generations. Although I gave up on grade school rather early, I still remember one of my teachers who explained that stories are about two things: there's what they are on the surface, but what they are really about is underneath. If you asked the men what *A Trip to the Gypsies* was about, they'd say it was about a woman who killed her three children. But if you asked them how my movie made them feel, I hoped they'd say it made them sad to think about how it's always the innocent who suffer when religion and greed hold hands.

My movie debut was so successful that the men asked me to make a sequel. I was overjoyed to have a new artistic project, and used the occasion to say that I had to stay in my room to write, but really I was exhausted. It's draining to be performing for seven days straight, and I needed a break. A vacation from nothing, if you will. I was brewing tea in my electric pot when I heard a soft rapping on the door. The new guard, the one I hadn't met yet, popped his head in. He was young, twenty maybe, with skin so fair he looked Caucasian. I noticed immediately that he was extremely tidy. Not a speck of lint on his uniform, and his hair was parted like a laser beam had just burned a line there. It was like he had just been taken out of the box.

"You tell a good story," he said, walking into my room. He sat down in my only chair and extended a cigarette. His jade eyes had an excited shine.

"Do you mind?" he asked.

I offered him a cup of tea, which was my way of saying I didn't.

"I'm Afshin."

"Najah."

"I know."

He was sitting there like he just wanted to talk, but you can never trust a guard, so I let him steer the conversation. You can learn so much if you nod instead of speak. Afshin was looking for a friend. After getting on someone's bad side at a prison in Tehran, he'd been reassigned to our little remote oven of the world as punishment. He didn't elaborate, and I didn't ask, but now he was forced to stand in one spot by the prison fence all day long, and he was colossally bored. He was looking for someone, anyone, to talk to, and figured I had the gift of gab after watching me perform in the yard. To be polite, I inquired about his family. His mother was a general manager in some type of manufacturing company, and his father was an intellectual, before the Revolution. I knew what that meant. "Intellectual" was often code for "disappeared" by the Islamic regime.

"The Iranian government killed my father," he blurted, crushing his cigarette butt with his heel. "I hate this revolutionary government."

My skin prickled. We were veering into dangerous territory, and he was either opening up to me or trying to trick me into thinking he was my friend so I would then say something that could get me in trouble. I wasn't going to take the bait. Guards griped all the time, but they didn't say treasonous things in front of the prisoners.

"Do you have any siblings?" I asked.

His dark look receded, and he reached for something in his pocket. His happy-puppy expression returned.

"Wanna see some pictures?"

He unfolded his wallet and wrestled out a photo of two teenage girls, posing with their arms around each other's shoulders, hair swept up in ponytails. I had not seen a female in so long that I had the same curious sensation as if I were looking at a photo of an exotic animal, like a zebra or a shark. It was strange and beautiful and frightening all at once. My brain overloaded with curiosity. What were their names, what did they like to eat, what music did they listen to, what did their voices sound like, what did they think about the war? I asked question after question, and he was only too happy to answer, and we stayed up all night talking about his beloved sisters.

Afshin returned the next night, and the next, and the next. Slowly, I started to trust him a little because he kept visiting without asking any-thing of me in return. He visited so often that he enlisted a second guard to keep an eye on his abandoned post and alert him if the bosses noticed he was missing. The other prisoners noticed our friendship forming and were pleased. The inmates felt, and rightly so, that Afshin's favoritism was like a bank account, and if we ever needed help in an emergency—a news report from the outside or help getting a message out to a family member—I could call in a favor. It was good to keep the enemy close.

That day came sooner than I expected. Afshin set his teacup down one night and told me he would soon be transferred back to Tehran. My heart fell an inch. I would miss him; our talks had made me come alive a little bit. I could tell he looked a little sad, too.

Then he lowered his voice. "If you need anything from me, tell me what it is, and I can bring it to you before I have to go."

I was prepared with my answer; I had thought of it the minute he set foot in my room and said hello.

"Bring me the smallest radio you can find," I said.

Three weeks passed, and then Afshin woke me up one night and pressed a battery-powered Aiwa transistor radio, about the size of half a deck of cards, into my palm. He took my other hand and wrapped my fingers around an earpiece. He might as well have placed the key to the prison in my hand.

"This is more precious to me than my own heart," I whispered.

"Good luck to you."

"Wait," I said, stashing the radio in the pocket of my jumpsuit. I gave him two date-pit necklaces and a bracelet carved by the prison artists. "These are for your sisters and your mother."

He hugged me and then walked away into the night.

My fingers trembled as I plugged in the earpiece and turned the dial. The static crackled, then I heard warbled sounds, and then I picked up a Saudi news broadcast. I plugged my other ear with my finger and heard the announcer say something about the United Nations Security Council and a ceasefire resolution. Our war had gone global! I squeezed my eyes shut to concentrate on the words. Saddam was willing to sign it, the reporter said, but Khomeini was balking. Tears of relief flowed down my cheeks. It wasn't just the prisoners of war who were praying for the war to end; the international community was with us—more than a hundred countries demanding peace! It was only a matter of time before Khomeini gave in. I felt a flutter—so small, barely a wisp of hope—tingle inside me.

My son must have been six years old now. I hoped he had her olive skin and inquisitiveness, and my athleticism and business smarts. But most of all, I hoped he would accept me back, his sudden dad.

I clicked the radio off to save the battery. I couldn't go back to sleep. Instead I scooted under my desk and started scraping the wood from underneath with my spoon. The shavings fell in sweet-scented curls in my lap as I patiently carved a cubbyhole to stash the radio. Then I removed a screw from one of the legs and positioned it to keep the radio from falling out of the slot.

The next morning, I walked the yard alone, slowly dribbling the wood shavings out of my pocket. I didn't tell anyone about my radio. When I had good, solid confirmation that the war was indeed over, I'd share the news, but until then it was too much of a secret to ask the others to keep. Something as priceless as a radio was a lightning rod in prison, something men would fight to have access to, and then it would only be a matter of time before the guards caught wind of it and punished all of us for my indiscretion.

It was July 1988, and while the loudspeakers at our prison kept telling us the war was still on and the Iranians were close to removing Saddam from power, I was hearing quite a different story. On an Iraqi radio station, during a speech marking the twentieth anniversary of the Baath Party, Saddam declared that Iraq stood on the edge of victory, after inflicting "material and moral damage" on Iran. Which didn't make a whole lot of sense because in the next breath he announced Iraq would give up all the land it had captured inside of Iran. He pledged to cooperate in peace talks, as long as he got what he wanted, mainly both countries to withdraw to their original borders, respect each other's political systems, Iran to guarantee Iraq's use of the Shatt al-Arab to export its oil, and an immediate prisoner exchange.

My heart leaped at the last item on the list. Saddam ended his address to the Iraqi people in typical fashion, with a threat: "If Iran refuses to start direct negotiations with us, it will be held once again responsible for spilling more blood and rejecting the honorable peace path."

A response came three days later from the old buzzard Khomeini, now eighty-eight, reluctantly accepting the ceasefire, after his advisers convinced him that it was his only remaining option.

He issued a statement with characteristic melodrama: "Happy are those who have departed through martyrdom. Happy are those who have lost their lives in this convoy of light. Unhappy am I that I still survive and have drunk the poisoned chalice."

And then, on August 20, I heard the news I'd been waiting for since I left Alyaa with our baby boy in her arms. Khomeini and Saddam had signed the ceasefire document. There were 350 UN peacekeepers spread out along the 740-mile border between the two belligerents.

This goddamn war was over.

I fell to the floor and held my hand over my heart, feeling it thrum with joy. I couldn't cry out or jump up and down; I had to find a silent way to explode. I put the earpiece back in, and to hell with the batteries, it was time for some music. I moved the dial until I heard the strains of an Egyptian harp, a Kaman violin, and an oud. Then the Arab diva Umm Kulthum's unmistakable voice danced between the strings. She was with me in my cell, with her diamond-studded cat-eye sunglasses, beehive hairdo, and flowing floor-length dress, calling to me. The lyrics floated into my ears, lifted me up over the concertina wire, and like a slingshot rocketed me back to my homeland:

My heart, don't ask where the love has gone,
It was a citadel of my imagination that has collapsed.

I mouthed the words in my mother tongue, imaging myself drowning my sorrows over a drink with Umm Kulthum until the song became fainter and fainter and then petered out. The batteries, after four months, had finally died.

Let's just say story time was especially captivating in the yard that day. When I told the men, we couldn't reveal what we knew, because it was business as usual inside Arak. I don't know if this was because the guards were too stupid and illiterate to know that the war was over, or if they were purposely keeping us in the dark. The command staff surely must have known about ceasefire Resolution 598, but they sure didn't let on. Some of the inmates wanted to riot and break down the walls, but I was able to advocate for calm. How would we explain how we knew? Officially, yes, the war had ended. But we were still captives, and we were not the ones with the weapons. Until the prisoner exchanges happened, we were basically still fighting our own hidden war. So we celebrated with winks and nods and grins as we went about our days. We laughed more and cared less when the guards were rude to us. And then little signs began appearing that told us we were about to be released. The guards started being nicer to us, telling jokes and asking about our families. All of a sudden a third meal appeared, and now we were getting lunch daily. Medical teams arrived to give us physicals and examine our ailments. Our crusty jumpsuits we'd been wearing for the last three years were taken away and replaced with new ones.

The euphoria didn't last. A whole year went by, and our new jumpsuits lost their brightness, same as our expectations. I'd tried asking the guards about the war ending, but they insisted they had not heard anything about it, and there were no orders to exchange us for Iranian prisoners. I still held out hope that they were lying and that it was taking a long time because Arak was at the bottom of the list for prisoner exchanges, and I was one of the few who kept a positive attitude. But even Sharshab had given up.

"Maybe it was wrong what you heard on the radio," he said, taking a seat next to me in the yard.

"It sounded real," I offered.

"Maybe it was true at the moment, but then Saddam or Khomeini changed their mind."

I sighed. All these maybes were giving me a headache. It was entirely believable that either country had gone back on its promises. Both were infamous for saying one thing and then doing another.

"It just doesn't add up, Najah," Sharshab said. "The Falklands War happened the same year ours did. It only lasted a few months, and within three days England and Argentina exchanged *all* their POWs."

"You're making me depressed," I said.

When a second year went by and one of the inmates in the prison for high-ranking officers next door started a rumor that Saddam had invaded Kuwait, I gave up hoping to be released. We were fighting two wars now? Or did this mean he'd moved on to a different war? Nothing made sense anymore, like we were human experiments in some twisted game of psychological warfare. I asked a different guard if he'd heard any news about Khomeini signing a peace accord, and he looked at me with a knot of confusion between his brows and asked me, in all apparent seriousness, if the Shah was no longer in power.

I was in Arak for five more years. I had long since stopped looking for answers when one night the guards shook us awake, told us to gather our things, covered our eyes with blindfolds, and relocated us again, to what I prayed would be a clearinghouse where we would finally be exchanged with Iranian POWs. When I could see again, I was in an outdoor pen enclosed on all four sides by a chain-link fence. There were concrete freeway lane dividers forming another fence around the fence, and behind those, armored tanks. We were in Tehran now, at a military base for the Revolutionary Guards called Heshmatiyeh. A paved walkway separated our pen from an identical one filled with other Iraqi prisoners who were waving their arms and hurling bloodthirsty insults at us. I looked closer and recognized some faces. These were the traitors from my first prison, Torbat-e Jam, the suck-ups who had denounced their country in order to save their own asses. These rats were the reason why we had been singled out and sent to the caves in Sang Bast for extra-special treatment. Every scar on our bodies had one of their names on it.

We responded in kind, telling them exactly where they could stick it, and soon the air above us was boiling with venom. Guards came and tried to placate us, telling us that we were about to have our long-awaited second chance at life, if we would just stay quiet and not cause any trouble. Their plan was to mix all the prisoners together and then send us back to Iraq when all the paperwork was done. I interpreted what he said, and my men blew up. They swore on the souls of their dead grandmothers that they would kill those treasonous Iraqi POWs the minute they had the chance. The turncoats curled their lips at us and spat, and the guards dragged everyone out of the pens, kicking and screaming, and separated the warring factions into large rooms of 200 men each, with four-tiered wooden bunk beds.

The prison command's quick fix to the unrest was to bring in a high-ranking military guy, who swept into the central courtyard with an entourage in a hurried fashion, as if he was irritated by this errand and had more important places to be. All the prisoners had to assemble before him, in our divided camps, with rows of guards with Tasers and batons forming a safety barrier between us. There were so many more prisoners than I had first realized, more than a thousand. The speaker scowled as he gave the assemblage the once-over.

"Iran won the war," he boomed. "All you Baathis; your lives are effectively over. You cannot go back to Iraq, and Iran doesn't want you. So that means you're mine, and you will do what I tell you. And I will tell you this: the first one who gives me trouble will be executed on the spot!"

The prisoners who had just arrived with me from Arak were having none of it. We knew that nobody had won the damn war, which had ended in a stalemate eight years before. We said as much, first raising our hands to speak, and when that didn't work, shouting over him. We demanded the truth, demanded to go home, demanded to know why the Red Cross hadn't saved us yet. And then he had to go and tell us to shut our big mouths.

The first shoe sailed through the air and clunked the speaker on the head. Then a second one hit the mullah standing next to him. The prison guards saw where this was going and started to back away. Someone threw a punch and then a full-fledged riot erupted between the brainwashed POWs and our guys as the speaker and his interpreter ran for safety. Guards in the towers fired into the air and prison commanders squawked threats over the loudspeakers in both Arabic and Farsi that they would open fire if we didn't cease and desist, but there was no stopping a thousand men from avenging one seriously long vendetta. I tried to reason with my friends, pleading with them that there were frail and elderly among us who could get harmed. But my shouts were useless, as I watched them knocking out the traitors with the very Bruce Lee fighting moves I'd taught them. The brawling lasted for five hours as so many years of pent-up rage roared out of everybody, and it probably would have continued until every last one of us was unconscious or dead had it not been for the Iranian TV news cameras that came bursting through the prison doors. As soon as the fight became a potential public-relations liability, Iranian police in riot gear showed up and started shooting from behind shields, aiming haphazardly into the crowd. Twenty-two men were killed.

As a punishment, we were locked in our rooms for three days without food or water. When the door finally swung open, a bigwig Persian military guy with three stars on his collar came in and greeted us with a warm smile.

"Salaam Alaikum."

When we didn't answer, he asked who could speak Farsi, and I approached cautiously and shook his hand.

"Son, we are very sorry about what happened. That speaker was insulting, and he was wrong and is being court-martialed now. You are Iraqis, you will stay Iraqis, and you will be returned to Iraq. We don't need new citizens." He chuckled. "We have enough people in our own country."

He said we would not be punished, but I smelled bullshit. The melee had made the news, and the United Nations had ordered envoys to come to the prison to check on our living conditions. This guy wanted to butter us up so that when the inspectors came, we would say nice things about our captors. So this is what I translated to my men, while the dumb guy stood there smiling. And then I used the opportunity to pump him for information. I did a little buttering up of my own.

"We are neighbors, we are two brother nations of Muslims. We have no feud with Iran; it's America and Israel that started the feud between us," I said.

The bigwig practically kissed me. I saw my opening and asked him when we would be exchanged back to Iraq.

"Don't worry, son. The UN is negotiating bilaterally. There should be an answer soon."

Eight months later, Iranian officials showed up and read some prisoners' names off a list. I peeked at the paper and saw that it said "International Committee of the Red Cross" on the top. During the war, the Red Cross had tried to document all the POWs, but they were denied access to many of the prisons in Iran. I'd never seen a Red Cross worker in any of the prisons I'd been in. The prisoners whose names were called today were the lucky ones who had been documented elsewhere, and now, because they existed on paper, they were being freed. Which begged the morbid question, what about the rest of us, who technically didn't exist? When the chosen ones got on the bus the next morning, were the rest of us going to be taken out back and "disappeared"? Nobody said this out loud, of course, but it's what we all were thinking when we shuffled back to our cells that night.

The world had forgotten us.

The men who didn't make the cut got busy writing notes to be delivered by the eighty men who were leaving. They carefully unwrapped paper from cigarette butts and, using syringes they'd stolen from the clinic and filled with ink made out of cigarette ash and soapy water, wrote notes to their families in miniscule script.

The next morning, the soon-to-be-free were lined up on one side of the yard, waiting for the bus. I joined the throng trying to thrust notes at them, but instead I looked each one in the eye and asked them straight from my heart, "Please, if you go to Basra, find my family. Tell them I'm alive."

FIFTEEN

GRAVESTONE

Sometimes when you pray for something, a different prayer gets answered instead. I had begged Mira Sahib to kill me, but I should've known he'd never get rid of his court jester. Prison camp in Ramadi was severely lacking in entertainment—there was no television, no music, and no women—so how else were the guards going to amuse themselves if they didn't have me to toss around?

I wished for the sweet release of death, but instead I got something better. I got resolve. It came after a dream. In it, some force was coaxing me to walk across a canyon on a tightrope. Fall, and I would be consumed by the flames below. Succeed, and freedom waited on the other side. I was terrified, because people ahead of me were falling and the rope was swaying perilously, but I lowered my center of gravity and duck-walked across. When I awoke, I felt like I had a magic force field.

Prison was nothing more than a silent battle of wills, and all my life I'd won that particular contest. All I had to do was outlast my captors, because this couldn't go on forever. Energy coursed through me as I rose, imagining a steel rod inside me, stretching from the base of my skull through my spine, and anchoring me to the ground. I took a step, then another. And what do you know—I, Zahed Haftlang, the drooling *chai wallah* from Masjed Soleyman, had shaken off his tremor. Just like that.

"I can walk!" I shouted, waking up the cell with syllables as clear as gongs. All my neurons were firing in the right order again. I silently dared the officers to toss me in the sewer again. I'd kick their asses—*with my mind.*

But I never got the chance. Just days later, the guards woke the whole camp up before sunrise. Normally, when you got a wake-up call before the sun, you were a dead man. Executions were always done before dawn, and you were lucky if you got a quick bullet because otherwise it was a beheading or a hanging, and not the nice, quick kind of hanging. They hanged you so that just your toes scraped on the ground and you died after you finally gave up trying to stand on your tiptoes. But surely they couldn't be planning to kill all of us?

We assembled in neat, single-file rows facing the platform in the courtyard, where Mira Sahib was pacing absentmindedly and moving a baton from one armpit to the other. Usually, during the daily count I stood in the back to avoid his gaze, but this time I stood front and center. To my left and right, men were trembling, whispering to Allah for mercy.

Mira Sahib blasted his whistle, and all sound stopped. Then he extended his right arm, palm up, and swept it dramatically in an arc in front of his chest, like he was Rumi himself about to recite a poem. He pronounced each word slowly and deliberately as if his sentences were being recorded for all eternity.

"Your imprisonment has come to an end!" he boomed. "May you be enlightened and aware for the rest of your life, so the steps you take never lead back to Ramadi. As of this moment, you are guests at this camp. In a few days, the Red Cross will release you to your homeland."

There was a split second of absolute silence, as everyone needed a moment to absorb the sentences to make sure they had heard them correctly. Then we became euphoria itself, one ecstatic whirling dervish made up of hundreds of interlocked arms as we jumped together, dancing and crying with joy. The sensation was like a free fall, the same weightlessness I felt jumping off a cliff into the river as a kid, my skin zinging with the anticipation of impact with cool water. I couldn't speak, but I could laugh. And I laughed and laughed and laughed. It was suddenly so funny to me how the universe kept trying to kill me, and I kept wiggling out of it every stinking time. We didn't ask why we were suddenly being let go, but I doubt it was because the Iraqis suddenly had a change of heart. If they had hearts at all, they would have let us go two years ago when the war was over. But I certainly wasn't going to argue. The International Committee of the Red Cross was coming to rescue us, and that's all that mattered. I clapped and sang and hopped with everyone else like I'd just been given a billion dollars. *Okay, assholes, you asked for a belly dance . . . well, here . . . it . . . is!* I shimmy-shaked all over that prison yard, moving to the beat of my own private mantra: two years, four months, seventeen days, eight hours, and twenty-three minutes. Two years, four months, seventeen days, eight hours, and twenty-three minutes. Two years, four months . . .

As if on cue, a white SUV painted with red crosses pulled up in the middle of our celebration, and I turned to see three men and a woman get out. The sight of a female—a non-Muslim female without a hijab, at that—took my breath, and I stared at her even though I knew it was impolite. Her blond hair and brush of pink lipstick were like magnets pulling my eyeballs. Even from far away I could glimpse the whiteness of her teeth and smell the rose petals in her perfume. We stopped dancing so we could follow her every movement while the Red Cross recorded our names, officially moving us from the missing-in-action column to the POW column. Apparently, our captors had fallen down on their international promises to provide the Red Cross with prisoner lists.

The workers gave us each civilian clothes and closed-toe shoes, soap, and shampoo. After I washed and it was my turn for a medical exam, I kept my eyes on my new shoes in the presence of the French female doctor. Those shoes reminded me that I wasn't dreaming, that my beatings had come to an end and I was going to get out of Ramadi, and I had to keep checking that they were still on my feet and this wasn't a dream. Also, I was self-conscious in front of a woman, and was afraid that if I looked up, I'd stare again. With Agha-ye Ahmadi translating, the doctor said my tendons were destroyed by hanging from my thumbs and I would need surgery. She must have thought I was an idiot, staring at the ground without a response.

"Comprenez-vous, monsieur?"

Her voice was happy and innocent, like the peep of a songbird, and when she called me "mister," my eyes filled with tears. I had forgotten what respect felt like, or that I was deserving of it. I had a flashback to my hospital room in Masjed Soleyman and Mina asking me what temperature of water I preferred. The doctor rested a manicured hand on my shoulder until my sobs subsided and I could explain that I missed my fiancée and why we would never be able to marry. The doctor took me in her embrace and gently rubbed my back while making a shushing noise, just like a mother would. I let her, desperate to feel kindness again, to feel safety. She said something that sounded like flute notes again.

"Compassion is what makes the human face lovely, and love makes the mind beautiful," Agha-ye translated. "Even now, compassion and love have roots in your soul because in spite of everything, you remember Mina."

I lifted my head from her shoulder and focused on the gold cross she wore around her neck.

"Merci," I said.

I took her words with me that night when I slept outside in the dirt, looking up at the stars. She might have been right, that somewhere, buried deep inside me, was a dormant seed of good that one day might grow again. I let myself ponder this, with my belly full of a Red Cross buffet of chicken and tomatoes and *sangak* flatbread. I stretched my gaze all the way to the bright pinpricks of light in the sky. Now that we were technically free men, there was no way I was ever going to sleep in a cell again and miss looking at an expanse as great as this.

It took four days for the Red Cross to process all our paperwork, and when it was finally time to board the twenty-two freedom buses that would take us to Iran, the Iraqi officers stood off to one side to watch us depart. Mira Sahib was there, and as I neared him, I lifted my gaze and looked for the first time directly into his eyes. Never before had I, or anyone, dared such a disrespectful thing. I needed him to see that I was a person, not property, so I raised my chin until we were facing each other man to man. His irises were golden, like the light of sunset falling on sand, and intensely arresting, like every part of his physique. It's almost as if he hypnotized me with them, because I stood in place and searched those eyes as if they could tell me why their owner could have such a twisted mind inside such a lovely body. I couldn't help but think what a waste of a perfect specimen he was. *What happened to you?* I wondered. *Did you have a father who beat you, too?*

Mira Sahib did not appreciate this. He wasn't about to let me go without reminding me of the pecking order. He leaned in so that we were nose to nose and growled, "That so, motherfucker?"

I jumped back, as if he had spit on me. All these months I had resisted the urge to fight back, but now there was no holding back. *Oh, no, Mira Sahib, you don't get to insult me anymore.* I unbuttoned my pants, pulled down my underwear, shook side to side, and waggled my penis at him, while pointing at it with both hands just in case he missed the message: "Get a ladder and climb on this!"

I didn't even have time to pull my pants back up. Mira Sahib lunged, and with a hand that could palm a watermelon, he hooked a finger in my nostril and his thumb in my mouth and flung me like a rag doll into a cinder-block wall. I felt my nostril tear and heard a sharp crack as my jaw collided with cement. I spat blood and a few teeth, and my ears rang louder than an army of mosquitoes. But this time, instead of stepping back to watch the beating, the guards formed a safety perimeter around me as Red Cross workers pulled Mira Sahib away and put him in handcuffs. My nose and jaw were broken, and the French doctor insisted I stay in Iraq for surgery, but I refused. I didn't trust an Arab doctor to take proper care of me, I protested, eventually convincing the Red Cross workers that I could survive on painkillers until I got into Iran. After much arguing, I finally got put on the last Red Cross bus in the caravan. I hobbled aboard to a chorus of cheers and applause and shout-outs to the Prophet Muhammad, and collapsed into a plush seat next to my surrogate grandpa, Amu Safar. Air-conditioning cascaded over my skin.

"You are a madman," he said, turning to examine my swollen face.

The drugs were kicking in, so I was able to manage a bloody grin. Amu Safar's eyes crinkled, and then he erupted in a full-blown belly laugh, the first time I'd ever seen him do that. He slapped his shins and shook his head, shaking hard like someone was holding him down and tickling his ribs, and it lasted so long that I worried the old guy's heart might seize. But it was glorious to behold, and it kind of took the sting out of my injuries.

"You're just lucky he didn't rip off your dick."

I giggled alongside him, drooling blood and making a general fool of myself, which only sent us on another laughing fit. What I'd done was totally stupid, yes, but also totally worth it.

As we got closer to the Iranian border, the singing on the bus intensified, and the passengers began shouting at our potbellied Iraqi bus driver to go faster. I think they were starting to piss him off, calling him "carriage driver" and telling him he needed to hurry up, because he peeled off the highway on a side street just outside Fallujah, abandoning the Red Cross bus caravan. We were supposed to take the less inhabited belt road around the city, which was a safer route through enemy territory. Now, we were heading directly into the mouth of the beast. As we looked out the windows, trying to figure out where we were, the Red Cross worker assigned to our bus began walking up the aisle to question the driver. But before she could get there, he inexplicably parked before a crowd of a couple hundred Iraqi men, women, and children gathered on a city street corner, bolted off the bus, and disappeared into the throng.

Suddenly the crowd outside turned into a militia. Bricks and rocks crashed through the windows of the bus, sending glass shards raining down on us as we scrambled to the floor for cover. I heard fists pounding on the sides of the bus and felt it start to rock from side to side on its chassis as the mob closed in, hurling epithets and calling us Majusis— pre-Islam fire worshippers. Once the windows were smashed out, they threw rotten tomatoes and rocks in. A plastic bag with a brown liquid sailed in and landed on Safar's back.

"What the hell?" he said.

I plucked it off and saw that it contained a foul mixture of dung and water. I lobbed it back out the window. By now the Red Cross worker was standing at the front of the bus with her Colt 45 pistol raised in one hand and her walkie-talkie in the other, frantically calling for help. The crowd was throwing blankets now over the broken windows, so they could climb in from the outside, and we took off our shoes and whapped their knuckles to fight them off. Some of the dung bombs burst, ruining our fresh clothes and filling the clean bus with a musty farm stink. Clearly, these Baathis had been waiting for us, and our driver had set us up. They had made their ammunition in advance, and who knows what else they had planned for us once they got inside. I was livid. No way was I going to survive war and prison camp only to be killed by a bunch of backward peasants with homemade weapons.

Mercifully, an Iraqi military jeep roared up with a mounted machine gun in the back, and all the officers had to do was fire a few rounds into the air and the locusts scattered. The whole thing was over in less than ten minutes. But that's all the time it took to turn us from clean-shaven back to stinky, bloody subhumans. An Iraqi admiral boarded the bus and spoke with the Red Cross worker, and he instructed her to have us driven to the nearest military compound so we could shower and wash our clothes. After we cleaned up as best we could, the military gave us a new driver and some medical kits, and we continued on toward Iran, shivering in our wet clothes and fixing our wounds with bandages and tape. This time, nobody harassed the driver.

The Iraqis would have to work harder than that to break our spirit. Each time we passed a road sign showing the decreasing distance to Iran, we let out a huge cheer. Forty kilometers, huzzah! Thirty kilometers, ho! The sun shone brighter and the air smelled sweeter the closer we got, and I'm not just being poetic. Everything really did become more enchanting as we neared the motherland. Finally, we reached the Mundharieh-Khosravi border checkpoint, where buses with Iraqi prisoners were parked, ready to be exchanged bus for bus with us. But before we could touch Iranian soil, we first had to be received by a bunch of political and military officials, and smile like national heroes as they hugged us and passed a Koran over our heads and gave praise to God, Muhammad, and his family. Helicopters flew overhead in ceremonial circles, and the Iraqi military was marching in formations. I don't know whom the show was for, because no one from the public was allowed to see the top-secret prisoner exchanges. I noticed that the Iraqis waiting to be exchanged wore suits and looked well fed and strong; they could have passed for businessmen waiting for a commuter train. We, by comparison, were gaunt and disheveled in ill-fitting donated clothes, with the faint odor of cow dung.

Then finally it was time to step out of the neutral zone to our respective sides. Amu Safar and I walked together, and he broke into a run the moment he spotted an Iranian guard.

"Am I on Iranian soil?" he asked.

The guard pointed. "A few more meters that way."

"Show me exactly," Amu Safar demanded.

The guard took Safar's trembling elbow and guided him a few more paces. There was no line or marker, just sand all around.

"Are we really here?" he asked.

"Yes, Uncle," I said. "This is Iran."

Amu Safar dropped to his knees and collected fistfuls of sand, letting it spill through his fingers as he swayed back and forth, his eyes squeezed tight, his head turned skyward. He keened with a sound halfway between a chant and a wail.

"Hello, Iran; hello, Mother; hello, Cyrus the Great; hello, my everything . . ."

His rapture multiplied all around me, as men kissed the ground and thanked their country for waiting for them. I exhaled for what felt like the first time since I was a small child. Amu Safar was now praying, bent over his knees with his forehead on the sand. I gave him a few minutes to get reacquainted with his country. Then I cleared my throat, overloudly.

"What are you going to do now, Amu Safar?" I asked.

He didn't respond.

"Amu?"

I nudged him with my foot.

I crouched down and shook him, then pushed him to one side and saw the all-too-familiar fixed stare. The old man's heart had thumped its last thump.

"Paramedic!" I screamed.

What happened next was a blur. I remember the red and white of an ambulance, a sheet being draped over my friend, and the sound of whirring helicopter blades as someone helped me board a helicopter. The chopper landed on top of a hospital in Tehran, where I underwent surgery on my tendons, nose, eardrums, and jaw. It took six weeks to recover, during which time I fell into the most exhausted sleep of my life, and then finally a Sepah military officer drove me home to Masjed Soleyman.

My house looked the same except for one of the courtyard walls, which looked like it had been hit by a shell and patched back up. I was about to knock on the door when a middle-aged woman with salt-and-pepper hair opened it.

"Yes?"

Even though it was obviously not Maman, I waited for this stranger to snap back into my mother. When my brain woke up again, I stammered, "Uh. Um. Sorry. I am looking for the Haftlang family."

"They moved away after their son was killed in the war," she said.

I blinked. She blinked. A look of concern crossed over her face and she started to close the door. I reached up and grabbed the door before she closed it all the way.

"But I didn't die."

Her jaw dropped and her hand reached up, reflexively, to cover her mouth.

"Praise God," she said, pulling my face toward her to kiss my cheeks. She took my hands, which were in casts, and led me inside. Everything looked exactly the same, dishes and pots stacked where we'd left them, even the position of the pillows in the sitting room was unchanged, and all of a sudden I was thirteen again, and a lump lodged in my throat, as if the ghost of my father was reaching out of the shadows to squeeze my neck. It was too claustrophobic and I couldn't accept the woman's hospitality because I had to get out. When she returned from the kitchen with a glass of water, I was already at the door. I waved, said "Thank you," and ran out the door and to Mostafa's house, but it was deserted. There was nothing left to do but get back in the military vehicle that was waiting for me.

"My family is gone," I told the driver.

I stayed in the military dorms while officers helped me search for my family. But before they could locate them, they found a clue. My neck prickled as two soldiers walked me toward a special sectioned-off area of the Masjed Soleyman cemetery reserved for war martyrs, where the headstones were larger and cleaner and surrounded by a lush green lawn. They stopped me before a granite slab with a framed photo propped up against it. I leaned in closer and saw that it was my elementary-school photo. Chiseled into the gravestone was a quote from Imam Khomeini, "The martyr is the heart of history." Beneath that, the words MARTYR ZAHED HAFTLANG. Beneath that, my birthdate. And finally, the day I died: July 19, 1988, in Sumar.

I howled at the universe and smashed the photo of me against the stone. My family didn't know what had happened to me, so why did they decide I was dead? Did they wish it were true? They were tired of me and didn't want me back? After all I had suffered, how could my family, my country, so summarily dismiss me?

My outburst drew the attention of two gravediggers who approached and demanded to know what I was doing.

"What the hell do you think you are doing breaking the picture frame of a martyr? Where is your conscience? They served your country, and you are mistreating their grave?"

"I'm still alive!" I shouted.

The two men surveyed the photo and then studied me. I laughed at them like a mad scientist.

"You made a grave for someone who is not dead! Who did you bury?"

The workers dropped the frame and hustled back to the cemetery office. Either they believed the superstition that martyr ghosts came to visit their own graves or they realized they were in deep shit for making such a mistake and they wanted to go destroy the records. I pawed at the earth with my casts, vainly trying to find out who was underground. The Sepah officer who had driven me to the cemetery gently placed his hand on my shoulder and said, "Son, it's time to go."

I stayed in the military dormitory for another three weeks until officers tracked down my family two provinces to the east, in the city of Isfahan. The army contacted my family ahead of time and told them there had been a terrible misunderstanding, and that I was in fact alive and coming home. I traveled to my parents in high style, in a military helicopter that touched down at the military base there. By then the story of me coming back from the dead had trickled through the community, and by the time the chopper wobbled down there was a huge crowd waiting to greet me. I spotted my parents and all nine siblings, but also neighbors and family friends and government officials and a bunch of local imams.

I stepped out, and I must have been a sight, with my bandaged hands and my face still swollen from Mira Sahib's attack. My mother ran to me first but stopped short, suddenly uncertain.

"Zahed?"

"Yes, Maman, it's me."

She tilted her head away from me and looked at me sideways.

"How do I know for sure?" she asked.

"Because I have a scar on my butt from where that dog bit me when I was a kid."

"Let me see," she said.

I turned around and let her pull back the waistband of my pants to inspect. I let her do this in front of everybody, because she was my mother, and mothers have certain rights.

"It's really you!"

We hugged fiercely, relief coursing between us.

"Why did you think I died?"

"They gave us your arm. They said that's all that was left."

I held up my arms.

"Which one? Left or right?"

She laughed, and it was glorious to see that she hadn't buried me out of spite after all. She was truly happy to see me.

"Really, Zahed, when are you going to stop with your antics?" she asked.

My father clutched his heart like he was about to pass out. I walked to him and grabbed him by the elbow to help steady him.

"Baba."

"Son."

He nodded as if to say he would talk with me later, once I was done greeting the huge crowd that had come to celebrate my reincarnation. Over the next weeks I was a celebrity. I received visitors at the family home around the clock, extended family and neighbors and people I didn't even know, all eager to lay eyes on the not-dead martyr. I was some sort of religious miracle, and even the local mullahs had taken a collection in the mosques to help me get back on my feet. Because I didn't have a bank account, Baba put the cash, about ten thousand dollars, in his own savings account for safekeeping.

Meanwhile, Maman, taking note of my sudden popularity, got busy searching for a suitable bride for me, and set her sights on the sister of a man who was engaged to one of my sisters. I had absolutely no interest in getting married, especially to a stranger, but Maman would not be deterred. Since her chosen bride was still in high school, I was able to slow her down somewhat by suggesting we wait until the girl finished her studies.

I had more pressing matters on my mind. Of all the dying wishes I had received as a medic, there was one in particular that was gnawing at me. A dying soldier had asked me to please visit his twin daughters in an orphanage, and in his last breath, told me the address and names of his girls. What struck me was that he didn't ask me to adopt his children, or to find another family for them, as if he knew that would be asking too much. He simply asked if I would visit the girls from time to time, and the pitifulness of his request broke my heart. I decided I would take the money the mullahs gave me and open bank accounts for the sisters. I found Baba outside washing his car, but when I asked him for my money back, he refused.

"I'm protecting you from yourself. You will throw this money away," he said, as if that was the last word on the matter.

"It's not your decision," I said.

Baba kept moving the rag over the hood of the car in tighter and faster circles.

"You have brain damage from the war."

Baba spoke to me with the confidence of one who is conning a thirteen-year-old. He was talking to who he remembered I was, not who I had become. A stillness came over me, as I took all the brutality that I had witnessed since I ran away and distilled it into one command.

"I am only going to say this one more time. You will write me a check for that money. Now."

He turned and faced me. Then he reached for a shovel.

"You do not want to do that," I said.

Baba held the shovel tight to his chest. "You should not come home if all you want to do is argue with me," he said.

"I am not arguing. I am telling."

We stood at an impasse, until he wilted under the heat of my stare. He must have seen how dead my eyes were, and known that I no longer feared him. He put the shovel down and lumbered into the house. I looked over his shoulder as he wrote a check—for a couple thousand less than I had given him. As if I wouldn't notice. But I was tired of fighting with him, and it was time to cut my losses.

"Keep the rest," I said. "You've had to feed a lot of visitors in the last two weeks."

Baba kept his back to me. His weary spine was curved like an egg.

"I'm leaving," I said.

"Get the hell out."

SIXTEEN

RELEASE

*Dear Alyaa: I'm sorry. I had every intention of keeping my promise
and making you my wife. I had no idea that a few weeks were
going to turn into sixteen-something years. I am an old man now,
forty-six. Our son, sweet Amjad of the powerful legs, is a teenager.
Soon he will be eighteen—please don't let him get conscripted into
the army. I hope that you both have moved out of Iraq so his life
won't end up like mine. Although it breaks my heart to even think
that you have married another, I wouldn't hold it against you if you
did. Because above all, I want you to be happy, and I want you to
be taken care of. Please, please be in a peaceful country, like Iceland.
I dream of you warm by a fire with a cup of tea in your hands and
a golden retriever curled up at your slippers. I see Amjad in a wool
sweater with snowflakes on it, heading out the door to his classes at
a university. Know that I love you both, and that when I am free,
I will come for you. Until then, I will write you this letter, over and
over, in my mind.*

I was in my fifth prison. It was another military holding facility in
Tehran, called Parandak. Because I was such a VIP in the Iranian prison
system, apparently, I now enjoyed more comforts—there was electricity
in our room, and a toilet, and we were given plenty of food. We did

have to go to religion classes, but the teachers refrained from insulting us. The nicest perk was my mattress. I almost couldn't fall asleep at first because that much softness was jarring, like the pleasure overload you get from being tickled just a second too long, but in the two months I'd been sleeping with cushioned support, I must say I'd adjusted to it quite nicely. Really, I didn't have any immediate complaints, just one lingering one—that they'd kept me locked up a full decade beyond the end of the war. If I thought too much about that, I'd go insane. It's the anger and sorrow that will kill you in a place like this. I'd seen men completely lose their marbles, babbling incessantly to an audience of zero, having arguments with people only they could see. Every day I practiced bending my mind away from its propensity to be outraged, instead turning it into a stream flowing around a boulder. Don't think for a minute that I was too weak to stand up for myself. I stayed calm for me. Because one day when I was free, I didn't want to be carrying a bitter old man on piggyback. I was preserving my middle-aged mind so that I could make the most out of the years I would have left. *Dear Professor Lee, I am* being *the water.*

I was meditating on gratitude for my mattress one night when soldiers burst into our room, blowing whistles and demanding all prisoners assemble in the courtyard. I wiped the sleep out of my eyes and felt under my bed for my slippers, wondering why they could possibly need to move us yet again to another prison. One of the lieutenants waved at me to hurry.

"What's up?" I asked.

"Shhh," he said, thrusting some papers in my hand. He led me before the crowd and asked me to read the paper. I looked down and saw a handwritten list of names. No Red Cross letterhead, nothing. Just someone's scribbles. Seemed most likely this was a transfer list to another prison, but there was always the possibility it could be an execution list.

"Tell them that if they hear their names called, they must gather their things and return to the courtyard," the lieutenant said. I translated.

Then I began calling out names. Those who heard their names gasped and put their hands to their hearts in fear. Some protested, saying they were too sick, or too weak, to go anywhere. One man, an amputee on crutches, shouted that they would have to kill him first, because he wasn't going to budge. I read thirty names, about one-quarter of the way through the list, then stopped.

"My name's on here," I said.

"Yes," the lieutenant said, looking away from me as he spoke. "And when you finish reading the list, you, too, gather your things and join the rest."

"But I'm the translator. You need me here."

The lieutenant acted as if he hadn't heard me, but I knew he had. The last time I had been singled out from the prison population, it had been to send me to the squalid caves of Sang Bast. This couldn't be good. I finished calling the names on the list, then returned to my cell and rolled up my sliver of soap, my plastic teacup, and my plate in my two blankets and joined the rows of men sitting cross-legged in the courtyard, their hands on their heads as instructed. The men whispered questions to me under their breath, as if I actually had answers.

"Arshad, what do you think is going to happen to us?"

"I don't know," I said out of the corner of my mouth. We had to sit like that for several hours, as the blood drained out of our arms, until three buses arrived. Again, the blindfolds. They tied our hands in front of us and forced our heads down so we wouldn't be visible from the bus windows. My head banged into the seat in front of me as the Iranian driver, I swear, gunned it over every pothole. Then I heard the Iranian guard riding with us start chatting with the driver, and I lifted my head to eavesdrop. After the usual pleasantries about families and careers, the driver asked the soldier what would become of the prisoners once he reached the border.

"I think they are going to send them to their families."

"You might want to lower your voice," the driver said. "One of them knows Farsi."

Did I just hear what I think I heard? My mouth suddenly went dry and my brain felt like it was tossing inside a washing machine. I strained to hear more, but the Iranians were whispering to each other now. My heart thumped like I was running uphill, and I gasped for air, suddenly realizing I had been holding my breath for the last thirty seconds. I envisioned Alyaa, my mother, and all my siblings, like it was just yesterday. I was panting now, and I couldn't stop. I nudged the prisoner next to me.

"I heard something," I said.

We bent down lower in our seats, so our foreheads were resting on our knees.

"The guard said we are going home to our families."

I heard my neighbor inhale sharply, and felt his body start to tremble.

"I hope this isn't your idea of a joke," he said. "You heard this? In Farsi?"

"Why do you think I'm hyperventilating?"

The men seated behind us overheard our conversation and quickly passed it on. I heard a sound, like the muffled hoot of an owl, growing louder as the message crackled like static electricity throughout the bus. I immediately regretted telling my neighbor. These poor men would not be able to handle it if I had heard wrong. The guard had said "I think." He didn't sound totally certain.

"Hey! Quiet down!" the Iranian guard shouted from the front of the bus. We stopped chattering but kept bouncing in our seats as we felt the bus turn off the highway into a honking city with stop signs and roundabouts. When our ten-hour ride came to an end, the guards took us off the bus, one by one, and removed our blindfolds. The sunlight was blinding at first, but when the black spots finally disappeared from my vision, I saw that we were standing at the back entrance to an enormous white mosque. They led us inside, where shafts of light beamed on a banquet table spilling over with tangerines, pomegranates, dried apricots, and dates, plus a huge bowl of yogurt and a shiny tea samovar. The Persian carpets felt like velvet underfoot as we padded over to the table to feast. In between hungry bites, the men pelted me with questions, and I had no answers, just that scrap of maybe-information I had overheard.

I tried approaching several soldiers inside the mosque, but each one put up his palm, telling me to come no closer.

I stepped outside, under escort, to smoke a cigarette. My babysitter seemed friendlier, so I tried again.

"What city are we in?"

"Ahvaz."

I knew that name! Ahvaz was the first Iranian city I'd been stationed in, right before being sent to fight in Khorramshahr. Ahvaz was near the border! I tried to bring the cigarette to my lips again, but my hands were shaking too much.

"Is this the border?"

"Yes."

I faced the soldier, imploring him with my eyes.

"Why did they bring us here?" I asked.

The cigarette had fallen from my fingers, and he snuffed it out with his boot.

"I don't know; I'm just a soldier," he replied.

Four more soldiers approached and ordered me to go back inside the mosque with the others. We gathered in rows before a decorated military man, a general or a colonel of some kind, who called me to his side to interpret: "We apologize for keeping you here for such a long time. Iran and Iraq have signed an accord, and the war is over. We are both Muslim countries, committed to peace. We are going to take you back to your families. We ask only one thing of you—when you are home, tell Saddam Hussein to free our prisoners of war. If he does that, we will release more of your people."

I only got through the first part of his message, because by the time I told the men they were going home, their shouts completely drowned out the guy's request that we press for the release of Iranian POWs. I embraced the men I'd been living with for seventeen years as if I hadn't seen them for that long. I alternated between weeping and laughing— weeping at the thought of walking away from all my brothers whom I'd shared every moment with for so long, and the thought of seeing my family again. Our complexions glowed and our faces ached from grinning. It was November 1998, a decade after the war had ended, and by some twist of fate that I will never know, I was going home.

Inside a Red Cross tent set up outside the mosque, we had a choice to file a refugee claim to stay in Iran or get on a bus for Iraq, and let's just say the buses filled up fast. As we boarded, the Iranians tried to hand each one of us a Koran as a goodwill gesture, but I just had to laugh. Arabs wrote the Koran, and now they wanted to give us a copy of it? We dismissed the offering and chanted for our country, right there on Persian soil.

> We are victorious, victorious!
> God's banner is with us.
> Who dares enter our lands?
> Who dares touch our soil?
> We are the ones whose arms can never be twisted.
> Paradise! Paradise is our nation!

This time, I looked out the bus windows. And I saw green again, the color of things that are alive. After so many years in gray and beige, green was a revelation. My eyes drank in the mountains and the palm fronds. We pointed out birds and dogs and cats, clamoring to see another creature as if we were touring a zoo. Unfortunately, we did not see any pretty ladies. As we approached the arched gate at the border, I saw a line of Iraqi guards and a huge crowd of civilians waiting behind them. Because our bus bore Iranian flags, we could not cross the border into Iraq and had to stop just on the Iranian side of the big gate. As we stepped out, trumpets in the Iraqi military band started bleating and I walked through the archway and received handshakes and hugs from some important military officials, one of whom put a bag of money in my hand. A heavy one.

Our names had not been released to our families, so the crowd that awaited us behind a waist-high police barrier was made up of regulars who showed up every time a prisoner release was announced, hoping their relatives would be freed. There was so much confusion as people shouted out names and prisoners hollered back, while other prisoners kissed the ground and splashed sand on their faces. Ecstatic screams of reunion mixed with the blaring of the band, and I stood off to the side and tried to get my bearings, slowly making my way toward the throng, when I heard a woman's voice cut through the noise, clear as if she had turned to me in the kitchen of Bruce Lee Restaurant and said "The eggplant girl is here." My sister Samera. I searched faces and spotted her, tugging on an officer's sleeve and talking intently to him. The officer turned and put both hands to his mouth and shouted over the cacophony: "Who among you is Najah Mohammad Hossein Aboud?"

"Me!"

Samera slid her eyes over my broken teeth, my sunken cheeks, and my beard, and shook her head as if to say, "No, you have the wrong guy." The brother she knew had a healthy ripeness to his body, but now I stood before her like a dehydrated and gnarled tree trunk.

"Samera," I said.

She jumped, as if I had pinched her.

"Najah? Is this what you look like now?"

Tears flowed down my cheeks as I took hold of the barrier with both hands and hopped over it and into her arms. She kissed my forehead and my cheeks and my nose, and I let myself collapse into her. It was a pink dream come to life, but I feared it would slip away and any moment I would wake up back in my prison cell. Then I felt someone tugging on my pants and saw a boy of about ten smiling at me.

"Uncle!" he said, reaching his hands out for a hug.

It would have been rude to deny him, so I obliged. Then like little chirping birds, I heard the words "Uncle, Uncle!" peeping all around me, as a chorus of little ones competed to hug me next. I looked up at my sister, who had been just a student in school the last time I saw her.

"Are they all yours?"

"I have seven!"

Each of their embraces was a little injection of painkiller. I promised myself I would do everything I could to safeguard their innocence.
Samera and her husband took me home to their house in Baghdad, and
we drove through a war-scarred country that I didn't recognize. Every
street had vacant, bombed-out buildings that had never been repaired.
My restaurant was now a weedy lot. Gas stations were closed, and when
I asked why there were so many empty shelves in the grocery stores, all
I got was a shrug and a vague answer about economic sanctions. I saw
beggars stooping over to pick up cigarette butts and shuddered at how
undignified poverty had made my people. Even the bag of money by my
side was a joke—the dinar was so devalued that what I thought was a
fortune turned out to be about fifty bucks.

Over the next few days, my life fast-forwarded through births and
funerals as I raced to catch up with all that had happened in my absence.
My family had assumed, after hearing nothing for so long, that I had
died in the war, and the shelling had gotten so bad in Basra that they had
abandoned the family home and scattered. My father, who had never hid
his opinion that Saddam was to blame for the war, fled to Jordan, where
he could say such things without fear of execution. My mother had died
of a heart attack, and whether that was because of the stress of war, we'll
never know. My older brother, Jasem, had emigrated to Canada, along
with my sister Fatemah and my brother Ali. Samera and Samir were still
in Baghdad, and in Basra just my sister Karima, the only one who knew
I had a fiancée and son. And she was dying.

A cousin gave me a ride to Basra, and it was just in time. Cancer had
eroded Karima's spine and she had withered to just a wisp of what she
once was, and I felt her bones through her bathrobe as she struggled to
rise from bed to hug me. Talking exhausted her, so I mostly stayed by her
side and held her hand, sadness swallowing me slowly, like a snake devouring a mouse. I selfishly wished I had been kept a few more months
in prison so I wouldn't have had to see her die like this. Whenever she
opened her eyes and smiled at me, I told myself I was bringing her comfort, but I could tell that having me there was also taxing her stamina.

After three days, I kissed her good-bye for what I already knew was the last time and left her in the care of her nurses. On the way back to Baghdad, I asked my cousin to drive past Alyaa's home, but I couldn't find it. The buildings were so damaged that nothing was recognizable anymore. We tried a few other streets in case I was on the wrong one and finally gave up. I felt the last string holding my heart together snap.

I moved into my brother Samir's one-bedroom house with his wife and three children, but without a job, I was constantly in the way. Commerce had ground to a halt in Baghdad, so I did what I've always done: I hustled. I took a shallow wooden box, attached some straps to it, and peddled cigarettes and candies and bags of chips on the street just to survive. At night, I sometimes slept outside rather than be a burden on my younger brother and his family. My life had become quite ironic. When I was in prison, all I had wanted was to get out, blissfully ignorant of what was waiting for me beyond the walls. Now that I was free, I actually longed to be cut off from the outside world, to have the certainty of regular meals and an assigned place to sleep. I was more despondent, and hungrier, than I'd been in the last few years.

Two weeks into my new career as a peddler, the military intelligence office tracked me down and called me in for an interview. Finally, I thought, they were going to compensate the POWs with military benefits. But that was before I knew "interview" was the cover word for "interrogation." I showed up at the appointed time and recognized dozens of fellow prisoners in the lobby. We were called together in a group before an Iraqi military officer, who eyed us warily. He wanted to know if we'd been subjected to Iranian "reeducation" programs while in prison. Basically, he wanted to know if we'd been brainwashed into becoming enemy sympathizers by all those forced religious classes.

"If you all are truly Saddam loyalists, why didn't you commit suicide before letting yourselves get captured?"

We were stunned into silence. When he got no response, he tried the question a different way. "Did you surrender so the enemy could take your tanks?"

He couldn't be serious. After seventeen years, he was accusing me of being a traitor? In Khorramshahr, I saw our own men running back to Basra, sprinting for the Shatt River and diving in. Those were the cowards who gave up, not the people like me who kept fighting and got captured. I boiled inside, but saying anything at this point would only make this guy even more suspicious. My God. We were the prisoners who had been singled out for torture because we stood with Saddam, and now instead of thanking us, Saddam's men were questioning our loyalty? This was a bigger blow to my self-esteem than being a prisoner, more devastating than fighting a war that had gone nowhere. I had given up everything for my country, and now my country wanted nothing to do with me. In Saddam's Iraq, you were either a martyr or a war hero. A POW was an embarrassing thing in between: a national disgrace at best, a spy at worst.

"The government is going through tough economic times," our interrogator said, explaining why we'd be getting no government assistance. "Once the sanctions are lifted, we will review your circumstances."

His words were bullets, and they lodged inside the last remaining granule of dignity I held deep in my chest. I left his office without any hope that I would be able to get back on my feet. I knew my family loved me, but it was humiliating to go from being the family success story, spoiling all the siblings with my restaurant fortune, to barely one step above a beggar, cajoling strangers to buy marked-up treats they couldn't afford from my wooden box. My brothers and sisters were barely scraping by themselves, and I was nothing more than a burden. I shoved thoughts of Alyaa and Amjad to the back of my mind, because I couldn't let her see how low I had sunk. I needed to be able to support my family before I could get my family back. Iraq was a dead end, and I needed to leave if I was going to survive.

The next morning Samir and I went downtown, with fifty precious dollars in my pocket, to bribe government workers to issue me a passport. We took our places in a fantastically long line at nine in the morning when the office opened, and three hours later, it was finally my turn.

The passport officer looked at my photos and my military papers, and I could see a question forming on his brow.

"Where have you been all these years?"

"POW."

He folded my documents and handed them back to me.

"We received orders that returning POWs are not permitted to leave Iraq for one year."

In other words, the regime was so paranoid that returning prisoners might be spies that it was keeping them under tight surveillance. He lifted two fingers in the air, signaling the person in line behind me to step forward.

"How dare you!" I shouted. I knew it wasn't his fault, but he was the only one there to hear my complaint.

He turned his attention back to me with a poison smile. "Sir, it's time for you to get the hell out."

Samir hooked me by the elbow and tugged me out of line. I was a rabid dog yanking on a chain, so angry I could already feel seventeen years of stifled rage connecting with that condescending bastard's chin.

"There's nothing we can do but wait," Samir said as he flagged down a taxi.

I slammed the car door and immediately began chain smoking, shouting to my captive audience.

"Our country destroyed us! Cut off our air supply! All those years in prison, for nothing!"

I paused only to catch my breath and take a drag on my cigarette.

"We stayed loyal to our country, and this is our reward? To be a suspect? We give up our lives only to be trapped like prisoners by our own government?"

The driver pulled to the side of the road, cut the engine, and turned his grizzled face to study me. I could tell right away that he was one of those older men who had had a prestigious job once, before the war. Iraq was full of taxis being driven by former lawyers and professors and scientists.

"Excuse me, may I ask you a question?" he asked.

At first I thought he was going to toss us out, but his expression was genuinely curious. The volcano inside me settled from boil to simmer.

"What happened to you, son? You seem to be exploding."

I told him my life story in three minutes or three hours, the words tumbling out in an unstoppable rush. When I finished, he opened the glove compartment and took out a piece of paper. He drew a cross, then a checkmark on top of it.

"Try again tomorrow. Give this paper to the same officer who denied you."

Samir and I exchanged glances, but I put the note in my pocket as if its message contained the meaning of the universe and shook the driver's hand as I got out.

"Looney bird," I muttered, watching him drive away.

"Hey, you got a better plan?" Samir asked.

He did have a point. Out of curiosity or desperation—take your pick—the next morning we handed the coded message to the same officer. This time, he snapped his heels together and saluted the paper, which I found comical yet also somewhat fascinating. He asked for my photos and for a phone number so he could call me when my passport was ready. I reached in my pocket to hand him the bribe, but he waved it away.

"That won't be necessary," he said. Then he lifted his two fingers again. "Next!"

We walked away, stunned. And sure enough, that afternoon, my brother's phone rang with someone asking for me by name. The voice on the other end of the line said he was calling on behalf of a General somebody—I was so astonished that I didn't catch the name.

"General? I don't know any generals."

The voice ordered me to go to the glitziest hotel downtown, the multistory one where the foreign dignitaries and journalists stayed that was encircled by a blast barrier. It was air-conditioned, for sure, and rumored to have a pool on the roof.

"Why?"

"Room nine. Now."

Then he hung up.

"You're going to need some clothes," Samir said.

We changed into the cleanest shirts he had and took a cab to the hotel, while my mind raced through the plots of American spy movies, where the unsuspecting hero walks right into a setup. I thought, *What if Iraqi intelligence is behind this, and I go in the room and they put a gun with a silencer to my temple and off me? I have no idea who that taxi driver was, what that cross and checkmark meant, and I quite possibly just handed over my own death sentence.* The taxi curved up the circular drive and stopped before a gilded entryway with bellhops flanking the door. My brother was about to go inside with me, but I put a hand on his arm and stopped him. He was innocent; he shouldn't have to die because of anything I was wrapped up in.

"Stay outside, away from the entrance," I said. "If I'm not out in thirty minutes, I want you to run away."

A look of understanding came over him, as if he just realized that this might be a trap. Then he looked at me as if he was memorizing my face. He hugged me tight, and I went inside.

The door to room nine opened a few inches and an army private peered at me through the crack.

"ID?"

I showed him my military ID card and then he slipped me an envelope. Inside was my passport, still warm from the printer. I tried to give him some money, but he looked away and shut the door. And within the hour, before anything could go wrong or be taken back, I was on a bus to Amman, Jordan, to find my father.

He was living in a run-down house with seven young men who let him stay there for free in exchange for housekeeping. As undignified as it was for a university-educated former port official to scrub floors on his hands and knees, it must have been equally as jarring for him to see me looking like an old man of his generation. But as soon as we embraced, I began to believe that I just might get through my own hard times. I promised my father I would get us both back on our feet, and his room-mates helped me find work buying leather jackets from Iraqi importers at the bus depot, which I then resold for a higher price on the streets of Jordan. Dad's roommates generously cleared a spot for me in the house so I could sleep on the floor. Within a week, one of my father's roommates let me use his cell phone to call my sister Fatemah in Canada. She said she would wire me money and then passed the phone to my brother Jasem.

"I'm coming to see you," he said.

I had forgotten what it felt like to have a support system. I didn't know how to ask for help anymore, so they were offering it first, slowly reminding me what a family was for. I handed the phone back and felt something close to hope again.

When Jasem showed up, I ran outside and we hugged and cried in each other's arms for half an hour before we could compose ourselves. He had changed for the better, and was clearly now the handsome one in the family. He agreed.

"Prison has ruined you," he teased.

That day was the first time I'd ever seen my father cry. Jasem took one look at our living situation and invited Dad and me to stay with him in a hotel for a few days of vacation. We had a warm meal in the hotel restaurant that night, and let me tell you, the whiskey went down quite pleasantly. On the fourth and final day of Jasem's visit, he and I stopped at a bar. He took a shot of whiskey and plunked the glass down and winked at me. I mimicked him with a shot of my own, and he nodded in approval. Then he raised his hand and ordered two more shots, then turned to me.

"Do you have courage?"

"Of course! I will kill half the people in Amman if you just say the word!"

"I just want you to be daring. I want you to save a life."

I put the second shot of whiskey back down and focused on what he was trying to tell me. Whatever he was getting at, it wasn't small talk. He put an arm around my shoulders and pulled me closer and lowered his voice.

"This is just between you and me. I'm going to give you my passport and you use it to get to Canada. Once you arrive, don't worry, I'll handle the rest."

"You're drunk," I said, tilting him back toward his own barstool. He tilted right back toward me.

"I'm sober. And this is the real reason I came to see you."

His offer hung in the air between us. Totally illegal. Totally dangerous and, just perhaps, totally brilliant.

"It's a real official passport issued by the Canadian government," he whispered. "Don't be afraid, just evade any questions you are asked at the airport. Once you get to Amsterdam and board a plane for Canada, destroy the passport on the plane. When you land in Canada, tell the border officials you are a refugee."

Jasem asked the bartender for a pen and then wrote refugee in Arabic on a napkin. Then, next to it, he spelled out R-E-F-U-G-E-E. He pronounced the English word slowly and made me repeat it back to him.

"Memorize that word. Say it when you land in Canada."

"But what about you? How will you get home?"

"I'll go to the embassy and say I lost my passport."

"Is that going to work?"

Jasem shrugged. I couldn't believe my ears. I wanted nothing more than a new life in a peaceful country with my brother—nothing, except for marrying Alyaa. It was time to confess that I had a secret family.

"You are at a crossroads," Jasem said. "Either risk your life and go back to Alyaa, or save your life so then you can save them."

If I could get refugee status in Canada, I could eventually sponsor Alyaa and Amjad to join me. I could give them a new, safe life with me. My Iraqi passport wasn't a true solution because I'd need to get a visa, and even then I'd only be allowed to stay in Canada for a few months. I heard myself telling my brother I would do it. Jasem ordered a third drink to celebrate.

"Don't tell Dad," I said.

SEVENTEEN

MARYAM

When you sleep in parks and shelters at night, you meet some interesting entrepreneurs with advanced degrees in street economics. And that's how, after being kicked out of the family home, I found myself working in the field of private collection services. The offer was simple, and right in my wheelhouse: make an unannounced visit to a rich man who had hired workers to tile his floors, and remind him sternly that he forgot to pay for it. Collect the overdue bill, keep a portion of it for my trouble, and deliver the rest to my new boss. And just between you and me, it was a nice change of pace from prison life to be the terrorizer instead of the terrorized.

I smelled barbecue as I approached my mark, and heard music and at least a dozen conversations floating from the courtyard. There was a big party in full swing, probably right on top of that expensive tile. The man who responded to my knock filled the door frame with his barrel chest and had to duck to keep from hitting the overhang as he stepped out to greet me.

"You owe some money for your tile work," I said, thrusting a bill for several thousand dollars into his hand.

He didn't even look at it. He picked something out of his front teeth, then kept his eyes locked on mine as he tore the bill into strips and let them flutter to the ground. He stepped back inside and started to shut the door, and I put my foot in the way to block it.

"Listen. I will be back in fifteen minutes."

He chuckled and shut the door.

I whistled on my way to the gas station, filled a can with five liters of fuel, and returned to the man's house, and this time I didn't use the door. I threw the gas can over the courtyard wall, then climbed over it and hopped down to crash the party. There were thirty or so people gathered around a long table that was covered in a white tablecloth, feasting on a banquet of roasted meats and trays of rice and fruit. I saw some of the women point at me, and as I approached with the gas can in one hand, they called out to their husbands in panicked voices. I unscrewed the gas cap, sprinted like a racehorse toward the table, and poured gasoline down the entire length of it, covering the food and splashing the guests. People screamed and poured their glasses of ice water on their skin to wash off the gas, and the men rose to chase me, but I stopped them in their tracks when I pulled a cigarette lighter out of my pocket and held it in the air.

"Nobody move!"

"What do you want?" somebody said.

"I need my money."

The man of the house lifted his hands in the air and told me to please wait, that he'd be happy to get it for me.

"Two minutes," I said, thoroughly enjoying this. There was no way I was going to burn all these people, but just the fact that they thought I would made me feel invincible, and somewhat of a mastermind. The man returned with cash in a bag. I checked it and it was all there.

"What about interest?" I asked. "This payment is two years late."

The man bolted into the house and returned with another stack of bills. It was so easy; I decided to go for more.

"Now I need my money. You've made me go to a lot of trouble."

"What will it take to get you to leave?"

"Double what you've already given me."

It was ridiculously easy. I was good at extortion. When you have killed as many people as I had, and had as many friends die as I had, you lose all sense of fear. And encountering someone who is not afraid to die to get what he wants can be terrifying. I thanked the wealthy man for his time and grabbed a kebab off the grill as I let myself out—this time through the front door.

With the money I made as a bill collector, I bought a bus ticket to Dehloran. I had my own debt I needed to repay, to one Mr. Yadollah for his prized ram. I bought dresses and shoes for his children, perfume for his wife, and a whole box of gaz nougat chews with pistachios. When I got to the village, it was more like a heap of rubble with a slum rising from it, not a solid structure as far as the eye could see. Yadollah had always said his cave was just a temporary refuge until the war ended, but looking around, he'd be better there than in this mess. I had no idea where to begin to look. Just as I was pondering a strategy, an armed bicyclist in civilian clothes who identified himself as "security" directed me to Yadollah's home. Although "home" is too generous a description. It had only one wall, made of stacked bricks without grout, and it listed like it was about to topple at any second. The other three sides were made from stretched canvas held in place with ropes and stakes, and the front door was a ratty burlap sack. It was a rubble shanty. There was nothing to knock on, so I shouted.

"Hello, Yadollah?"

A leathery hand with swollen knuckles parted the curtain, and Yadollah, hunched over and blinking like a mole, peered out at me.

"Yes?"

"Do you know who I am?"

"Your face is familiar, but I don't see so good anymore."

"I'm the sorry runt who stole your ram."

Yadollah stepped into the light and threw his thin arms around me.

"My dearest son Zahed; I'm so happy that you are still alive!"

He took my hand and brought me inside, and the children, a little taller now, still rushed up to me like bouncing baby goats, jostling for the presents in my arms. They tore through the box of candies, and wax paper fluttered like snow as they devoured the treats. His wife looked just the same, although her hair was more salt than pepper now. The family was still living without electricity or a bathroom. Yadollah showed me proudly that he did have running water in a tap in the backyard, where I also spotted a handful of thin sheep snoozing in the soft mud.

"Where is your flock?"

Yadollah winced, and I regretted asking. Sore subject.

"I made a mistake. I herded them into a minefield and lost many. Now all I have left are what you see here."

"Have you tried asking the government to help you rebuild?"

He shrugged it off, and invited me in for yogurt and bread. I pressed again. I'd heard that there was some funding to help people who had lost their homes in the war.

"The army boys helped us build this," he said, gesturing at his leaning shack.

"No, Yadollah, did you apply for a construction grant? The government might help you."

"I'm old and illiterate." He sighed. "I don't know where to go for those kinds of things."

So I began my next job assignment. I set out to become a royal pain in the ass at the Department of Water and Electricity in the nearby city of Ahvaz, demanding the staff send construction workers to Dehloran. I even called in a favor of a former Basiji who was now working in the government office in charge of rebuilding broken neighborhoods in the war zone. Within five months, the road was paved in front of Yadollah's house and electricity was restored on his block. I used my ill-gotten monies to help rebuild Yadollah's house with proper walls and a real door. It wasn't like I brought the ram back to life, but it was what I could do, and I swear he stood up a little straighter when it was all finished.

"You are a good man," Yadollah said once the work was finished. We were talking late into the night after the rest of the family had fallen asleep. Yadollah liked leaning against his new walls, saying it helped straighten his back.

"No, I'm not," I said.

Slowly, haltingly, I told him that I had become a common criminal, a thug hired by bigger thugs for extortion services. I told him about the time I scared a whole family by pouring gasoline on their dinner table. That I beat people up, and I'd been arrested and thrown in jail more times than I could count, due to my chosen profession. I was nothing more than a brute who would do anything to get by.

Yadollah took my hand in his and didn't say anything for a long time, letting his tea go cold. His hands were gnarled and shaky but still had strength in them.

"The war has taken so much from you, from me, from all of us," he said. "We are all just getting by, but you don't have to hurt people to do it. Don't chase money, Zahed; it will take you over a cliff every time. Poverty is not lack of money; it's lack of friends and lack of happiness."

He stood up, spread his arms wide, and turned in a circle before me. "Look at this beautiful house," he said. "I am your friend and forgave you, and you did this for me. Put good deeds out in the world, Zahed, because good deeds eventually come back to you. Put evil into the world and it will come back to devour you."

Yadollah was right about one thing. His forgiveness made me happier than I'd felt since childhood. Helping him was like a medicine that temporarily took my anger away. I'd never known contentment, but maybe this was what it felt like.

"I'll try to be a good man."

"Promise?"

"I'll do my best."

Yadollah didn't look convinced. He needed proof, so I found myself telling him that I would like to help more people. I mentioned my promise to visit the twin sisters in an orphanage in Isfahan.

"Inshallah, Zahed, inshallah."

I found Laleh and Elaheh in a knot of kids in one corner of a barren recreation room, pushing and hollering over something of great interest on the floor.

"Don't touch it!"

"I want this one!"

"I'm telling; you already had your turn!"

After explaining in a low voice at the front desk that I was a former army medic fulfilling the last wish of a dying soldier, I was allowed to visit the children. My army boots slapped the linoleum, but the children were too absorbed in their argument to notice me. When I got closer I could see they were crowded around a twelve-inch black-and-white television, and bickering over which cartoon to watch. But the sweet smell of the tray of *zoolbia*, saffron rosewater doughnuts, I carried caught their attention.

"Happy New Year!" I said.

The children encircled me and began shoving anew, and it was impossible to line them up neatly because they were so worried there wouldn't be enough for all of them.

"Are you a real soldier?" one of the boys asked. I noticed his teeth were yellow.

I was wearing army fatigues, because that's what I bought when I got out of prison. They were comfortable and familiar, plus they had great pockets for concealing all manner of self-protection implements.

"I used to be, but the war is over and they don't need me anymore. I just wear these because I like them."

"Cool," the kid said, grabbing for a second doughnut.

Laleh and Elaheh looked to be about eleven. They had straight black hair that fell to their mid-backs, and they used plastic barrettes to keep it from falling into their eyes. All the orphans, toddlers up to teenagers, were there because of the war in one way or another. Some had fathers killed in battle or in prison; others lost parents in bombings or in political executions during the Revolution. Some had parents who fled during the regime change but for whatever reason left them behind. I did not tell the girls that their father was killed by a sniper, or that he died with his head in my lap in Shalamcheh, nearly seven years before. Instead, I said I was "Uncle Zahed," and kept them company, as their father had asked. I read stories, colored in coloring books, and played enough games of hide-and-seek to last a lifetime. Eventually the sisters opened up to me and told me they were picked on by the other kids because they were Afghani, so I had a few private words with the bullies. I used what was left of the homecoming money the imams had given me and opened two savings accounts, one for each of the girls. As I was currently un-employed, I had a lot of time to visit the orphans, and I found it so soothing to be surrounded by their innocence that I was soon stopping by almost daily. I realized that I was having a hard time adjusting to ci-vilian life after the war, and going back to childhood gave me a beautiful escape from the hypocrisy and greed of the "real world." When I became a regular at the orphanage, I began noticing little things that needed im-provement. This was a government-funded orphanage, after all, so why weren't there enough blankets or toys? Just like I had done with Yadol-lah, I rattled some cages and donated some of my own money for basic supplies, as well as a couple more televisions so the kids wouldn't have to fight over programs. I searched until I found a dentist who would check and clean the children's teeth for free. Helping these kids helped keep my mind off the fact that I was an orphan, too—an orphan without the blessing of a place to live.

As I was leaving the orphanage one day, I passed two young women on their way in. They were wearing black chadors that covered all but their faces, and one of them turned back to look at me just as I snuck a glance at her. I saw just the flash of her rosy cheeks before she caught me, and I quickly shuffled off to find a secluded doorway or thick bush where I could sleep for the night, floating with the sudden exhilaration of a new goal. The next day I asked around at the orphanage, very casually, and learned that her name was Maryam and she was friends with one of the sixteen-year-old orphan girls. A bell went off in my head like I'd just answered a quiz-show question correctly and won a prize. This meant I was all but assured to bump into this lovely Maryam creature again.

And when I spotted her a second time, I made sure not to ignore fate. I strode over and boldly looked her in the eyes, and then realized I had absolutely no good pickup lines.

"I'm Zahed. I'm twenty-two," I stupidly said.

She looked puzzled, like she thought I might be a little . . . slow. "Is this how you come dressed to an orphanage? Like G.I. Joe?"

I turned to the window and looked at my reflection. Oh my goodness. I only owned one pair of pants, and it showed. They doubled as daywear and pajamas, and after months of indoor and outdoor living, they'd collected a mosaic of dirt and stains that might as well have been a billboard screaming in bright lights: Loser! And my hair hung in greasy strings. My skin was ruddy with windburn, and my five o'clock shadow had its own five o'clock shadow. I'll be the first to admit it: I was not very pretty.

"You are very pretty," I said, again stupidly. Then I hustled out the door to get some air and kick myself. And then I marched straight to a barbershop. From there I went to a clothing store and picked out a fresh pair of military pants and a camouflage shirt. I was down to my last few bills; I would need to get a real job soon.

"Excuse me," I said to the shop owner. "Is this a good outfit to pursue a woman?"

He discreetly put my choices back on the rack. "If I were a woman, I wouldn't take a second look at you."

I was a grown man who had never purchased real clothes. As a boy, my mother gave me outfits to wear. Then Mostafa dressed me. Then the military. I kept wearing fatigues because that's what I knew.

"So what should I wear?"

The owner thought I was joking and started to laugh, but then realized I seriously did not know. He put his arm around my shoulders.

"Haven't you ever lived among regular people?"

"Tell me what to do," I begged.

"Come with me."

He locked up his shop and walked me three doors down to a different clothing store for businessmen. There they put me in a black suit and a blue shirt with buttons, and a tie. I turned to the mirror and couldn't believe how phony I looked, like I was someone in a movie playing someone he only wished he could be. The tie, especially, looked like such a useless bit of decoration. It made me feel like a pansy.

"Forget the tie," I said.

That night I slept at a friend's house and changed into the suit in the morning. I felt like such a clown, but when I saw Maryam's eyes shine at my makeover, I didn't care one whit about my outfit, nor that it bankrupted me to buy it. She was impressed that I had listened to her complaint and followed her advice.

"I had to look twice to make sure it was you," she said.

"Take a good long look, then."

We began making plans to meet on deserted streets after our orphanage visits, so we could talk without being seen. I learned that she was seventeen, came from a home with thick Persian silk rugs, servants, and crystal dinnerware. Her friend at the orphanage was unhappy because she was arranged to marry a man whom she didn't like. Maryam was trying to use her family connections to help her. During our secret walks, Maryam confessed that she felt something for me even before my new look. She thought it was sweet that I always brought something for all the kids, new sheets or crayons, noticing the small ways I tried to improve the place.

"I can see that you are kind. But you should know, people are afraid of you."

I was jolted. How could she know about my not-so-legal freelance work? I certainly hadn't told her.

"Afraid of me?"

"You do bad things."

"Bad things?"

"People say you are like an enforcer or something."

"That's not really true anymore. I mean, it's been a long ..." My voice trailed off.

Maryam eyed me sideways. "And ..."

"And?"

"You smoke too much."

I quickly dropped my cigarette to the ground and snuffed it out. I'd picked up the habit not long after joining the Basij. Was I that gone over this girl that I was willing to give up the one thing that calmed me?

"All gone," I said. "That was the last one. Ever."

She almost smiled, but then thought better of it.

"Good. It's made your teeth yellow. And your hands smell."

The more she insulted me, the more I liked her. I figured Maryam must really have the hots for me if she was going to this much effort to scrub me clean and make me a presentable husband. She was good for me; she could teach me some of the social graces I'd never learned while I was growing up in the army, help me get along better with people. I glanced at the black grime caked under my fingernails and quickly curled my fingers into my palms to hide them from her scrutiny. We continued like this for several months, me flirting and she scolding, until eventually I met her standards as a suitable, sanitary mate, and we agreed to marry. But there were two roadblocks: my mother and her father. Maman still wanted me to marry the schoolgirl she had chosen because the girl's family came from the Bakhtiari tribal line, like ours. Maryam's family was Isfahani, which Maman said wasn't a pure ethnic group because they were a mix of Turks and Afghanis, and a lower social class to boot. Maryam's father was dead set against his daughter marrying an unemployed, hot-tempered former POW. I was not much of an asset to her family's wealth portfolio.

"We'll elope," I said.

"With what money?"

"I'll steal it."

As soon as I'd said it, I wanted to swallow it back down. It was pure habit, a natural reflex to use the quickest route to get from point A to B, and I'd blurted it out with all good intentions, but Maryam didn't see it that way. She recoiled.

"No way," she said, her voice suddenly flat. "No robbery, violence, or aggression. I want someone who is going to earn a living. My future husband is going to work and come back in the evening. Like a *normal* person."

She was right, and I knew it. It's one thing to wash the dirt off the outside. But I had a pretty bad reputation in Isfahan, and therefore it was highly unlikely anyone would give me work. I told her I'd have to move to another city where nobody knew me and save up the money for our wedding.

"What skills do you have?"

"Mechanics. I can fix things."

"Okay, then. What are you waiting for?"

I left my fiancée at the bus station and rode nearly four hundred miles south toward the oil refineries on the Persian Gulf. Pretty quickly, and with the help of my POW card, I was hired to help monitor sulfuric acid production in the Abadan refinery. The massive complex was heavily damaged during the war and only back to half capacity, yet still it was one of the largest oil refineries in the world, located just ten miles from Khorramshahr, where I had saved that Iraqi. I thought of him every time I went to work, wondering what had happened to him. More than likely, he was dead. If he was alive, he probably wouldn't remember me. I didn't even know his name.

Adjusting to the nine-to-five world wasn't easy. I found polite society extremely frustrating because it was so . . . polite. People never said what they really meant, and low-level workers like me were supposed to just take abuse from our bosses, and that sort of powerlessness didn't sit right with me. I was meek in prison, and I was damned if I was going to be like that ever again. I guess you could say my stint as a "street enforcer," as Maryam called it, was my way of taking my power back, of using my freedom to be the oppressor for a change. Now, I was willing to admit that two wrongs didn't make a right, but that didn't mean I had to take shit from anybody. I was no longer taking money to threaten people, but I certainly was going to speak my mind if the situation called for it. Not surprisingly, I rubbed my superiors the wrong way.

For example: My job was to check the levels and temperature of the sulfuric acid in the tanks and adjust the valves or add water to keep things running smoothly. Well, one day a coworker dropped a bottle of sulfuric acid and was horribly burned. I demanded to be transferred to a safer position. They moved me to polymer, where plastic pieces are made. It smelled horrible and I put up with it for several months but then demanded another transfer. This time it took more arguing, more answering questions about why I thought I was special, blah, blah, blah, but eventually I got my way and was transferred to transportation. Now this was a good fit because I was back in a mechanic shop, fixing company trucks and cars. Still smelled something awful, but petroleum at least didn't stink as much as plastics. The foreman was a massive labor-faker, prone to disappearing for long stretches and taking credit for other people's work, but I did my best to ignore him.

Every three weeks or so, I traveled to Isfahan to visit Maryam and show her my growing bank account, and after I'd been at the oil refinery eight months, she consented to marry me. We decided to have the ceremony at one of my sisters' homes, with or without our parents' blessings. I hadn't been able to save enough for a big wedding party, but I told Maryam that the refinery would give me a loan. I went to the company credit union, but the teller was a total asshole. I didn't qualify, apparently, because I hadn't been on the payroll long enough to get a loan. I couldn't be *trusted*.

For nearly a year I'd been working hard every day in toxic-smelling jobs, getting paid peanuts. I could steal more in a day than they paid me every two weeks, yet I was choosing to do this manual labor because it was the honest way to live, and the one time I asked for a favor, a little help, I got told I was not worth the company's trust? He had no idea I could take him out with two fingers to his throat if I wanted to. Instead, I told him what I thought of him; he disagreed, and we were about to settle it with our fists when some company security guards intervened and saw fit to kick me to the curb.

When I told Maryam I'd been fired, I felt more like her child than her lover, and I was so ashamed that I kept my eyes on my shoes as I confessed. But she said exactly the right thing. She said she believed in me. Then she suggested we have our ceremony right away, because so few relatives were going to attend and we wouldn't need to host a big party anyway. In the end, three of my sisters showed up, as well as Maman, even though she frowned through the whole thing. No one from Maryam's family came. But we were happy, and that's all that mattered.

Maryam and I found a one-room apartment for rent in the poor quarter of Isfahan. I looked for work but found that my reputation preceded me. There were openings, as long as your name didn't begin with Zahed and end with Haftlang. It didn't take long, a little more than a month, for my refinery savings to dwindle to rock bottom, so that eventually I broke down in tears in a taxi, realizing I couldn't pay the driver. In our desperation, Maryam and I went to visit the mayor, hoping there would be some sort of benefits I could get as a former POW. But Mr. Big Shot wouldn't see us, so we protested on the steps of his office, and then got a free ride in handcuffs to the local police station.

But just when I thought things couldn't get any worse, fortune intervened. The arresting officer at the police station was a former Basiji I'd served with at the front. He was willing to listen to our story, and he was willing to place a phone call. And we walked out of the station with a new career for me: undercover airplane security guard. I would get paid to fly from Isfahan to Tehran four times a week. Yadollah's words came back to me, that wealth is about friends and not money. My good deed helping to restore Yadollah's house had just boomeranged back with a favor for me when I most needed one.

I was thrilled, until I took my first flight. Sitting in those tiny seats jammed in with all those passengers was claustrophobic, just like being crammed in a prison cell. I got immediately queasy when the attendants locked the plane door with a clank. When the plane took off, I had to bend down and put my head between my knees to keep from passing out, which is not the alert and ready position you want in a security guard. And then nobody told me about turbulence—that a plane can buck just like a boat in a storm. I gave it my best shot, really I did, but one summer of that and I had to quit. My timing was not ideal. I was about to become an unemployed father of triplets.

"You'll find something else," Maryam said.

"I think I've run out of options on land."

"What are you saying?"

Lately, I had been thinking about finding work on one of those huge cargo ships. I thought I would feel safer out at sea, away from cities and noise and all the shadows of my past misdeeds. There was something purifying about the thought of being out in the middle of nowhere, with nothing but water in all directions and no sound. Plus, I liked sunsets. It would be a sacrifice; I'd be away for months at a time. But I was running out of ideas, and this seemed like an income, plus a form of detox for my cigaretteless, anxious self. I needed a job that was away from people, that let me be alone with my thoughts and could help me ease back into society. I pictured myself with my own cabin, with a porthole, working on my poetry and writing love letters to Maryam in between my mechanic duties on the ship. This just might work.

I was given a trial run as an engine technician by the Islamic Republic of Iran Shipping Lines, a private Gulf Coast shipping company contracted by the government to import and export all manner of things such as wheat, copper, fertilizer, and pistachios. The ship revitalized me like a new frontier, and I was hired on full-time. I left the other sailors alone, and they did me the same favor. In between engine work, I had plenty of time to resume my interrupted education. At each port, while the rest of the guys went to the bars or to find women, I went to bookstores. I devoured history and literature and poetry.

I made sure I was back on land when the babies were due. Waiting in the hallway outside the delivery room, the hair on the back of my neck lifted. Every muscle was poised, ready to spring at the first sound of a human cry. When the nurse finally approached, her expression was blank.

"I don't know whether to say sorry or congratulations."

"Has something happened to Maryam?"

"No, that's not it."

Whatever she had to tell me next, I could handle it as long as Maryam was there to help me with it.

"I'm sorry, the two boys are not well. Specialists are working on them in intensive care, but it doesn't look promising."

I blinked and was back in Halabja, staring down at the torn sleeve of my protective suit. Those chemicals; they must have done this to my boys. A second nurse approached and placed a bundle in my hands.

"Your new daughter, sir."

My baby calmly examined her surroundings, then locked eyes with me. I had seen hundreds of human beings take their last glance at the world, yet never had I witnessed the miracle of a person seeing the world for the first time.

I felt her tiny spine through the thin blanket and had the sensation that my fingertips were fusing with her bones. It would take more than dynamite to separate us.

We could already speak without words. And this is what I said to my new universe, my Setayesh: "I will never scare you. I will never do anything to make you want to run away from me."

EIGHTEEN

REFUGEE

I strode into the international airport in Amman a week before Christmas 1999, playing the part of a businessman eager to get home to his family, walking with purpose and just a touch of ho-hum to the ticket counter. The clerk waved my brother Jasem's passport under an ultraviolet light, flipped through it, and handed it back.

"Have a safe trip home," he said in Arabic.

Before I walked through a doorway that led to the security screeners, I turned to get a last glimpse of my brother, who was standing near the baggage claim, pretending to wait for his suitcase. I brought my hand to my heart, and he did the same. *Thank you.*

I tried not to look at the wall clock too many times as I waited for the boarding call. I was leaving Jordan with everything I owned: one change of clothes, a shaving kit, 150 Canadian dollars that Jasem had given me, and one cocktail napkin inscribed with the word "refugee." I'd left my Iraqi passport with my father in Jordan for safekeeping. So many things could go wrong that I'd had to knock back a shot—or two—of whiskey to make myself go through with this. At any moment I could get discovered masquerading as my brother and be deported back to Iraq, where government forces were already primed to think I was some sort of spy. Even if I made it all the way to Vancouver, what if Jasem's idea to report his passport stolen at the Canadian embassy in Jordan didn't work? What if we simply ended up switching places, me taking his life in Canada and him getting trapped in the Middle East?

When I finally buckled my seatbelt and felt the engines engage one after the other beneath my feet with a rumble similar to the inside of a Russian battle tank, I accepted that there was no going back. As we soared off the ground, I felt little pieces of the hopelessness I'd worn like a coat for the last few months begin to crumble away from me, falling off like the beginning of a rock slide.

The plane was aimed toward Amsterdam, where I would wait three hours for a second plane to take me to Vancouver. These were the facts printed on the paper ticket in my pocket, and all I had to do was find a connecting flight named KLM 452. But when I stepped off the plane in Amsterdam, I was swallowed by a human river, as people of every nationality poured through the corridors, speaking rapid-fire in a million languages at once, some of them with earplugs in their ears, having conversations with ghosts. Unaccompanied women were everywhere, stomping confidently in high heels with their hijabless hair flowing behind them. They were so beautiful, wheeling their bags expertly through the crowds, showing off their shoulders and wearing shirts with deep *V*s in the front. I even saw a few ladies with shirts that didn't go all the way to the tops of their pants, and one of them had an earring in her belly button. I stood in the swirl, transfixed by this new planet, trying to figure out where to go. Everywhere there were illuminated signs screaming for my attention in every language except mine. Most of it was English, those squatty neat letters that had absolutely no grace or movement to them. There were so many gates, and just one mistake and I'd get lost and miss the plane. I ducked into a duty-free shop and wandered the aisles, trying to come up with a plan. I pretended to read magazines while I calmed myself down, then gravitated toward the only thing that was comforting and familiar—the cigarette aisle. They didn't have my Baghdad cigarettes, so I chose a box of Kents and handed the cashier one of Jasem's bills, trusting that she gave me the correct change.

I took a long, slow walk, searching for my gate, and eventually located it. But I didn't wait there in one of the chairs, because I didn't want to give anyone time to notice me. I carefully mapped out a circular route and paced for the next two hours, while memorizing how to pronounce "refugee." I didn't stop to talk or eat anything, because I wanted to be invisible. Somewhere along the way, I took the napkin with the word "refugee" printed on it and tossed it in a trash bin. I had it down cold.

When it was time to board, a line formed behind a policeman who was checking passports and tearing tickets. When my turn came, he looked from Jasem's photo to my face, then said in English, "This isn't you."

I understood him and immediately pretended I didn't.

"Thank you," I said.

"This. Is. Not. You."

"What? What?"

The policeman put my ticket aside and began flipping through the passport pages now, studying each stamp. Behind me, someone groaned and dropped their bag to the floor with a frustrated sigh. I was terrified but had to act like nothing was wrong. Thankfully I had perfected this skill in prison, steeling myself from any emotion while being tortured. I looked at my watch, as if I was concerned about missing an appointment.

"Where in Canada do you live?"

Easy one. "Vancouver."

"What street?"

He stumped me, but I could use the growing irritation behind me to my advantage. So I argued.

"Not your business."

The officer grinned. He seemed to be enjoying this.

"You're right; none of my business." He reached in his pocket and pulled out a handful of Canadian coins. He plucked a gold-colored one with a duck on it and held it up.

"What's this one called?"

I smiled.

He waved over two female airport officers to join our little party. The policeman pointed to Jasem's photo. "Is this the same guy?" The women examined it, but I could tell they weren't sure.

"Which newspaper do you read in Canada?" one of the ladies asked. At least I think that's what she said, because I only understood the word "newspaper."

"Oh, come on!" a passenger shouted from the back of the line. It was like a traffic jam now, and people were honking with their mouths.

As she waited for my answer, I started acting insane. I bugged out my eyes and kept looking around, like something was wrong with my brain. If they thought my only problem was that I couldn't speak English, they'd just pull me out of line and find a translator. But if I were mentally disabled, that would add a huge layer of complexity to the situation. I began to hum a little song softly, like I was oblivious to the seriousness of my predicament.

"Plane's gonna leave in three minutes!" another passenger called out.

I started rocking methodically from side to side and muttering. The policeman rolled his eyes, snapped the passport closed, and handed it back to me. He waved me through to the jet bridge, where I kept it up, bumping into the walls and babbling incoherently, until finally a kindly stewardess helped me to my seat, as if I were a lost child. When the plane door closed, I relaxed back into the seat and waited for my pounding heart to resume its normal tempo. Now all I had to do was wait for the man next to me to fall asleep, so I could destroy the passport.

When his snores fell into a rhythm, I pretended to read the airplane safety card. I hid the passport inside it and tried to rip out the pages. I don't know what they make passports out of these days, but some sort of plastic was mixed in the paper, so that sucker wouldn't rip no matter how many ways I tried to tear it. I cursed under my breath. The stewardess appeared to check on me, and I slapped the safety card closed. She smiled sweetly and said something in English that I didn't understand. She was gorgeous, but I really needed her to go away. Now.

"Beer?" I asked, holding up two fingers.

"Bottle or can?"

"Can," I said.

When she returned with two cans, I held out a fistful of Canadian coins so she could pluck the correct amount from my palm. I'm certain she took only the correct amount because no one that beautiful steals. I pulled the tab off the first beer, gulped down half of it, and looked out at the clouds, waiting for inspiration to strike. I would figure out how to dispose of the passport; I just needed a drink first to relax. As I set the can down, I nicked my finger on the edge of the curled pull-tab sitting on the foldout tray. And then I laughed out loud.

With the tab, I sliced out a page of the passport in one swift stroke. I rolled the page and dropped it into the nearly empty can of beer. I added a second page and then crushed the can in my fist. You could almost hear the James Bond music playing in the background as I did this. I drank half of the other beer and concealed two more pages in it. That left sixteen more passport pages to go, plus the cover.

I was going to need more beer.

I ordered two more beers and repeated my steps, hiding the crushed cans in the pocket of the seat in front of me. As you can imagine, it didn't take long before I had to pee. On my way down the aisle, I passed through a small galley and spotted the boxes of beer. After I finished in the bathroom, I swiped one of those boxes and returned undetected to my seat, the proud owner of four free beers. When I was down to just the passport cover, a litter of squished cans at my feet, and a pretty nice buzz, I dug my heel into the number printed on the passport cover until it was unrecognizable. Then I ordered two more beers and got rid of the cover and drank the last beer, all to myself, to celebrate my genius. Then I fell into the most gorgeous sleep.

I dreamed of Alyaa, with streaks of gray in her hair, standing with me on the second-story balcony of our enormous house in the forest, as we watched our posse of children running in and out of the trees. I knew every board and nail of that house, because I'd built it for us, to the exact specifications we wanted. There were ten bedrooms, to fit all the kids, and an enormous farm table where we all gathered for dinner. There was even a special room for watching movies, with a huge screen and theater seats.

I woke to an announcement over the speakers, and a cup of sobering coffee from the same stewardess who was keeping a special watch over me. Out the window, orange afternoon light blazed over the tops of the tallest buildings I had ever seen, and a network of waterways, like snakes, twisted through the land. I collected all the crushed beer cans and put them in the now empty beer box, and as I walked off the plane, I slipped the box into the recycling bin as I passed through the airplane kitchen galley. I stepped off the plane and into a skyway, where four immigration officers were blocking the walkway, standing elbow to elbow with their feet hip-width apart. They let everyone pass by but kept their eyes locked on me. I was ready with my rehearsed word.

"Sir, may we see your pass . . ."

I smiled and, with upturned palms, pleaded my case: "Refugee!"

I was waiting for handcuffs, or at least someone to yank me by the arm or something, but then the strangest thing happened: the officers treated me with respect.

"Welcome to Canada. This way, please."

One held my hand, like we were a couple, and guided me to a nearby room with a couch and a television and a table, upon which was a tray with oranges and cheese and crackers. They asked me to empty my pockets, and I showed them the coins and a crumpled Kleenex and a scrap of paper with my sister's phone number on it. They emptied my small sack and examined my one change of clothes, then they checked the rest of me, patting me down in great detail, until they were convinced I had nothing more with me.

"OK, sir. Wait here. Help yourself to a snack. Coffee?"

As far as interrogations go, this one was starting off on an exceptionally high-class foot. I declined the coffee but held up an unlit cigarette, and one of the female officers lit it for me. I exhaled with a long, steadying breath and decided this wasn't going to be so bad after all. They couldn't feed me and give me cigarettes and call me sir if they intended to torture me, could they?

Over the next two hours as I waited for something to happen, I practiced finding the one good thing again, to calm myself down. It was good that I had made it all the way to Canada. It was good that I had family on my side. It was good that I had food, water, and cigarettes. When an officer finally returned with a phone and an Arabic interpreter on the other end of the line, the first thing they asked me was why I came to Canada. My answer took three hours. I told them about Bruce Lee Restaurant, the war, the child soldier who saved me, and prison. I told them Iraq was in shambles, my family had scattered, and I had no more life there. That I had a sister in Canada who was going to let me live with her. I told the absolute truth, except for the part about how I got on the plane. I said I paid a smuggler ten thousand dollars to get me out of Iraq.

"How, exactly?"

"I paid him. He brought me to the plane in Jordan. I boarded. He left."

"You boarded without a passport?"

"He had connections."

"What language did he speak?"

"He was Lebanese, or maybe Syrian."

The Canadian officials took my picture and my fingerprints, then handed me a refugee claimant form with my photo on it. They tried to give me twenty-five dollars, but I said no thank you; I already had money. They welcomed me again to Canada, wished me luck, and then shook my hand and let me go. I walked in a daze until I found a pay phone at the airport and called my sister Fatemah.

"I was just talking about you with my girlfriends," she said.

"Fatemah, I'm in Vancouver."

"Yeah, right. Seriously, tell me, do you need anything? Can I send you more money?"

"Look at the number I am calling you from."

She paused and then screamed so loudly that I had to hold the receiver away from my ear.

"Is this for real? Where? Where are you?"

"At the airport."

"Grab anyone you see around you and hand them the phone."

I saw a tidy-looking Canadian man in a polo shirt and khaki pants nearby and held out the receiver to him.

"Talk. Talk," I said.

He looked puzzled but curious and decided to take the phone. I heard him say "OK" a few times, and then he returned the phone to the cradle.

"Come," he said.

The man walked with me to a taxi, said something to the driver in English, then closed the door and waved as we pulled away. Canadians, I decided, were astoundingly friendly.

Vancouver was like a tape on fast-forward. As the taxi driver careened through downtown, I saw that every living thing was moving at warp speed. People drove actual race cars in Vancouver, Italian things that were flat like stingrays, in neon colors with howling engines that ricocheted off the mile-high apartment buildings. And the skyscrapers stretched so far up they made permanent shadows on the ground, so it was always dusk on some streets. Bicyclists in tight shiny pants whipped through the commute backup like traveling bullets, swerving just in time to miss pedestrians run-walking in the crosswalks. Was everyone in Vancouver late for something? I noticed immediately that there was some sort of organization behind the speed. Cars took orderly turns moving through intersections, and people crossed the street in marked places. Even the flowers on the medians were evenly spaced apart. Where I came from, it was like a still lake, and people moved in any direction they wanted to, making one big mess of things. Vancouver was a rushing river, and you either got in the right flow or you got knocked over by it. We drove over bridges and overpasses and yet more bridges. I looked down at a huge bay and saw a pod of rowers on skinny toothpick boats, racing one another like it was the Olympics or something. Along the shore, more people were running. Such an urgent place, Vancouver.

So when Fatemah opened her front door and I smelled falafel and samoon bread, I wept with relief. I had told myself I wouldn't get emotional and sloppy, but to see her face with features like mine, to know that I could rest under her wing until I learned to fly through the city solo, was overwhelming. Scent unlocked a sense of family that I'd had to forget to survive.

"It's OK now," she whispered. "You're safe."

I felt safe. But security and survival are two different things. I could stay with my sister, but I didn't want to become anybody's dependent. Could I reinvent myself, could I start over as a new man?

"We have to call Jasem," I said.

Fatemah dialed, and when she connected with my brother, she rather melodramatically let him know that "the package has arrived." And ten days later, Jasem landed in Vancouver with a temporary travel document issued by the Canadian consulate in Jordan. Shortly after that, he made space for me in his small apartment. Fatemah's husband found me work at a recycling plant. With my siblings' help, I figured out how to navigate the public bus two hours each way to get to and from my new job, where I worked from five in the evening until three in the morning, unloading trucks that came in with bottles and plastics and other recyclables, putting the cargo into huge compactors, and crushing it down into raw material.

My coworkers thought I was odd because I always showed up thrilled to be at work. My body ached for movement after so long in prison, and my pride ached to bring home a paycheck again. This was my second chance, and I worked full-throttle, which pleased the manager but made the crew a little ticked off, like I was making them look bad. But I didn't need friends. I needed a second chance.

My chance came a year later, when my refugee hearing finally came. I went to the Immigration and Refugee Board offices next to the big library downtown with my brother and an attorney, and told my story through an interpreter whom I liked immediately because he had a Buddha smile and a soft manner of speaking. This time, I told no lies. I started with the Iran-Iraq War, being saved by that child soldier, and described life in five prisons, the police interrogations when I returned to Iraq, and the truth about whose passport got me to Canada. I showed them my document from the International Committee of the Red Cross, which confirmed that I was a prisoner of war for seventeen years. The tribunal needed only thirty minutes to decide my case, as opposed to the typical three or four weeks. They declared on the spot that they believed me and that I could stay and work in Canada as a "protected person," and later apply for permanent resident status and, eventually, citizenship.

Next I got my driver's license, so I could drive my sister's car to the recycling plant, cutting my commute in half. I got my first cell phone and spent a long time choosing a ringtone, finally settling on the chicken because whenever it squawked it reminded me of my old neighborhood in Basra. I was getting used to strangers smiling at me as they passed me on the street, and remembering that it was polite to smile back and say hello. I still shied away from people because I didn't speak the language, but I was beginning to build on my early English vocabulary lessons in Sang Bast, and after venturing into a few shawarma shops, I had discovered there was a sizeable Arabic community in Vancouver. I was adapting to this cosmopolitan city, learning how to move swiftly, and starting to feel like my own person again. And my own person was getting a little testy that after a year I was still the lowest-paid employee at the plant, despite being constantly praised as the hardest worker. When I asked the boss about it, he made this puffing noise with his lips and turned his palms up and shrugged, like he was in a bind of indescribable proportions.

So that's why, when a load of bottled soda with six months remaining before its expiration date rolled up to the compactor, I got a business idea. I convinced a coworker in security to shut off the closed-circuit monitors for fifteen minutes, and liberated a few boxes of perfectly good, about-to-be-destroyed soda and stashed them in my sister's trunk. The next day, I drove to a few downtown restaurants with Arabic names and found owners who were quite pleased to buy the soft drinks at my reduced rate. Over the next months, I continued to pinch a few boxes of commodities here and there to supplement my income, and then one day I hit the mother lode when we got a huge shipment of mislabeled gin from England. All the employees were warned not to touch the alcohol, but this was too good to pass up, for personal as well as economic reasons. I bought a van. It was a wheezing old jalopy with rust spots and a tendency to pop out of gear now and then, and it was nothing to look at, which was exactly the disguise I was going for. That month, my income doubled.

Not long after, I discovered this wonderful thing called a flea market. I could expand my wares beyond drinks, eliminate the need to deliver my product all over town, and simply put out a table and let the customers come to me. With my own flea market stall, my skimming blossomed into full-scale stealing, and my side job became so lucrative that it surpassed my plant paycheck, requiring me to hire an employee. I even organized my vacations around particularly appealing inventory that came into the plant, so I'd have enough time to unload it all. One day my niece and I were making such a brisk sale in large plastic planters, the kind that you put trees in, that I told her to hold down the fort while I drove a friend's truck back to the recycling plant for a second load. The green and brown pots were from Seattle and were supposed to be ground up at the plant and returned to the customer as raw material, but they were commercial grade and hard to find in retail stores in Vancouver, so that's why they were selling for fifteen dollars a pop.

When I returned to the flea market, I weaved my way through swarms of bargain hunters, and it seemed every third person was carrying one of my garden planters. I inched toward my stall while doing a little giddy math in my head, multiplying the number of pots times fifteen, subtracting what I would pay my niece and spend on gas and our lunch, when in the distance I saw the recycling plant manager in a heated discussion with my niece. I sidestepped behind a taco truck and peeked around the corner. I saw my boss take out a camera and snap pictures of my van with its back doors open and the pots inside, then squat down to get a clear shot of the license plate. I waited until he was gone, then ran to my niece.

"What did he say?"

"Who the hell was that guy? He was totally rude."

"That *guy* was my boss."

"Uh-oh."

"What did he say?"

"I didn't tell him anything."

This conversation was revealing no information. I tried again. "What did he want?"

"He asked where the pots came from."

"And?"

"I said the auction."

"And?"

"Then he called me a liar. Then he took pictures and left."

I plopped down in a folding chair and put my head in my hands. "Shit. Shit, shit, shit, shit, shit."

"Uncle?"

I was going to be fired, that was for sure. That didn't worry me; I've always been able to figure out a way to earn money. But if the boss reported me to the police, I might lose my special status as a protected refugee. I wasn't sure Canada considered thieves all that special and might want to deport me. I had just started to put a little money away, always with Alyaa and Amjad in mind so that I could one day afford to go looking for them, maybe even bring them back to Vancouver with me. And now I'd thrown it all away for a few effing garden pots.

"I gotta go before he sees me," I said. "Sell them for five bucks. Or whatever you can get for them, and keep all the money for yourself. They all have to be gone by tonight."

On the way back to my brother's apartment, my cell phone chicken-squawked and I almost swerved into a parked car as I fumbled to wrest it from my pants pocket and flip it open. Of course, it was the company manager.

"Your vacation is ending early. I want to see you first thing in the morning."

He hung up before I could answer.

All I could think when I showed up at work the next day was that shame felt worse than fear. Never before had I been embarrassed to be me. All through prison I'd refused to submit to "reeducation" by my Iranian captors specifically because I couldn't live with the shame of turning on my country just to save myself some pain. Life was full of shortcuts, but it took the most brave to ignore a devil's bargain. But look at me now, so weak that I had succumbed to quick cash. I was so far behind men my age, men who already had careers and stability, that I justified cheating a little just to catch up. Now, I couldn't even look at my manager, the one who once praised me for being so diligent, so hardworking, so *trustworthy*. He knew bits of my story and felt genuine compassion for me. Why couldn't he have just fired me on the phone?

"Najah."

His words were stripped of feeling, like they were computer-generated.

"Listen, don't lie; we know you stole those pots from the company and sold them at the flea market, so there's no use denying it."

I nodded. Right so far.

"There's only one solution. I will prepare a document showing that you resigned two months ago. I will also file a police report about our missing inventory. But if anyone questions you, police or others, you tell them you resigned two months before the stuff went missing. I will back up your story. Understand?"

I knew a huge favor when I saw one. He obviously felt that what I had done was stupid but not grounds for ruining my future with a criminal record and possible deportation. He slid a piece of paper toward me. My resignation letter, dated two months before.

I thanked him, signed the paper, and walked out the door.

NINETEEN

MAN OVERBOARD

Working as a ship mechanic was the one job that stuck. As I traveled the world over the next five years, I turned the job into my own floating school. I was making up for lost time, studying history and geography textbooks, devouring literature and comparative religion, even reading the Bible, trying to make sense of the Islamic Revolution that had so altered the course of my life. I was discovering that there was a much bigger world than Iran out there, and there were many different interpretations of faith.

Turns out, I had a way with words. I transformed what I was learning into poems, and by poems I don't mean the little pert ones that use only a few lines. I wrote seven-thousand-word epic poems about the nature of man, the question of religion, and the corruption of power. My poetry was secular; I wrote about nature and love and freedom as more powerful forces than God. My work provided an alternative view to the religious education that the crew and I grew up with, but this did not sit well with the ship's command staff, which required we follow Islamic doctrine on the ship and pray several times a day. My bosses also took note that I skipped prayers regularly.

The ship captain had gone to college and was book smart yet life stupid. He knew absolutely nothing about what it was like to fight for his country but acted like he was the biggest patriot aboard. It irked me that he didn't even seem to appreciate how lucky he was to have had that fancy education, whereas people like me had sacrificed our chance to go to school. He didn't take too kindly to me correcting his bold assertions about stuff he was totally ignorant of, like what kind of rifles were popular on the front lines or some such thing. He went on and on about how we should praise the war martyrs, and I gritted my teeth. Those "martyrs" were little boys who had been sacrificed in the minefields for a God that did nothing to save them when their bodies were blown to bits—so many of them that the sand turned pink with their blood.

My way of blowing off steam was to host little poetry readings in the cafeteria. My poems took the guys from the tedium of the empty ocean to imaginary tours of Masjed Soleyman, my words conjuring the chime of goat bells and the smell of flatbread warming on stone inside Bakhtiari tents. A rumor got back to me that the captain said my writing proved that I was a pagan, which amused me.

One day in the summer of 2001, while loading the ship with wheat at a huge grain silo at the Port of Vancouver in Canada, the captain interrupted one of my recitals.

"You're going to have to put that away now," he said, reaching for my poem.

I yanked the paper out of his reach.

"Is there a rule against art on this ship?"

"Don't question me. I am the captain."

"Unfortunately, yes. But I am the captain of the soul of this ship," I said, sweeping my hand toward my audience. "No one on this ship is morally superior to another," I added.

If I could sum up everything I had learned in my self-study to that point, it was that man has a right to free will, but too often he gives it away; his free will has been corrupted throughout history by indiscriminate power. Growing up, I followed what I was taught to believe by my culture and so did not protect my physical or mental freedom, and I paid for it dearly. Now that I was a self-appointed academic freedom fighter, I was not about to back down again to some snot-nosed punk who insisted I pray to his chosen god.

To emphasize my point, I tore a framed photo of Ayatollah Khomeini off the wall and smashed it on the ground, and my poetry fans took this as their cue to vacate the cafeteria/performance space. I felt a rush of adrenaline and took a swing at the captain, landing at least one of my windmilling punches. An officer from the ship's Islamic ideology department intervened, stopping me with a choke hold as I kicked and spewed hateful words, something about the captain's mother being a woman of ill repute. When I had quieted enough that he could get a word in edgewise, the officer holding me down told me to expect a one-way ticket to prison once the ship returned to Iran.

I stayed in my cabin for two days, subsisting on canned food and nuts, and staring out the porthole thinking about how many months it had been since I'd seen my family. Seven. Every time I came home on leave, Setayesh pattered after me everywhere, not even letting me go to the bathroom in private. I don't know how Maryam explained to her where I went or why. But it was getting harder to leave them both each time. I was so tired of waiting for my real life to start. How much sacrifice is enough for one man before life starts getting a little easier? That's all I wanted, just to be with my family. But when I wished for something, why was the answer always no? I refused to return home to my wife and baby girl as a criminal. I was tired of the job, of my homeland, of always butting heads over politics and religion. With the exception of Maryam and Setayesh, I could truly say there was nobody worth a damn in the whole world. I hated everybody, and just about everything. And I refused ever to be locked up again.

So while the ship was still docked in Vancouver, I left during a permitted leave and hid my ID and all the Canadian money I had, $150, in a small bag and stashed it underneath the bottom step of a staircase attached to one of the grain silos. My plan, if you can call it that, was to wait until the next week, when they did the final head count before departure, and then sneak off the ship and make a run for it. My options had whittled down to two: prisoner or fugitive.

Only we pulled away from the dock a day early. I was caught off guard, and the gangplanks had already been removed by the time I realized there had been a change to the schedule. I ran to the bow and watched as we pulled away, away from the silos, and away from my freedom. Stunned, I grabbed the railing to steady myself. Was this God punishing me for my pagan poems? I saw myself walking off the ship in Iran in handcuffs, and Setayesh running up to meet me and raising her pudgy arms to be picked up, and me unable to grant her wish. I would have to call Maryam and tell her what had happened, that I'd failed to heed all her warnings to keep my temper in check and now I wouldn't be coming home. The Iranian government could lock me away for the rest of time if they wanted to. I was queasy with fear and self-loathing.

A shadow crossed over my face and I looked up at the underside of Lions Gate Bridge as we entered the open expanse of English Bay. From my vantage point, I could look down at people sunning on yachts and see sailboats racing one another in the wind. There were kayakers bobbing in their bright boats, and fast things like water motorcycles bouncing over the chop; everyone playing and having fun in this natural water park nestled between islands studded with forests of fir and cedar. I wanted freedom like that. I wanted to have a whole day in front of me with nothing more to worry about than which direction to point a boat and whether I remembered to put on sunscreen. All these adults were out having a day of leisure, oblivious to the doomed man gliding right by them. I begged for some miracle to switch places with these carefree Canadian boaters. And when it didn't come, I swung one leg over the railing. Then the other.

Then I jumped.

A million microscopic icicles stabbed every surface of my skin and I instinctively opened my mouth underwater to scream, then surfaced choking on salty, oily brine as my lungs tried to remember how to exhale. The water in Iran is cold, but I'd never felt a flash-freeze like this. My jeans and running shoes were like heavy chains on my legs, pulling me down as I fought to stay above the whitecaps, floundering against a strong current. I scanned the shoreline and saw a cluster of buildings and tried to swim a clumsy freestyle in their direction, stopping every three or four strokes to tread water and catch my breath. But each time I stopped swimming, the surge carried me back a few more feet, so that I was essentially being carried out to sea. The last of my energy was draining away, and I could feel the water winning. The only way I'd make it before exhaustion and hypothermia set in was if I made a major push to get within shouting distance of the boaters. I put my head down and cranked my arms through the waves and gave it everything I had. When I looked up again, I was maybe fifty feet closer at best.

"Komak!" I screamed into the wind, then realized that nobody knew what that meant. My teeth were chattering uncontrollably.

"Help!" I tried again, waving one arm. "Help me!"

Nobody heard me. My chin sank below the waterline, and I tilted my head back to keep my mouth and nose out of the water. I kept my eyes on the tiny dots of neon color in the distance, willing one of those kayaks to come my way. Then I felt something grab the back of my T-shirt. I sputtered and looked up at a kayaker who had a white triangle of cream on his nose.

"I got you, man!" he said.

I lunged for his arm and nearly flipped him upside down on top of me. He pulled out of my grasp and maneuvered the kayak so the back of his boat was pointed at my head.

"Grab here!" he said, pointing at black ropes that formed X's on the back deck behind his seat. I reached with both arms and clutched the ropes. My head and shoulders were safely above water, and I rested one cheek on the hard plastic of the kayak and went limp.

"Up, up!" he said. He wanted me to hoist myself out of the water so that my belly would be on the back on his kayak. I tried, but I was too exhausted. The man took a loose piece of rope and looped it under my armpits, and then tied the ends to a handle on his kayak, securing me to it with my stomach and legs trailing behind in the water.

"Stay still," he said.

He hauled me that way, like a big game fish tied to the stern, all the way to a small West Vancouver beach next to a marina filled with dozens of small, white one-person sailboats. Once on shore, he helped me walk to a spot in the sun where I could sit down and try to stop shivering.

"You OK?" he asked, handing me a bottle of water from his pack.

"OK," I said, gulping it down. "Thank you."

He said something in English that I didn't understand.

"No English," I said.

He tried again, with fewer words.

"Stay," he said, extending his arm in front of his body and holding his fingers out like the number five. "Telephone."

This nice man was trying so hard to be helpful, but he couldn't go call someone. I wanted to escape, not to be found. I needed to hide until my ship was safely out of Canadian waters, at least five thousand miles away, before I could go to the refugee office. Otherwise, the government could return me to my ship by helicopter, and stick me with the bill.

"No. No."

He looked confused. I searched my brain for the English word for "escape."

"Run away," I said.

"Wait here," he said, jogging off toward his cell phone, probably.

Not an option. As fatigued as I was I got up and I shuffled in my waterlogged jeans along the shoreline for a good thirty minutes until I reached the grain silos and retrieved my ID and small roll of cash. *Now what?* It was late evening, and there were only a handful of workers left at the dock. One of them, a tall Latino man, was standing next to a red-and-white GMC truck that was sputtering exhaust. As I neared, I could see the tread on his tires was wearing unevenly; truck probably had a bad suspension. I approached him because he had a kind face, and maybe I could help him with his truck, and then maybe he could tell me where the hell I was and where I could sleep for the night. The run had warmed me, and my clothes were more or less dry, save for my underwear, when I approached.

"Help me, please?"

He said something fast in English, and I took a step closer. I put my hand to my chest. I chose him because he looked like a regular working guy with dirt under his fingernails, like me. Not like some pansy rules follower who would report me to the police.

"Refugee. Persian. Help. Please."

The man quickly did a 360 scan of the corporate yard to make sure we weren't attracting attention and then placed a call on his cell phone. He talked for a few minutes and then handed the phone to me. It was his Iranian coworker, who asked me to explain who I was and what I wanted. A faucet turned on in my mouth and I poured out Farsi words, then handed the phone back to the truck owner. I saw him nod yes a few times, then he handed the phone back to me.

"Don't worry, this man's name is Jack and he will help you," the voice said. "There is a motel down the street and he will take you there and give you eighty dollars for a room."

I showed Jack that I knew how to say "Thank you" in English. Over and over and over, all the way to the motel. I cried more than I slept that night, soaking my pillow with tears of relief, fear, and exhaustion. I must have dozed eventually, because at noon someone woke me with their urgent banging on the door. I recognized the woman from the front desk, and by the shaking of her head and the tone of her voice, I learned that eighty dollars only bought me one night.

I quickly set about the vital tasks of securing food, shelter, and transportation. I made my way on public transportation to downtown, where I spied an unattended bicycle in an alley. I did a quick scan of the area and hopped on, apologizing silently to its owner that I needed it more than he or she did. I cycled all day, trying to figure out where I was. I pedaled through an enormous park called Stanley Park that had neat lawns and flower gardens with blooms placed in perfect rows, like some sort of botanical theme park. It was so large that it had its own lakes, forests, and a beach that tourists could reach by foot, car, or horse-drawn carriage. I took a mental note to sleep in Stanley Park if I couldn't find anything better.

When I came upon a huge downtown library with a shopping center on the bottom floor, I stashed the bike outside and, as if by divine intervention, walked into the Holy Grail of food. Inside, clustered at tables under an atrium, were people in business suits eating falafel, sushi, burritos, pho, curries, and fried rice from a dozen different international fast-food restaurants. I studied where people paid and where they sat and where they got their drinks and also where they threw away their plates. I noticed that people often left their food unattended. Sometimes they went back into the store to get a drink. Sometimes they left half-eaten sandwiches for the employee wiping down tables to toss. Or for Zahed to eat.

I waited until I spied an abandoned sandwich, then walked over and, fast as a switchblade, reached out and swiped it under my jacket. Then I bolted out the door, onto the bike, and gobbled it down while pedaling as if a dozen police cars were chasing me. I didn't even give myself time to taste what kind of meat was between the bread. Over the next few days, my bicycle became my trusty getaway car. I found produce markets that stacked their fruits and vegetables outside the store, right on the sidewalk, and became expert at whisking an apple or an orange as I flashed by. Sometimes people saw me, but all they could do was shout as I rounded the corner and out of view.

While I had solved the food and transportation problems rather quickly, housing was trickier. I inspected a homeless shelter on the seedier side of town, but when faced with a choice between sleeping alone in a secluded grove in Stanley Park or on a cot in a large common room with one hundred other men in various states of criminality, addiction, and hygiene, I chose to fly solo. That night, I returned to the park and put my bike in the public bike rack, then hid in plain sight, in a cluster of flowering bushes overlooking one of the park's shoreline parking lots, tucked under a thick tree canopy, just steps from the groomed walking path and public washroom. I made a bed out of leaves and listened to the animals scratch around at night until I fell into a deep sleep.

I woke with red bumps all over my skin that itched like hell.

Mosquitoes. With my greasy hair, dirty clothes, and pockmarked skin, I probably looked like an ogre who eats children. I felt my pocket, and the money was still there. At least I hadn't been pickpocketed overnight. I was going to need a job, and my search for work took me to East Hastings Street. Every city has a street like this, dotted with check-cashing places and soup kitchen lines and bartenders serving drinks called corpse revivers to the previous night's customers. But it's also the place where you can get hired off a street corner, no questions asked. Maybe I could find a construction or auto repair job so that I could get a little money to stay more than one night in a motel. The sound of East Hastings Street was like a drunken United Nations conference, so many languages at once, but much of it was slurred or in some type of heated spat. It all blended together like TV static, but when I heard the clear bells of Farsi on one block, I headed straight for the voice and practically knocked over an Iranian man in my excitement to talk to someone who could understand me.

"Hey, man, easy," he said. "What are you looking for?"

I explained that I needed a place to stay and a job. He told me he could get me a job selling drugs, and I declined, but as luck would have it, he said I could stay in his studio for one hundred dollars a month, just down the street. I had barely one hundred left, but thirty days was plenty of time to find a job. I took the short walk with my new friend to a seven-story brick building with a rusting neon sign out front that said Hotel Empress. Sheets were haphazardly tacked over apartment windows in lieu of curtains, and a police car was parked in the alley, with officers inside keeping watch on the back door. I followed the Iranian through a musty bar on the bottom floor, toward the pool tables in back, to a stairwell, and as we made our way to his third-floor apartment, I noted some of the rooms didn't have front doors but a steady flow of visitors who looked like zombies at rush hour. A few ladies in very small dresses made kissing noises at us as we passed.

But my new friend's place had a locking door, a couch, and running water. I gladly gave him one hundred dollars, and the second he was gone, I took the longest shower of my life. I had just gotten dressed when I heard the doorknob jiggle and in walked a man I had never seen before, a man who looked just as stunned to see me. He yelled at me, and I didn't have to speak English to understand—I had invaded his space. I tried in my broken English to explain that I had paid for the room, but I didn't know the words for "rent," "landlord," or "tenant," and this guy didn't seem like a patient person. He jumped on me and we rolled on the floor, hollering in our respective languages and drawing the neighbors. In the melee, I heard someone ask who the hell I was in Farsi. I screamed in Farsi to please translate for me, and the Farsi voice said something in English that made the intruder stop pummeling me. My savior was a Persian neighbor who carefully took me into the hallway and explained that the man I was fighting with was a very dangerous drug dealer who lived in the room.

"How did you get in there?"

My story sounded so stupid, but it was true.

"This man said I could stay there for a month for one hundred dollars."

"What man?"

"I don't know his name. He was about this tall . . ."

He sighed and shook his head. "Look, brother, you can't stay here. I will explain to everybody what happened. But for your safety, you should leave right now."

I walked out into the night, homeless again. And, of course, my bike was gone. The fat clouds opened up, and suddenly I was in a downpour. You know how you sometimes see a person sprawled out on the street, totally given up on life, and you wonder what in the world happened to that guy? Well that guy probably did what he was told all his life, worked hard, had a family, and one day he finally admitted that all he was doing was running in place, and he simply stopped moving his feet. I know that guy. After ten days of sleeping in the park, that guy was about to be me.

When I was down to my last fifty cents, I approached a hot dog vendor who looked Iranian and offered him the coins.

"Hot dog, OK?" My stomach was empty, and I hoped he would take pity.

"Are you Iranian?" he asked in Farsi.

"Yes! I'm sorry, this is all the money I have; I was hoping to pay you back."

He lifted the lid and reached into the depths of his cart where the hot dogs were kept warm, then placed three in my hands, waving away the money.

"On me. Are you new here?"

It was so thrilling to have someone to listen that I told him everything, from Masjed Soleyman to saving the Iraqi soldier to Ramadi camp to jumping ship and living al fresco in Vancouver. He listened for two hours, pausing only to serve a customer, nodding knowingly and occasionally uttering a word of sympathy and understanding. It was like I had been waiting for this man my whole life.

"Are you a refugee, then?" he asked.

"Yes."

"Then why are you homeless? The government can help you, you know."

I had yet to fill out an application for refugee status. It was probably safe now, but I didn't know where to begin. I asked the vendor what I should do. He offered to call someone who could help me and opened his cell phone. He spoke in English, and I worried he might be calling the police, but something made me trust him.

"My friend says you can stay with him and he will help you with your refugee claim."

Ten minutes later, a man drove up to the hot dog stand and waved me into his car. I was frightened, but the alternative was sleeping outside in the rain again. The stranger let me stay in a room in his house for several days, and took me to a government office where I told my story to an immigration officer with the help of an interpreter. The officer already knew my name and a little bit about me, because the ship captain had reported me missing.

"Your captain reported you are an honest man and not a thief in Iran. Is that correct?"

"Correct." The officer didn't have to know about my brief stint in debt recovery services in Iran.

"Did the captain tell you that I was a child soldier? That I was tortured as a prisoner of war?"

The officer shuffled through his papers. "No, there's nothing about that here," he replied.

"How much time do we have?" I asked.

I began with running away from home at thirteen. Three hours later, I finished with the story of the hot dog vendor. At the end of it all, he asked me to sign my name to a promise I would not commit any crimes in Canada, then gave me two hundred dollars and a letter of introduction to a place called Welcome House, where I could stay temporarily with other new immigrants while I looked for work.

I went directly to the address and found a corner building made of beige bricks, with offices below and two floors of apartments above. I pushed open the glass door and walked to the receptionist, who to my delight was also Persian. She read my letter from the immigration office and then took me down a hallway decorated with children's finger paintings, past the cluttered offices of social workers, and up a flight of stairs to the apartments. She opened the second door on the right, and I found myself in a small room that was divided into a kitchen and a living room. There was a faded foldout couch and a big television, and if I turned left, I faced a miniscule bathroom flanked by two bedrooms, each with three cots inside. Only two of the cots were taken, both by Iranians: Akbar of the Ray-Ban sunglasses, a reedy guy with sharp cheekbones who was about my age and had been in a different battalion in Khorramshahr; and roly-poly Hamid with a receding hairline and no military experience and the irritating air of someone who dismisses anyone younger than himself. He was about a decade older than Akbar and me, and a Communist who made no attempt in my first week at Welcome House to disguise his opinion that we were political rubes. I liked Akbar, and we ganged up on Hamid by silently farting in the living room whenever he was watching *Gladiator*, which was like every third day.

But as far as roommates go, I was a dud. Now that my fight-or-flight-response could recede with my indoor sleeping arrangements, I had time to really think about my life. And it was a depressing picture, to put it mildly. Here I was, thirty-three, living with two strangers in a barren sub-sidized apartment, not knowing if I would ever see my wife and daughter again. I missed them so much that I would cry spontaneously through-out the day: in the middle of brushing my teeth, while boiling an egg, while watching my clothes tumble in the dryer, in the middle of a dream. Akbar and Hamid tried to cheer me up, bringing me glasses of water and Kleenex, but I was inconsolable. They tried to get me out of the apartment to get fresh air, but I couldn't find anything more appealing than sleep. I had fallen into depressions before, but this one felt like I was buried in a crucible of hardened lead. I was a man composed of nothing, a profes-sional loser who had let his job, his money, his motherland, his wife, and his daughter slip through his fingers. I wanted to work, but that would require me to learn English, and right then, that seemed like one more mountain in my way, perhaps one that I just didn't have any more strength to climb.

So I wallowed in the valley, letting the days go by without calling Maryam. She did not marry the person I had become, and I couldn't let her find that out. Setayesh would have a jailbird for a dad if I returned to Iran, and it would kill me to watch her admiration for me slowly melt away as she grew up and realized her father couldn't give her everything she deserved. My own self-hatred I could live with; it was their disap-pointment in me that I couldn't bear. So that is why, in early July, I began venturing outside to root around in the Dumpsters until finally I found a good piece of rope. I tied it into a noose and hid it behind the children's climbing structure just outside my apartment door, and thought about it. And after a couple days of consideration, I came to this: It would be a relief to both Maryam and Setayesh if I didn't exist. That was the only thing left that I could give them. I could spare them from getting dragged down with me.

"You sure you don't want to go with us?"

Hamid and Akbar were on their way to the waterfront to see the fire-
works. All week there had been Canada Day celebrations for the country's birthday. I rolled on my cot to face the wall and waved them away.

"Suit yourself," Hamid said.

I listened to them clomp down the stairwell, then I walked to the
narrow crank window in the living room, too small to fit through, and
watched them round the corner out of view. I dragged two chairs from
the dining room table and positioned them side by side under the
living-room light fixture. I stood on one arm of each chair, unscrewed
the fixture from the ceiling, and removed the light, revealing a hole in the
popcorn plaster and exposing a wooden ceiling beam. I looped the rope
over the beam and secured it. I took a deep breath, put my head through
the noose, and kicked the chairs away.

I heard a crack like a walnut shell being crushed, and realized with
horror that the sound came from my neck. As the rope constricted my
throat, currents of pain radiated through my body as if I had just been
shocked with a megavolt. My lizard brain suddenly woke from hiberna-
tion, and I realized that I wanted to live. I kicked and thrashed, trying
to reach one of the chairs with my foot, but they were mockingly out of
reach. The sound of my pulse became louder and louder in my temple,
like a drumbeat counting down to my death. The dirge inside my head
intensified, like my own regret was knocking to get out, then my whole
body began to convulse with the tempo.

Fuck me, I thought.

And then Akbar had his mouth on mine. I opened my eyes, and the
first thing I saw was his crooked nose, bent from being broken so many
times during the war. I was on my back, and he was blowing air into my
lungs. He had come back for his sunglasses, found me swinging, and cut
me down. The middle-aged neighbor from Afghanistan was also in the
room, and when she saw me open my eyes, she slapped me across the
face.

"Stupid! What'd you do that for?"

It was what my own mother would have done, and I instantly loved her for it. Then she dropped to her knees and rocked me in her arms as I wept.

"Don't cry. I lost two sons; I lost my husband, my sister, my brother, my mother. They killed all my family. But life goes on. You still have your wife and daughter. Why would you go and kill yourself?"

If I could have stopped crying and formed words, I would have told her that I realized that now. I'd come to the same thoughts while struggling for oxygen, right before I blacked out.

Hamid huffed into the room, and my roommates each took an elbow and helped me walk to the emergency room at St. Paul's Hospital, about fifteen minutes away. Nurses gave me fluids and kept me overnight for observation, and in the morning a doctor said I could be released on one condition: that I go immediately for psychological counseling at an immigrant help center called VAST—the Vancouver Association for Survivors of Torture.

TWENTY

ANGELS

Getting fired from the recycling plant was the best thing that could have happened. Self-employment has always suited me better, and it didn't take long before I had charmed the flea market overlords into giving me the prime stall next to the entrance, and my customer base grew so quickly that buyers began showing up at four in the morning when I arrived so they could cherry-pick.

My inventory was top-notch, and that was because I had started a moving company with my van, and to my great delight I discovered that often customers hired me to clear out homes and storage lockers after the owners had died. They often didn't want to hassle with the contents and asked me to haul them to the dump, so I had a steady stream of nice antiques. I watched this American television show with my brother called *Antiques Roadshow* to learn about the provenances of paintings and jewelry and furniture, to make sure I never let anything go for less than it was worth. I had found a house to rent near some organic farms outside of downtown Vancouver proper, and I was on my way to finishing the paperwork to become a permanent Canadian resident. My ultimate goal was Canadian citizenship and a passport, and then I would fly back to Basra and search for Alyaa and Amjad. And for the first time since I left her with our baby in her arms, I started to truly believe that we'd be together again. The old pride I felt when I ran Bruce

Lee Restaurant was coming out of the deep freeze now that I had my own business, employees, a roof over my head, and money in my pocket. Every day I woke up tickled pink that I was alive. Behold the return of the Falafel King!

Even Dad was with me again. Jasem and I had convinced him to move from Jordan to Vancouver, where we could take care of him, now that his heart was giving him trouble and he was starting to lose his memory. We assumed he would love Canada as much as we did, but the adjustment was harder on an old man set in his ways. He complained of the noise and the rainy weather and refused to learn English words or eat anything that didn't come from Fatemah's kitchen. My brother and I started worrying that he was becoming depressed, so we arranged for him to get counseling once a week at an immigration services agency. Jasem would translate between Dad and a therapist, and because my brother has poor eyesight, I drove them and waited in the lobby until they were finished.

It was Dad's third or fourth therapy appointment at the Vancouver Association for Survivors of Torture, and I filled a Styrofoam cup with coffee and took my usual seat on the run-down leather sofa in the waiting room. There was a guy sitting in a chair across from the sofa in a short-sleeved shirt with one of those intense stares that gives you the heebie-jeebies.

"Salaam," I said, to be polite, then picked up a magazine to avoid conversation and pretended to read it.

"Salaam," he answered.

The man cleared his throat, and even though I didn't look up, I could feel his eyes on me and sense that he wanted to talk.

"Are you Iranian?"

Oh, buddy, you couldn't be more wrong.

"Yes," I said in Farsi, hoping he would leave me alone. I kept my eyes on the pages and waited for the next stupid question.

"Where in Iran?"

"Tehran."

"Why are you in Canada?"

I pulled out my cell phone and checked my messages. "Work," I said.

Mr. Chatty wouldn't let it go.

"I don't think you're from Tehran. Your accent sounds like you are a villager."

Busted. I laughed it off. "I was just pulling your leg; I'm not Iranian."

"Afghani?"

"Iraqi."

He still didn't believe me. "But you speak good Farsi."

"I spent a lot of time in Iran."

"As a tourist?"

"No. Prisoner of war."

That ought to have shut him up. But instead he leaned forward in his seat and drilled his eyes into mine so that I couldn't look away.

"I was a POW, too."

Now this strange little man had my attention. I leaned in toward him. "How long?"

"Two years, four months, seventeen days, eight hours, and twenty-three minutes."

He was telling the truth. Only a real POW would have an answer like that.

"Did you serve in the military in Iran?" I asked.

"I was in the Basij. I participated in the liberation of Khorramshahr."

I dropped the magazine on the floor. "I was in Khorramshahr. That's where I was injured and taken prisoner."

The man clapped his hands together and squeezed them as if begging for something. He asked me to tell him more.

"I don't remember much. I was in a bunker. The Iranians were killing all of us. Suddenly a child soldier, too young to have a beard, came and saved me. He was like an angel sent from God."

The man jumped to his feet, his voice rising. "What year?"

"1982."

"Was it May?"

"Yes."

"Did you have a Koran in your pocket?"

Now I stood up. "I did. And it had a photo in it."

Then the strange man finished my sentence for me:

"Of a woman holding a baby."

Now the man was looking at my teeth.

"Your teeth, are they missing because someone hit you with their rifle?"

Now we were shrieking.

"You! You were the one who saved me?"

"That was me!"

I heard people running and saw my brother, father, and the entire office staff running toward the lobby, certain a fight was breaking out, but instead they found two sworn enemies wrapped in a fierce hug. I was overcome with a tremendous sense of destiny, like a connection to something larger, more powerful and mysterious than any religion, something from the deep past that will continue forward for eternity.

Some people call this God or fate or Mother Nature or karma or magic or the will of the universe. There are many words for explaining what we cannot explain.

I call it humanity.

My angel and I may not be brothers by blood or nationality, but we are brothers in the human spirit, and that lasts longer than any culture or tradition or history, and will continue to exist long past life itself. The war destroyed so much—entire towns and families and battalions are now gone. But this one act of grace survived.

When we finally pulled apart, I asked him a question I'd been holding onto for nineteen years: "Angel, who are you?"

EPILOGUE

Zahed and Najah were living just ten miles apart when they bumped into each other in Vancouver in the summer of 2001. Since then, they have become as close as real brothers, with blended families and shared histories. Their reunion gave Zahed a reason to live again, and it gave Najah the chance to finally repay Zahed's act of mercy on the battlefield. Both men now have Canadian citizenship.

Zahed opened his own auto shop in Vancouver, Best Man Auto, and was able to bring his wife, Maryam, and his daughter, Setayesh, to live with him in 2004. They had a son, Niayesh, two years later, who has grown to become something of a karate sensation in his community. In 2014 Zahed announced on his stepforpeace.ca website that he is fund-raising for a 3,500-mile peace walk across Canada to New York, where he plans to present the United Nations with signatures collected along the way calling for an end to war and weapons manufacturing. He has had some skin cancers removed from his arm where he was exposed to chemicals in Halabja, and today is very proud of his physical comeback, which he will gladly demonstrate by doing thumb push-ups—a feat more impressive than the great Bruce Lee's push-ups on a finger and a thumb. During the writing of this book in 2016, Zahed and his father, Ali Askar, reconciled over many difficult phone conversations. His father apologized for his abuse, and Zahed began the long process of forgiveness.

Najah lives alone in his home filled with merchandise he plans to fix and sell at his flea market stall. He was outfitted with prosthetic teeth, but they never fit well, so he decided against them, saying, "My face tells my history; I can't run from the mirror." His Best Deal Moving Company is thriving, and he spends his off hours eating home-cooked meals with his relatives and growing roster of nieces and nephews. He was finally able to return to Iraq in 2016, where he confirmed what he had begun to suspect, that he should stop holding out hope for finding his fiancée and son. A cousin in Basra confirmed that Alyaa and Amjad had been killed when their street was shelled during the Iran-Iraq War. Najah traveled with Zahed, who returned to Ramadi prison camp, where he checked to see that his name was still scratched into his former cell wall. Najah has made peace with his fate, and enjoys his new position as an accidental ambassador between Arabs and Persians. He is thankful to all the Iranians and Iraqis in Vancouver who recognize him from the media coverage and, inspired by his story, invite him into their homes and make him feel like a movie star.

ACKNOWLEDGMENTS

MEREDITH MAY

Behind every book is an army of friends, coaches, editors, and idols who deserve as much credit as the author. My first bow of gratitude goes to Zahed and Najah. Thank you for your openness, your honesty, and your patience with my fusillade of questions. It was a gift to study you, and your friendship has made me a better person. I am forever in awe of your resilience and unyielding compassion.

Without interpreters Hossein Talebian, Mehrnaz Ghaffari, and Jasem Aboud, we would never have been able to communicate. I am deeply indebted to your masterful translation of Arabic and Farsi into English and back, and for sharing your firsthand experiences of the Islamic Revolution and the war. Not only are you translators, you are professors of Middle East history, religion, and culture who helped me understand the significance of Najah's and Zahed's words.

To my beloved agent, Heather Karpas at ICM Partners, I am beyond grateful for your unwavering belief in me, your advice, and your laser-sharp manuscript reads. I truly won the writer lottery.

More applause for Regan Arts CEO Judith Regan, who realized this story should be a book, then rallied her superhero team behind it, led by executive editor Alexis Gargagliano. All the credit goes to Alexis for making this look easy. Thanks also to the rest of the Regan Arts team, especially Mia Abrahams, Lynne Ciccaglione, Max Anzilotti, Richard

Ljoenes, Nancy Singer, Tamar McCollom, Zainab Choudhry, and editorial assistant Lara Kleinschmidt who brought the project to Regan Arts. Copy editor Laine Morreau, I owe you big.

Sincerest thanks to my scribe tribe at the *San Francisco Chronicle* for getting my long-form legs trained for this: David Lewis, Meredith White, Ken Conner, Julian Guthrie, Sam Whiting, and Carlos Avila Gonzalez. And high fives all around to the numerous friends who said exactly the right thing at the right time, and who gave me a quiet room to type: Mag Donaldson, Barbara Byrnes, Josh Mohr, Rima Karaman, Sarah Pollock, Shobha Rao, and everyone at the eco-magical Hedgebrook writers' residency on Whidbey Island.

Last, a never-ending hug to my wife, Jenn. Every day you remind me that love always wins in the end.

ZAHED HAFTLANG

This book is a tribute to friendship. I learned on the battlefield that compassion is more powerful than mortars and machine guns. I can kill you with a punch, but I can change you and the world with kindness. It's a message parents must instill in their children, so that we can break the cycle of atrocities and learn from the horrors of the past.

Najah, you are the other half of my heart, and our bond is the most precious thing to me. We saved each other not once but many times over, and you have become a brother to me. Your smile turns a light on inside me, and I thought of you often during my captivity to help me survive.

Thank you to Meredith May for writing this book. Your passion for sharing this story equaled ours, and also you are *so* picky about details that I knew I was collaborating with a like-minded soul. Thank you to Zainab Choudhry and everyone at Regan Arts for pairing us together.

Sincere thanks to Mehrnaz Ghaffari, whose truck broke down near my auto shop one day, and in the years since has become my interpreter, my confidante, and my dear friend. You and your partner, David Dyck, are like family to me.

I began putting my life story to paper more than twenty years ago while working on a merchant ship. Since then, numerous people have helped shape and translate my writing into English, most notably: Ramin Bahrami, Marjan Kh, Babak Yusafei, Mehran Sharifpour, and Robert Matas.

A forever thank-you to my beautiful wife, Maryam, who saw the good in me before I could see it myself. To our children, Setayesh and

Niayesh, I hope this book will help you to understand me and guide you to become good parents one day.

My gratitude, also, to my family, and in particular my late grandparents and my parents. Only now do I understand that you also lost so much during the Iran-Iraq War. Baba and Maman, I wish we could have communicated better when I was a child, but I am thankful that at long last we are talking about the past and starting to heal.

NAJAH ABOUD

Some force beyond human comprehension drove Zahed and me to be in the same place at the same time during the war. It is the greatest and most humbling mystery of my life. Zahed, I thank you in my heart every day for removing your finger from the trigger. You may not be my brother by blood, but you are my brother in humanity, which is indestructible.

Certain aspects of my story I have never before told publically, because they are too painful. Thank you to my attorney, Cindy Silver, and her associates at Silver Law in North Vancouver for helping me decide that this was the right time to open up. And to Zainab Choudhry at Regan Arts, thank you for coming to me with this book project.

Collaborating with writer Meredith May was as therapeutic as it was intense. Thank you for letting me relive my glory days before the war, and for being sensitive during the tearful moments. Talking about my loss was difficult at times, but during the interviews there was also a lot of laughter, and relief, and plenty of delicious shawarma sandwiches.

Thank you to Hossein Talebian for bridging two languages so Meredith and I could understand each other. You were a gracious host, and your personal knowledge of both Iran and Iraq put my words into context, which was invaluable to our three-way conversation.

I want to also thank filmmaker Ann Shin, who took great care to bring our story to the screen. To my family in Canada, brother Jasem and sister Fatemah, thank you for reminding me what family is for. Your support, from the day I got out of prison to today, is the earth under my feet.

Despite the violence still raging in the Middle East, my story is proof that humanity is still alive and well and will never die. Thank you to everyone who helped me spread this message of peace.

Most of all, thank you, Alyaa. My heart is locked, and only you have the key.